JOURNEY OF THE TALL HORSE

MERVYN MILLAR

JOURNEY OF THE TALL HORSE

A STORY OF AFRICAN THEATRE

OBERON BOOKS
LONDON

First published in 2006 by Oberon Books Ltd.

521 Caledonian Road, London N7 9RH

Tel: 020 7607 3637 / Fax: 020 7607 3629

info@oberonbooks.com / www.oberonbooks.com

A catalogue record for this book is available
from the British Library.

ISBN: 1 84002 599 9

Cover photography: Mervyn Millar and Damien Schumann

Printed in Great Britain by Antony Rowe Ltd, Chippenham.

Contents

FOREWORD

THE STORY OF THIS PRODUCTION BEGAN IN THE '70S IN Botswana, where my partner and I lived for three years.

Adrian worked at the university, I at the museum. Certain items required at work were unobtainable locally and buying trips to South Africa were rotated amongst those members of staff who were allowed to enter the country. On one such trip Adrian saw what seemed to be an African puppet in the window of an art dealer in Johannesburg. He couldn't afford it, but put down a deposit. Six months later it arrived by post in Gaborone.

Inside the parcel was a simple, refined and elegant yellow-painted figure which moved with a commanding grace. Its maker was clearly a master puppeteer. Bewitched, I wrote immediately to the gallery owner, Vitorino Meneghelli, asking for more information. It turned out that the puppet came from Mali and that he had a small collection. The museum asked him if he might be prepared to send them to Botswana for an exhibition. I'll never forget the unwrapping process when they arrived: such a wonderful variety of shapes, colours, mechanisms. Antelope horns, with rows of little human figures perched all the way up, their arms articulated by strings that led down through the horn to the puppeteer below; twin water sprites with flowing black hair; farmers with hoes; a weaver with a loom; marabou storks…

It turned out that the dealer was prepared to sell the exhibition to the museum and suddenly I found myself the curator of 36 wonderfully joyful puppets. Around then I discovered Mary-Jo Arnoldi's small but highly informative gallery catalogue on the Bamana Puppets of Mali and steadily the significance of the puppetry of Mali as Africa's oldest and most fecund puppetry tradition became apparent.

Some months later, when Adrian suggested facing a return to South Africa to start a puppet company there, it was my growing awareness of this authentically African tradition that allowed me to support his crazy plan.

In a very real sense then, the Bamana puppets of Mali were an inspiration behind the formation of Handspring Puppet Company. We knew very little about them of course and what we knew was second hand. However, they did influence the style of our version of *A Midsummer Night's Dream*, produced in 1987, and were a constant 'background radiation' in the development of our work.

Imagine how thrilled I was then, when Alicia Adams, Vice President, International Programming and Dance of the John F Kennedy Center in Washington DC proposed a collaboration between ourselves and Yaya Coulibaly, director of the Sogolon Marionette Troupe of Mali. The vehicle for the collaboration would be the story of a 19th century giraffe's epic journey from the savannah of Africa to the royal menagerie of France.

Adams' initial proposal came in June 1999. The Kennedy Centre put together a creative team that included a number of Americans: script writer, set designer, composer, script adviser, researcher, and so on. Whilst attempting to raise money to mount the production, they utilised funding from the Doris Duke Foundation to organise meetings of the creative team in Mali, Cape Town and Washington. Meanwhile, through a chance meeting I made contact with AngloGold Ashanti, who had mining interests in Mali. Bobby Godsell, their CEO, loved the project, took time off work to fly 1500 km to spend a day with our creative team in Cape Town and the upshot was that he offered the Kennedy Center a substantial donation towards the production costs.

However, the basic funding was not forthcoming and at the end of 2002 I received a phone call from Alicia Adams informing me of the cancellation of the project. It was a very sad moment. Two and a half years had passed since the original proposal. A lot of thought and enthusiasm had already gone into it. But soon after this Steve Lenahan, one of AngloGold's directors, called. It was 8 am. The night before we'd opened *Confessions of Zeno* at the Centre Pompidou in Paris and I was feeling bleary.

'We heard Kennedy has cancelled.'

'Yes.'

'You're not going to give up are you?'

'Yes.'

'Why?'

'Because even if you gave Handspring the money you were going to give the Kennedy Center, it would still not be enough to make the show.'

'Then make a proper budget and we'll talk.'

AngloGold Ashanti have mining interests in Mali and I think they appreciated the difficulties and the rewards of working between two very distant African countries. They really wanted to support our initiative. Indeed the physical, temporal and cultural distances that this project were about to bridge, were formidable.

The first thing I had to do was to downscale the project and make the logistics more workable. This meant finding a South African composer, rather than an

American, and asking Kohler to become responsible for the design of sets and costumes. Having the designer, composer and director in Cape Town immediately made the project more practical. We also reduced the number of people on stage from the projected 20–25 to 12. Kennedy had always seen the production as something of a spectacular with Broadway potential. We had no idea of how to serve such an audience and it was with some relief that the downscaling exercise helped us move away from that ambition.

Nevertheless, taking on this show as the producers meant that we had to negotiate fees and draw up Dollar and Euro contracts with highly experienced and canny agents, handle complicated and cripplingly expensive flight schedules from Bamako via Ivory Coast, Ethiopia, Zambia to Cape Town. (Fortunately, the French Institute in Johannesburg provided funding for this.) There was also a major linguistic challenge: all contracts and written communications with French speakers had first to be translated by people who were qualified to do legal translation and charged accordingly. I complicated our lives by deciding to bring a selection of sixty puppets from Yaya's family collection for exhibition in Stellenbosch, Cape Town and Johannesburg and found extra funding from BASA and AngloGold to make this happen. Accommodating a cast and crew of 17 in these cities was also a major organisational task and basically I and my very able assistant, Estelle Randall (funded by the National Arts Council), were hugely overstretched.

It was only after the artistic team was in place that the person who was to lead us came on board. This was Marthinus Basson, the famously talented, playful and hugely energetic Cape Town-based director. It fell to him to draw us together and create the show that became *Tall Horse*. His gargantuan and masterful process has been wonderfully documented by Mervyn Millar in this book.

Millar came to the production as an observer and chronicler. However, as a result of his deep knowledge of the theatre, his resilience and tenacity, intelligence and sensitivity, and above all his supreme sense of diplomacy, Basson enrolled him as his assistant director.

Indeed in this account of the switchback ride that *Tall Horse* became, Mervyn doesn't properly indicate what an important part he himself played in making it happen. He rehearsed small groups of puppeteers when Marthinus and Koffi were on the main stage, he translated, he took photographs, and he often acted as a mediator between actors and the creative or management teams. Many times, he and Enrico Wey worked into the early hours painting puppets, finishing props, sewing harnesses and generally taking up the slack. We thought of him as the production's resident angel. We owe a huge debt of gratitude to him, to the Arts

Council England, to the Puppet Centre Trust in London, who funded his trip, and to and his publishers, Oberon Books, who have made this account possible.

However, perhaps the final word of thanks should go to AngloGold Ashanti, a remarkable company, and their staff including notably Mark Pool and Cheryl Smith in Johannesburg and Madani Diallo in Bamako who have given so much of their time and financial generosity to support *Tall Horse*. Especially in moments when we ourselves felt least confident in our ability to pull off this production, they have been our staunchest champions.

Basil Jones
Producer, Handspring Puppet Company

1

KALK BAY HAS, FAMOUSLY, THE BEST croissants in Cape Town. The Olympia Café, on what is very accurately called Main Road, is a patisserie and restaurant that manages to be both bustling and laid-back, spilling over with satisfied customers. Outside, Main Road stretches along the waterfront. On one side is a short patch of beach and the warm Indian Ocean. On the other, the hills start to lift up towards the rocks inland. Not many miles away, on the other side of town, facing the Atlantic, a village like this would be full of tourists on a hot day in February. But nowhere in Kalk Bay is as busy as the Olympia, and looking along Main Road to the East there are a few folk, of various colours, moving between the antique and bric-a-brac shops, the supermarket, ice-cream parlour and a Cuban-themed bar on the beach. The sandy beach is strewn with kelp washed up days before. It's not a glamorous town, although it seems well-heeled, and alongside the posh harbourside restaurant there are working fishing boats and a homeless family living in the shelter of the promenade. There's a relaxed, comfortable quality to this sun-bleached African Riviera.

I'm here to attend a development workshop for a new show by the Handspring Puppet Company, Kalk Bay's other celebrated asset. After many years in Johannesburg, Basil Jones and Adrian Kohler moved their base here, and now occupy a purpose built house and workshop a little way up the hill (but within an easy walk of the Olympia). Kalk Bay is a pleasant place to encounter these two men, especially in the summer (although they insist the wind is very high for this time of year). They are calm and focused as they approach this new piece of work – a reflection of the international esteem they are held in after taking seven productions to several of the most prestigious theatre festivals in the world.

The new show is a co-production with the Sogolon puppet troupe of Mali, and like all of Handspring's most recent shows, will combine actors, large puppets, video projections and sound to create an epic piece of theatre. This week, the various creative contributors to the project will come together, many for the first time, and start to sketch out what will be rehearsed five months later.

Basil and Adrian are from Kalk Bay, but it's an international team: Yaya Coulibaly, the puppet-maker and director from Bamako in Mali, Koffi Kôkô, the celebrated choreographer from Benin, and Khephra Burns, a writer from New York, as well as Marthinus Basson, Jaco Bouwer and Warrick Sony, the director, video artist and composer, also South Africans. It's fitting: the story the show will tell is about the giraffe brought from Africa to Paris in 1826 to furnish the menagerie of the King, and its handler, Atir: a global story about the meeting and comparison of cultures and values. The story is explicitly about the exoticism of the 'Dark Continent', brought to the enlightened Europeans in the person of Atir, a freed slave who is the only person the giraffe will trust, and, in the giraffe herself, the first time since the Romans that such an extraordinary creature had been seen in Europe. The story is political too: the giraffe is a bribe from Mehmet Ali, the Ottoman Viceroy of Egypt, to prevent the French involving themselves in the Greek War of Independence.

The show will tell the story from an African perspective, using traditional Malian puppets, combined with Handspring's own carving style, to represent an African view of the French aristocrats who fawn and flutter over their living curios. Handspring are an African company, and a lot of their past work has been set in Africa or has explored the possibilities of an African culture that draws on both indigenous and colonial components. As well as their recent *Chimp Project*, set in Africa, their celebrated productions with William Kentridge recreated European myths through African perspectives, as in *Woyzeck on the Highveld* and *Faustus in Africa!* Here, the company will apply the African perspective to a slice of history.

This workshop week sees all of the key collaborators coming together for the first time, and it will be the first chance for the director, Marthinus Basson, to get a sense of what and who he will be working with. He has set out some targets for the week: exploring and developing the script, testing out some of the visual set-pieces, and giving each of the key collaborators an opportunity to present their work to each other. The end of the week will see a presentation of some of this work in development to key funders: among them representatives of AngloGold Ashanti, the company who are the main supporters of the project.

Yaya Coulibaly has come from Mali with fourteen large, heavy and mysterious bundles – each one packed with figures he has carved specifically for the production. The Bamana puppetry tradition is a grand one, and so the bundles contain the heads of cattle and antelopes, numerous elegant human heads, birds, canoes, and several small ornamental figures to decorate the major characters. Coulibaly does not draw designs before he carves, and so it is the first time any of the other collaborators have found out what many of the characters will look like.

The opening of the bundles is subsequently described by Adrian Kohler as 'one of the great moments of this collaboration'. Each larger than a man, the fourteen bundles had arrived at Handspring's home and office wrapped in plastic sacking and bound tightly with strips of inner-tube rubber. 'I remember that night, I think it was one of the lowest nights of the project. There were fourteen bundles of puppets on the stoep at home. And me, too scared to open them, and Yaya, not knowing yet that they'd arrived. Sitting in his B&B, and he's not sure if they're going to arrive in time.' Kohler and Jones hadn't dared imagine what was inside. Waiting for Yaya to reveal his designs was one thing. But to have them there, wrapped up, with the workshop in a couple of days, was quite another. What if the puppets weren't what they expected? Jones and Kohler can have a tendency to worry and that night they had worried very hard. That anxiety made Adrian's response to the puppets themselves much more powerful. Even now, he can't talk about his relief without feeling the exhilaration again: 'The next morning, opening those bundles and seeing what was inside them, and seeing the correlation between the characters he'd made and their use within the piece, it was…it was…it was…so exciting. It was so exciting.'

The response to the carvings is unanimously positive – and it staggers everyone how much Yaya has produced in the few months he has had available. He is still working on some of the figures, and there are chances to see him carving using a set of adzes on a tree stump. The finished piece will include upward of sixty puppets, many of them very large, as well as some of the masks from the Bamana tradition.

In the spirit of community that seems strong in Kalk Bay, the local church hall has been provided for this week-long workshop. There's a raised stage at one end, but it won't be used except for storage; the floor space of the main hall area is closer to the size of the stages this production will play on. A lot of the week will centre on the Hunt. The sequence will eventually involve Handspring's puppeteers Fourie Nyamande and Basil Jones, on stilts and wearing Malian-style puppet/head-dresses to play mother giraffes, being chased and taken down by Ousmane Coulibaly and Téhibou Bagayoko, of the Sogolon troupe, in traditional Malian lion costumes. It's set to music and will draw on Koffi Kôkô's ability to combine stylised movement and dance.

On the first day, the priorities are to identify the story and atmosphere of this section. Composer Warrick Sony, who works with instruments from African, Western and Oriental traditions as well as electronics, samples and found sounds, has put together some rhythms and textures that explore possible moods for different parts of the scene as he has imagined it. Marthinus and he estimate the lengths of each part of the sequence, and Warrick goes back to edit the piece for the next day's work. Although Marthinus is the director and the decisions flow through him, he is aware that as well as the writer Khephra Burns's shaping and

Some of the puppets that Yaya Coulibaly brought from Mali, laid out with the giant head of Mehmet Ali made by Adrian Kohler

vision of the piece, he also has Adrian and Yaya here. These two, with Basil, have conceived the piece and been with it from its inception, and as the makers who are physically carving many of the characters from wood, they have an investment in these characters which would be unusual in many other contexts. Kohler is also the set designer. The decision-making process here in the workshop is open and discursive, with Basson effectively inviting voices from across the floor. There are two puppeteers here from Handspring, two from the Sogolon troupe and two actors.

As the second day begins, work on the Hunt sees the introduction of stilts, which have been made overnight in Handspring's workshop. No one has any more than the most rudimentary stilt-walking experience, but Basil and Fourie volunteer to try them out. The next three days of the workshop will see the stilts go through several versions. The first set are the most dangerous – although not high, they taper to a small point of contact with the ground. The second set, found in Handspring's archive, left over from a fancy-dress party some years previously, are much heavier, but are supported at both heel and toe with hinged joints and inner-tube rubber, giving a flexible stability. After working through – and developing confidence on – a couple of different designs, the two men learn to lope, skitter and even kick out at their attackers on an adapted version of the original stilts

Some of Yaya Coulibaly's puppets, including boats, and the head and horns of a cow

(with a larger, non-slip footprint). This is all the more surprising and impressive considering what they are wearing on their heads.

Most of the Bamana puppetry in Mali takes place in the open air, and many of the puppets are held high above the head for ease of viewing. Some of them are worn on something like a backpack made from dried, twisted branches, woven together and strengthened with string. The backpack is tall, curving from the waist up to the wearer's crown, where a padded extension rests on his or her head. Fixed onto this simple frame is a beautifully carved head on a long, long neck. The bottom of the neck-pole is carved into a flat shape drilled with holes, which allows it to be woven tightly into the backpack frame. It's an elegant, delicate, precarious vision of a giraffe – the first of several versions of the shape that the audience will see in the final show. Both Basil and Fourie quickly begin to explore a range of walking movements. Most of the spectators' eyes are on the large piece of heavy wood they are wearing a foot or more above their heads, waiting for what seems (but it turns out is not) an inevitable overbalance and topple. By the end of the week, the Hunt has a real sense of shape and story, with the giraffes tracked and then attacked first by lions and subsequently by the human hunters who slaughter them and take their calves. With or without music, the range of tone is fascinating, and the initial image, of the mother giraffes grazing peacefully, is one of the strongest: as Koffi Kôkô says, 'Before the violence we want to see something

– comment vous dit? Tendre.' The international language of Mali, and of Benin, is French. We are lucky that Koffi Kôkô has some good English to go with it.

It's a trademark of Handspring's style that puppets interact with actors on an equal footing; but it's a new possibility for Marthinus Basson, who is keen to see how it looks in practice (and in rehearsal). So one of the scenes which receives attention has Atir (played by an actor) in Marseilles, flirting with Clothilde (a puppet, manipulated by two puppeteers). Neither Handspring nor the Sogolon troupe try to hide or disguise their puppeteers on stage with black hoods or outfits – so care needs to be taken to direct the focus of the scene towards only two of the four figures. These puppeteers have lots of experience in maintaining a neutrality on stage and directing their energy towards the puppet, and the scene quickly shows its potential, with even Lulama Masimini, the actor playing Atir at this workshop, expressing surprise at how easy he found it to forget that he was playing opposite wood. Atir is one of only two main characters in the play to be represented by actors, and he is the giraffe's constant companion. As he and his charge move from place to place, he is a flesh-and-blood man among wooden sculptures. Another question is whether the robust, almost processional quality of the Malian puppets will be able to play against actors in a theatre. Everyone is conscious that these traditions and designs are intended for a less contrived setting outdoors.

One of Basson's strengths is his ability to co-ordinate short bursts of work, moving quickly on to a new section before discovery and experiment turn to repetition. It's a good system for a workshop and there is an exploratory atmosphere throughout. So each day sees some work on the script, with the actors trying out a scene and Khephra and Marthinus looking for alterations and cuts. Khephra Burns has built up great trust in Basson. Later on he says: 'I recall that first week of meetings in Kalk Bay (October of 2003, I think it was), with Adrian, Basil, Marthinus and myself, and the great promise it held out for the collaborative process. Marthinus was key. I had worked on the story for months with another director, and Adrian and Basil had worked on it for many months longer than that with Yaya, Koffi, Alicia Adams and others; and still all we had was an epic collection of scenes. Marthinus took what we had, suggested consolidating some scenes and eliminating others, and by the end of that week we all could see, for the first time, the outlines of a play.' The budget was only able to cover Burns visiting Cape Town once – either in October or now; and the decision was made to bring him earlier for this reason. He has paid his own travel to attend this workshop. The week's work has a number of major punctuation points. Kôkô's

I was very keen to get involved because I'd never worked with puppets. So it was rather wonderful.

Marthinus Basson

Some of Adrian Kohler's drawings of puppets in Yaya Coulibaly's collection

I would like to help more African companies to meet, for their own cultural benefit, but also for a better diffusion of African culture. Because we have arrived at a time in African history when the finest intellectuals and academics do not have the truth. We are in an age of technology. And I carry what is essential, the truth. And that reduces the frontier.

Yaya Coulibaly

arrival on the Wednesday is one, but what everyone has been waiting for is a sight of the giraffe.

Handspring's productions always seem to have an animal puppet that has a vitality and presence that set it outside the show. In *Faustus in Africa!* it was a hyena. In *Ubu and the Truth Commission* it was a crocodile suitcase. In *The Chimp Project* they went all out and filled the stage with chimpanzees of all types, from curious young cubs to aggressive, wild adult males. Here the giraffe will take some beating (although I hear there's a cat in the offing which will have a go). It stands thirteen feet high and its graceful neck can curve in all directions, even bringing it right down to the ground. Two operators 'wear' the body, both standing on stilts (again) – and the one in front supports on his chest the weight of the neck and head. Its appearance encapsulates the Handspring aesthetic: the operators

Koffi Kôkô   Photograph by Enrico Wey

Being there, not only to see how the words work, or not, in the mouths of the actors and puppets, but also to see how the puppets are made and even participate in their making, was invaluable.

Khephra Burns

> For me, it's my first time making choreography
> with puppets. And that is a very important and
> exciting experience.
>
> *Koffi Kôkô*

are completely visible but completely part of the puppet. The body section is a lightweight structure made of bent canes and hung with patches of fabric that instantly convey a sense of the pattern of giraffe hide. But between the patches you can see right through the beast to the human beings inside it. The giraffe stands twice this week – it's the first time on stilts. The second time, in the final presentation, it moves gracefully around the room and interacts naturally with actor Lulama Masimini, playing Atir. The puppeteers inside the giraffe on this occasion are Adrian and Téhibou – one of them a founder of Handspring and the puppet's designer; the other a youngster from Mali on his first visit to South Africa, who first saw this puppet only a few days ago but takes to it with an irrepressible enthusiasm and a natural touch.

The final presentation sees the giraffe in action, of course. And the company is able to show pieces involving all of the performers giving some of the varied flavours they have planned for the production: a satirical French soirée in which discussions about science and anthropology are thin masks for innuendo and social backbiting; a short solo by a puppet representing a French fashion designer; the King and Queen of France promenading in their pleasure gardens, given a surprising new spin by their representation, through African eyes, in the form of the traditional royal puppets of the Bamana tradition: the King as a hunter and the Queen, massive, riding a huge cow.

The visitors, not only potential sponsors but also some friends of the company, are also given a taste of Warrick's range of compositions and some idea of the show's video content. Throughout the workshop Jaco Bouwer has sat with a laptop, soaking up the development of his colleagues' contributions whilst continuing his own, which uses a distinctive cut-and-paste style to animate certain sections of the story, and using the grid lines that are a motif elsewhere in the production to create patterns, shapes and structures – an accompaniment to the stage action which often becomes a focal point in its own right.

Téhibou Bagayoko spraying the plastic 'grass' on the *castelet* frames in Handspring's garden in Kalk Bay

In the Café des Arts the following day, the creative team reflect on what lies ahead before they can return to begin rehearsals in July. It's almost unheard of for two African companies to collaborate on this scale. The involvement of an international choreographer and writer shows the ambition that lies behind this project. Koffi Kôkô's schedule is busy and it will be good fortune if he's available throughout a seven-week rehearsal process. The men of West Africa, Kôkô and Coulibaly, are obviously used to making speeches – both are gracious, generous and courteous in their appraisal of their colleagues and their experiences. Khephra Burns is confident that these puppets can convey what he has written in his script, and he clearly values the opportunity to meet Yaya especially – until now he has had more opportunities to spend time with Handspring than with Sogolon.

Marthinus Basson is genial, businesslike and optimistic. Basil Jones, the producer, is positive too. The week has been a success and the feedback from his funders and visitors has been positive. Both Yaya's beautiful carvings and Adrian's epic engineering of the giraffe have dazzled.

One thing that still needs to be achieved is picking a title for the show. Yaya Coulibaly is asked what the word for giraffe is in the Bambara language. There's some discussion – I think there is more than one way of expressing the concept. He responds with 'Sogo Jan'. *Sogo* in Bambara means animal or horse. It is also the name used for puppets and masks which represent animals. *Jan* means tall. Yaya explains that many animals have names constructed in this way. *Sogo Jan* would be a possible name. Discussion turns to whether audiences might think the production is in Bambara. When the team leaves the table, the rather unwieldy title proposed is *Sogo Jan: The Journey of the Tall Horse*.

By the time the group come together again, it's been abbreviated to *Tall Horse*.

2

ON THE NINETEENTH OF JULY THE FULL
company assembles at the H B Thom Theatre in Stellenbosch. The 430-seat proscenium arch theatre, part of
Stellenbosch University, takes its name from a former rector,
and was run for a time by a couple of European actors who
settled in Stellenbosch: professionals who once worked in the
University's Drama department, as Marthinus does now.

Stellenbosch is on South Africa's winelands tourist trail – named after the first
governor of the Cape, Simon van der Stel, it is one of the oldest colonial towns
after Cape Town. The central part of town is full of grand colonial architecture,
nowhere more so than at the University: a campus of several blocks, exclusively
filled with huge white behemoths. On one corner sits the Drama department and
this theatre.

Most of the twelve performers are lodging together and have met the previous
day – some live in Cape Town and will commute every morning. Two, Fezile Mpela
and Bheki Vilakazi, are dedicated actors who won't be doing puppetry. Both are
South Africans from Johannesburg. Fezile will play Atir and have the unenviable
task of sharing the stage with various versions of the giraffe – puppets are notorious
among actors for their ability to upstage. Bheki plays the eminent French scientist
St-Hilaire, who supervises the giraffe's travel from Marseilles to Paris. Handspring
and Sogolon each provide four performers. Busi Zokufa and Fourie Nyamande are
with Basil Jones and Adrian Kohler from Handspring; and from Mali, Yaya Coulibaly
and Téhibou Bagayoko – who attended the workshop in February – are joined by
Yacouba Magassouba and Nana Kouma. Tehibou and Yacouba are both nephews
of Yaya as well as experienced members of his company. Nana is a dancer. The final
two performers are from Cape Town: Craig Leo and Zandile Msutswana. Craig
is an actor, puppeteer, director, designer and stiltwalker. Zandile, a bright and
beautiful young actress, will be making her first acquaintance with puppetry.

The puppets are spread all around the stage, in and out of large flight cases,
although some (notably both sections of the giraffe) are too large to fit in cases.
There have been significant modifications made to most of them since February,
and there are many more of them; as Adrian says, 'In the studio at Handspring
there was so much stuff we could barely move.' Later in the week, racks will be
assembled to hold them. Until they are hung up, the performers will need to
watch their step.

Bheki Vilakazi in the wings of the H B Thom theatre
Photograph by Enrico Wey

The theatre was built in the 1960s. Most of the (traditional, dark red velvet) seats are downstairs, and there is a small balcony level. The stage is raised by about three feet. There's no grand decoration in the auditorium; but the foyer is a tall, narrow, carpeted room with high windows, which the company will sometimes use as a secondary rehearsal space. Upstairs is a third available room (the private bar) and another foyer area, which has been equipped with that rehearsal essential: a hot water urn, coffee and teas. It's a major asset to the production process that the company will be able to rehearse in a theatre rather than a rehearsal room. The theatre has enough height and size to accommodate the set, and has facilities which will eventually allow for rehearsal with video and lighting. At the moment, the set is laid against the back wall of the theatre, a confusing stack of stained, slatted wooden platforms and lengths of timber. In comparison to the puppets, it's not attracting much attention.

Traditionally, the first day would include a read-through of the script, but Marthinus has decided to start by engaging with the puppets. He has been holding off making decisions until he can see the puppeteers bring the figures to life. 'I actually find watching how the puppet functions, what their limitations are, and what is possible, far more illuminating,' he says when I ask if he has read up on the Malian Bamana tradition. He's read the books, of course. But it's no substitute for seeing the tradition in action.

The first things that are presented are the stilts. Yaya has made them based on those made for the workshop; stout and strong, with large feet, in a variety of lengths. They lash on to the leg in the traditional way, with four long pieces of strapping criss-crossed around the foot and calf. Zandile and Nana are the most likely candidates to play the mother giraffes, and although Nana has had experience of walking (and dancing) on stilts before, it is Zandile's first time. Everyone's conscious that they will need plenty of practice on the stilts if they are to be confident in choreographed movement. They're strapped in. Tall Craig is a veteran of circus, and one of South Africa's outstanding stilt-walkers. He and Yaya give some instruction to an enthusiastic if apprehensive Zandile. There's a difference between their teaching styles. Craig is calm, asking for gradual, controlled improvements; Yaya, more animated and cheery, demands that his students leap straight in, finding their balance by being left standing isolated. The company are impressed and enthused by Nana's apparent comfort on the stilts as she sways her hips to accentuate her movement. Zandile isn't able to watch: she's taking tuition from Yaya, who needs some translation from his French: 'Are you right or left handed? Don't lean forward. Look ahead, not down.' After lunch, Nana is keen to teach Zandile the balance that keeps her steady in her dancing. Zandile already seems remarkably comfortable. As time goes on Yaya will introduce a method of showing the walkers how stable they are (and keeping them alert) by kicking at their stilts while they're standing on them.

There is a language obstacle within the company, and at tea breaks the cast tend to coalesce into their respective language groups. This means the four Malians together, speaking French, or more normally Bambara. All of the South Africans speak flawless English, although in many cases it's not their first language – frequently during the process conversations will take place in Afrikaans, Xhosa or Zulu. It's during this first week that the choice of language used feels like a defensive barrier, to keep thoughts relatively private, or as a refuge for comfort – you'll often find Marthinus and Jaco Bouwer discussing the developments of the video design in rapid Afrikaans. But the will to converse and communicate is strong. At this point Adrian has pretty good French, and Basil and I have a little. Yaya has some English and can often follow what's being said. As the process continues, all of the South Africans will pick up some conversational or practical French – and everyone will be astonished by how quickly Téhibou and Yacouba pick up English.

For me, I personally like to just put myself one step back, and try and understand what Basil and Adrian's view has been, over a very long period of time. And I mean, it's not that difficult, because we sit out in the auditorium and we see the same things.

Suddenly you can hear Adrian go, 'Aha, ja, that!' and they say something, and 'Aha,' you say, 'that!' – and you feel that you are aligned.

Marthinus Basson

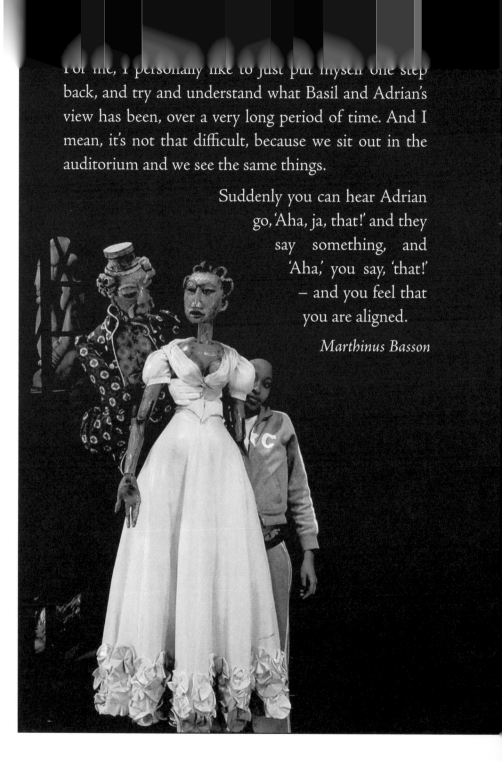

Count Grandeville-Largemont, the Prefect of Marseilles, and his wife Clothilde;
Zandile Msutswana peeping out from behind and holding her up

'For me, the language barrier does not exist,' declares Yaya. 'It's not a problem. My father told me: even when we don't understand the language, we can understand the sense. And the most important thing in the meeting of humans is the heart. When you have a good heart, and when people want to work together, there's no reason why they can't.' It's a typically rhetorical appeal to the special spirit of this collaboration. There will be times when the wordless connection between people sweeps away boundaries – and there will be times when it doesn't.

Each of the puppet types is demonstrated. The traditional *marionnette à tige* (Malian rod puppet) is a single carved head, shoulder and body piece which can be held in the hand of the puppeteer, with two arms loosely tied at the shoulder and hinged at the elbow. There are stout rods lashed visibly to the hands of the puppet. The puppeteer will hold one or both of these rods as necessary. In the *meren habitable*, the head and shoulders piece is mounted on a frame which is worn on top of the head and across the operator's back, so that the puppet's head and shoulders are up above and behind those of the puppeteer, leaving both of the puppeteer's hands free. The puppet's costume obscures the whole of the puppeteer and the arm rods are inside the costume – the effect is that of a very tall puppet character.

The Handspring puppets usually have a shaped handle set at the waist level of a carved polystyrene and plywood body section. In front of this handle is a rod, which can be turned to rotate the neck, and a string control which allows the head to be lifted or nodded on the neck. The arms have naturalistic joints at the shoulder and elbow. The hands will either be controlled with slender wire rods attached to the palms (in which case there is a wrist joint), or with a rod running through the forearm which is controlled from behind the elbow, allowing rotation of the hand. Sometimes this control is supplemented with a pair of strings which allow the wrist to bend. In both cases the puppets are between three-quarters and full life size. On first acquaintance these two types of puppets seem very different. The Handspring designs tend to keep the controls as discreet as possible (though they, like the operators, are visible). Moreover, they are relatively mechanically complex and are designed to be able to articulate very subtle and complex human movements – a tiny turn of the head or incline of the wrist. In comparison, the Malian puppets, with their thick wooden rods and inflexible necks, flaunt their

One of the *merens habitables*

artificiality. More daunting still are the Malian *castelets* – stylised antelope and cattle. They are constructed from a frame about a metre and a half long made of thick roots, with a large, heavy carved head on a neck at one end, and a tail poking up from the other. The body is covered in brightly patterned Malian cloth, and grass hangs down from the fringes to obscure the legs of the operator. There is no movement of the head, neck or tail relative to the body – although in some cases the jaw closes and the ears can be wiggled with strings. It will turn out that they are very heavy and uncomfortable to work in.

One of the principal questions facing (and prompting) this collaboration is whether these puppets can be made to work together. Handspring's puppets and Sogolon's puppets are, of course, developed in response to different environments.

Sogolon's puppets bear the authority of having been developed over generations of usage. Yaya Coulibaly is very conscious that when he carves a puppet he is the custodian of a tradition as well as being a working theatre artist and sculptor. The tall, long faces of the Malian puppets are a feature of the way they are carved: first, held in one hand on a tree stump, using crisp, controlled downward strokes with an adze; later, using a knife for detail. The puppets are smoothly finished with strong, minimal featuring, although sometimes with surprising details. They are stylised – in many cases the necks are very long and sometimes curved; the lengthened face is often topped with a formalised carving representing an ornate hair-do; the hands at the end of the long arms are flat, with the palm splitting into five identical and parallel 'fingers'. Yaya describes and later shows a video of the type of performance that takes place in Mali – outdoor shows surrounded by people drumming, talking and eating on all sides.

'I'm a hybrid puppeteer,' says Adrian Kohler. 'I have my Japanese stuff, I have my Central European stuff; some of the controls I use are German. And you know, string puppets were what I grew up with. I basically use what intrigues me with the

One of Adrian Kohler's early designs for Mehmet Ali, with multiple arms
and a *castelet* adapted to be a city, armoury and throne

puppets.' Like Yaya's, his puppets also have heads, necks and hands made of wood, but the wood, like the inspiration for the mechanisms, is sourced from abroad: it's jelutong, soft and light Indonesian timber. It's not available in large enough pieces to make the heads Adrian carves, so two or three sections are glued together and the resulting block is carved using chisels before being hollowed out. Adrian works to a rough finish in which the concave curves left by the deep-gouge chisels create complex shadows and lines on the puppet's face, emphasizing that this is wood. The artist and director William Kentridge, a long-time Handspring collaborator, describes it as using 'speed and imprecision' to achieve the 'definitively imperfect'. The productions in which Handspring have developed their puppet style over the last twenty years were made in small- to medium-scale theatres, using theatrical lighting, recorded, atmospheric music and performed to a very focused, literary audience. Their puppets often speak text in a 'Western', more or less naturalistic style, and have always interacted directly with human beings.

But the two forms have a fundamental connection. In fact, before Handspring was even established, Basil and Adrian, as young graduates working in Botswana to avoid the draft, found themselves inspired by a small yellow Bamana puppet. 'They're all rod puppets,' Adrian will say – and he has as much respect for simplicity

　　　　　JOURNEY OF THE TALL HORSE

Mehmet Ali with Drovetti. Téhibou Bagayoko on Mehmet's
left arm and Fourie Nyamande holding Drovetti

of design as he does for intricate engineering. The work of the puppeteer is the same. Holding the spine of the puppet near where the puppet's waist would be, one hand gives the figure breath and direction. The other ornaments and clarifies intention by moving or positioning the hands relative to the body and head.

The company approach, and handle, the puppets. Many of them have variations from the basic design. Some of the Handspring puppets have built-in tricks. For example, the Prefect of Marseilles, Count Grandeville-Largemont, has a door in his chest which holds a bottle of cognac that he will offer around the party. Another puppet, Drovetti, has legs which are separate from his body and can run about the stage independently. As the puppets are demonstrated, it's clear that adjustments will need to be made to some of them. Marthinus takes one look at the King's minister and wants him to be able to bow lower. Instead of legs, he has a single sprung foot, like an elegant, elasticated pogo-stick, with which he bounces onto the stage. If he is to bow lower and still look up, there will have to be wood cut away from his head to allow the nodding angle to be widened. Puppets like these attract a lot of enthusiasm at this point for the intricacy or wit of their mechanisms. Basson in particular is exercised by the possibilities: 'I was very keen to get involved,' he remembers, 'because I'd never worked with puppets and it's really exciting. So it was rather wonderful.' At the end of the day, he's satisfied: 'Just from an afternoon's workshop, you can already see: this puppet has a certain feel, that puppet doesn't; in that manipulator's hands it takes on a slightly different meaning.' The love affair between Basson and the puppets has begun.

Pride of place goes to the giraffe. Téhibou and Yacouba, who will operate it, practised briefly last week. They put on their stilts and strap themselves into the body. As yet, the legs have not been attached, and Adrian isn't sure about the way they look. The giraffe's design, especially the framework of the body, is inspired by the *castelets*. Téhibou, working the front, hoists up the long neck and braces it on the chest pad of his harness. The boys walk onto the stage, and the head looks around. It gives the right impression. It's extraordinary. The smooth curve of the neck works with the nonchalant flicks of the tail, and although the giraffe is awkward today, it has an unmistakable grandeur even now.

Also here is Philani Mbana, a dancer and choreographer from Cape Town's JazzArt Dance Theatre, who will work as an assistant choreographer to Koffi – due to arrive on Tuesday from Berlin. Leigh Colombick, the company stage manager, will be one of the most important members of the team, overseeing the scheduling of rehearsals and the sourcing of the props and materials that the company will need. She'll be on hand in the rehearsal room throughout the process, not only keeping the urn filled and hot, but making sure the 'book' – the master copy of the script – is up to date. Subsequently this copy will be used to call the lighting, sound and video cues in the show's run. Handspring have a regular backstage team who are all working on this production. In addition to Leigh, there's Wesley France (both production manager and lighting designer) and Simon Mahoney (sound engineer). The three have years of experience working together which means that they've found a way (perhaps they've had to) to crew the productions themselves: you'll usually find Simon helping to load and assemble the scenery along with Wesley, or shopping for props, allowing Leigh to remain in the rehearsal room. They're a tight team with a lot of trust between them. Basil reflects later that Wesley has worked on all of Handspring's shows. I find them at their happiest when everyone's gone home and they are on their own, fixing up some bits of scenery or technical equipment. You get the sense that they'd be even happier if they didn't have to wait for everyone to go home first, but the hierarchy of theatre means that technical work can only rarely assert a claim to the stage over rehearsal.

The day finishes off with a production meeting for Marthinus, Adrian (in his role as set designer as well as puppet maker), Basil (who is also the producer),

Yaya, Wesley and Leigh. With Koffi expected tomorrow, Marthinus is keen to allow him time to make an impact on the company, and to see the way he works. The two do not know each other beyond the couple of days they spent together at the workshop in February, and their relationship will need to develop on the job. Wesley France wants to know how early it's possible to put up some of the set, and a provisional schedule is worked out. There is sound equipment to install so that Koffi can work with Warrick Sony's music, and a plan for some shadow puppetry sequences to be filmed so that Jaco Bouwer can integrate them into his projected video – a plan which impacts on Adrian's time also, as it requires him to design and make the shadow puppets for these sequences. Marthinus offers that some of the technical students at the University will be able to help with the making of shadow puppets and props. There are longer-term considerations too; Basil needs to keep an eye on promotion and to schedule the shooting of a short video of the show to send to overseas promoters and venues. The show will play at three venues during this run – Cape Town, Pretoria and Johannesburg – and there's a little discussion as to which would be best. Wesley is concerned about the limited wing and backstage space at the Johannesburg venue – he also needs to plan transportation, for which he will need to know exactly how much is travelling with the show.

The first day of a project is often characterised by a bubble of enthusiasm. Today's pace has been more like the exploratory, inquisitive style of a development workshop. Or is this an example of the famous 'African time'? It's my first visit to Africa and I'm particularly curious about how things might be done differently here. The jokes about African time-keeping are many and old: on Robben Island the guides tell you: 'In Switzerland you have clocks; in Africa we have time.' Marthinus will say later that he dislikes stifling their natural enthusiasm by putting the actors straight around a table. Today he's been laughing and bubbling over with ideas for how the puppets can be used – and his joy in the process has infected the puppeteers and actors.

The second day of rehearsals is Basil Jones's birthday. No one knew except the long-standing Handspring members, but they've organised flowers and a cake. Yesterday's enthusiasm has carried over, and everyone is enthusiastic about reading the script together. Most of the company have seen at least parts of the script – Basil and Adrian of course have been involved in its development. The

French-speakers have their own version and will speak their lines in French. This makes a lot of sense, but causes some confusion for the rest of the day – especially since the two scripts are laid out differently and there's no correlation between the page numbers. Two languages will be used in performance, too, although there is some debate about this along the way. Forcing the Malians to learn their lines phonetically in English seems unreasonable, but the play is being performed to an English-speaking audience: will they be able to follow what's going on? Handspring are familiar with the use of surtitles: they have taken their shows (in English) to countries across and beyond Europe. This may be the way to keep things clear for the audience while still allowing the Malian actors to perform in a language they already know.

In a number of scenes there are crowds: museum assistants, scientists and a variety of French townspeople. So there are plenty of occasions when English and French voices mix in quick succession. Busi Zokufa, one of Handspring's puppeteers, who will be playing the Queen of France, has decided that she will play this role in French. At this stage, Busi speaks no French at all.

One of the peculiarities of this piece is the number of characters it involves. Adrian often describes it as a 'road movie': Atir and the giraffe move from place to place encountering new characters everywhere they go. As well as requiring Yaya and Adrian to make a vast number of puppets, this will test the puppeteers' versatility too, as each will be playing several characters. Most of the roles are allocated during the read-through. Some have already been decided. Most of the performers come away with at least one major speaking character that they can invest in. The others know that their roles are less verbal – particularly, of course, Yacouba and Téhibou, who for a large part of the show will be operating the voiceless giraffe.

The afternoon session sees the puppeteers get back to working the puppets; a workshop led by Adrian. His style of teaching is not prescriptive. The first instruction is: 'Everybody grab a puppet. Just explore what it can do.' It had been hoped that Koffi would have been able to come and see this, or even lead some of it, but his flight has been delayed and he will now not arrive until tomorrow afternoon.

This is the first opportunity to compare the puppets in action. The script is written mostly naturalistically, as if for human actors, so the puppets will be required to perform alongside humans in a natural relationship, as well as in more poetic and heightened ways which can challenge and transform that reality. Adrian's style of carving brings out the subtler emotions: lots of his puppets look like they are about to say something, lips just parting to express hope or sadness, mischief or derision – and often a combination in the same face. Yaya's carvings (and this is borne out as part of the tradition in some of the other Malian puppets he has brought to form an exhibition) are also pregnant with emotion, perhaps more so because of the precise simplicity of their faces. The company will learn more about the difference between them later, but for now Adrian is keen just to get puppeteers working puppets.

'I want to see how they breathe. What does breath mean in the puppet?' Five years ago, I took a workshop with Basil and Adrian in London that has indirectly led to me being here documenting this process. They arrived with some puppets and told the group, not that they were going to instruct us in the mysteries of their craft, but rather that they needed some help in solving a problem they had been having. It was that of breath. They also mentioned a project they were hoping would come off: a collaboration with a company from Mali. 'It'll be pretty amazing,' I remember Adrian saying. Here in Stellenbosch five years later, as part of that collaboration, Handspring are asking the same question of these puppeteers:

Zandile Msutswana with Clothilde   Photograph by Enrico Wey

what does it look like if this puppet breathes? What does it mean if this puppet breathes?

It mustn't be too much: 'It's very still... Less... Less...' Adrian invites the puppeteers to make the smallest movements within their range, and a movement at the heart of the puppet, where it has no joints. This breath can be given to any object, from a stone to the most complicated marionette. It shows the puppeteer how little they need to do to make the puppet live. This first session will form the basis of all the puppetry work. Fourie knows this routine, and every time he picks up a puppet over the next few weeks, you'll see him studiously concentrating on giving it a breath, before he tries anything else.

'In...out...in...out...in...out... What happens to your chest?' A row of puppets across the front of the stage come to life. 'In, and look to the right.' The movement of each puppet is very different. More first principles come from Adrian: 'For the puppet to look completely natural, the puppeteer looks completely unnatural.' Indeed, the puppeteers' bodies lean in towards the puppet, stressed across the diagonal lines of the body, in tension just as the puppet is being given life. And then the breathing figures are allowed to move. 'For the next in-breath, everybody rise up on your toes.' And then: 'Take the smallest little jump, on an in-breath.' The puppets try little breaths and big breaths, turning to look in each direction. Little jumps. None of the puppets being used in this workshop has legs, although some have dresses that reach down to a realistic level. Adrian is interested to see how they look, and how they feel to the puppeteer, at different heights. But the puppets are heavy and the puppeteers need regular short breaks or to exchange puppets, to vary the pull on their wrists and shoulders. Adrian is also thinking as a puppet maker, trying to identify difficulties that can be fixed with simple mechanical adjustments. They now focus on the puppets' arms – again, using very simple movements, finding the smallest, simplest means of communication – and finally move on to a little 'walking'. The puppeteers will need to spend a lot of time working on their puppets' walks. Without legs, they need to move the puppets at the waist to simulate (and sometimes slightly exaggerate) the way this part of the body would move if it had legs. It's surprisingly convincing. Each puppet has a different walk according to their character, and, of course, each character's walk varies according to their situation.

The Malian puppets really begin to show their potential in motion. You might expect that their stiffness – the distance from the grip to the top of the head is about a metre of uninterrupted straight timber – would make their movements awkward. But used skilfully, this line serves to accentuate the economical and delicate movements of the puppet's 'breathing'. These movements are made

[Yaya] did say to me, a couple of weeks ago, 'With you, I'm the student. When you come to Mali, you'll be my student.' [*Laughs.*]

Adrian Kohler

Fourie Nyamande with one of the Soirée puppets

crisper, often funnier (which is no bad thing), and certainly more expressive. The Malian puppets – wise-looking long-necked men and tall, solid-browed women – become proud, skittish and threatening. The Handspring puppets, which held the attention more firmly during the initial breath control exercises, fall into the background as these begin to move. Again the emphasis is on exploration – Adrian doesn't single out puppets for special attention, and the puppeteers take whichever puppet they fancy. They learn as much from watching one another experiment as from listening to Adrian's commentary. A few hours ago some of this group had never even held one of these puppets. Now they are attempting improvised scenes (and most of the puppeteers have gone for puppets they know they will find difficult to manipulate). Adrian lines them up opposite one another and each puppet approaches and wordlessly encounters its opposite number. It's one of the simplest improvisation exercises possible; and the restriction of not using words forces the puppeteer to tell the story visually. Today, the group begins to find ways of using the puppets together and having them interact. But all of these puppets present challenges. Kohler's sophisticated controls take months to handle comfortably and years to master. Yaya Coulibaly's figures are easier to make an impact with, but the judgment and sensitivity that are required to convey subtle thought take just as long to learn. It's a process that will continue to develop right up to and beyond the opening night.

3

YAYA COULIBALY IS A FATHER FIGURE for his company, the Sogolon Troupe, and takes his responsibilities to the generations that will succeed him as seriously as he does those to generations past. He's a direct descendant of Mamari Biton Coulibaly, the greatest king of the Segou region of Mali in the 17th century. It was Biton who unified those people who practised animism in Segou and who later became known as the Bamana, or Bambara.[1]

Denise Paule's entry on the Bambara in the *Dictionary of Black African Civilization*[2] gives the story succinctly:

> The legend explaining their origins tells of two brothers who came from the East and managed to cross the Niger near Segou on the back of an enormous catfish, which earned them the nickname of Kulubali, meaning 'no boat'... Mamari (Biton) Kulibali (c.1660–1710) was their greatest king. He conquered his neighbours and unified all the Bambara of the Niger Valley. The range of Bambara art extends from almost pure abstraction to comparative realism and is one of the most important in all Africa.

Mali is a republic now, but the name Coulibaly still carries some weight. Yaya is the seventh generation of puppeteer in his family, and those members of the company who have visited his home in Mali talk with awe of the puppets, many very old and rare, piled up on every available surface and in every available space. A selection of these have travelled with Yaya to South Africa to form an exhibition, and he and Basil have hopes that someone will be willing to invest in setting up a permanent collection in Bamako to preserve the collection in the country of its origin.

As I haven't yet been to Mali to see Yaya's company at work in their most familiar environment, I am dependent on others who have seen Bamana performance first-hand to explain it. Janni Donald's essay 'Sogo: Puppets and Ritual Objects in Bamana Culture' in the brochure for her exhibition of puppets from Yaya Coulibaly's collection is an excellent guide to the subject. I also refer extensively to Mary Jo Arnoldi's book on youth masquerade in the Segou region, *Playing with Time*.[3]

Puppets and masks have an important role to play in the culture of the Bamana, and there are strict codes regarding who can handle these traditional figures –

some are only for mature men, most are denied to women. According to Arnoldi, the tradition extends back at least six centuries and precedes the arrival of Islamic culture in Mali. Janni Donald writes about four different contexts in which puppets and masks are used. The first is a non-demonstrative use in pure ritual – initiations and animal sacrifices. The second is that of initiation rites for young men and women which may also include semi-sacred performance. The third is traditional theatre performances, where a troupe would perform to a wide audience at a celebration: a wedding or funeral, or at New Year. The final category is the popular festival, where many of the restrictions of the other contexts are relaxed. All of the young men in the community are involved in the creation of the spectacle. These festivals will take many hours, with performances involving the community's best-loved mask characters. There are masks, puppets or *castelets* of many animals, genies and spirits, each of which have their own dances and songs to perform. Janni Donald writes that 'the comic and light nature of the material allows the community to laugh at itself';[4] Mary Jo Arnoldi that 'like folktales and other theatrical forms, these performances throw cultural values and social relationships into high relief and open them up for public scrutiny'.[5] A character might dance for five to ten minutes to ensure that all of the crowd are able to enjoy the detail. The emphasis of the puppeteer/performer is on the movement characteristic to the character – which Arnoldi describes as 'highly abstract'. There is also a strong element of innovation and experiment at these events – the traditional work is accompanied by new departures and ingenious designs and characters.

> Within Bamana communities in Mali…individuals are classified as belonging to one of three social categories. These categories include the *hòròn*, freemen, the *nyamakala*, blacksmiths and bards, and the *jòn*, descendants of slaves.[6]

The puppet theatre is where the blacksmiths and the bards come together.

The puppets are traditionally made by the blacksmith, one of the most important figures in a community. The blacksmiths and the performers, who between them prepare the figures and masks for ritual activities, occupy a special (and ambivalent) status in Bamana society. Yaya's family were puppet performers, but he is the first in his family to combine this life with that of the blacksmith. He works alongside his own smithing teachers in training the next generation of smiths and giving them an understanding of the needs of the puppeteer in performance.

While Yaya certainly carries with him the knowledge of a traditional style of work, it would be wrong to suggest that he is a traditionalist. His company also present contemporary puppet shows, including educational pieces about AIDS and female sexual health and political satires. Atypically for a puppeteer in West Africa, Yaya was fully educated at school in the former colonial period and subsequently went to Charleville-Mézières in France, to study at the Insititut International de la Marionnette. He returned to Mali with an interest in string puppets and has introduced string-puppet versions of traditional Malian characters – the blind sage, the hyena – into the work of Sogolon. While often bringing Bamana puppetry to the outside world by touring internationally with his company, he also works to introduce the young puppeteers of his company to the practices of the Western theatre. He's been careful in his selection of personnel for this experiment, too: all three of the younger Malian performers are hungry to work and exchange with the South Africans.

Yaya distinguishes between the Coulibaly family's work with Sogolon and some of the other performance activity in Bamako. 'Mine is a family which preserves. And the puppets of my family are working puppets [*les marionnettes fonctionelles*]. In contrast, the puppets of other companies are free puppets – you can work with imagination to make all these – undirected.' Coulibaly is careful not to claim that his traditional work is better than the 'free' puppets, but he wants to underline the distinction. 'The fundamental difference between the puppets of my family and the other puppets is this: for me, before I cut the wood, there is a ritual – a sacrifice. There's a sacrifice to do.' For the puppets to fulfil their ritual function properly in society, it must be seen that they are created with a suitable ritual of their own. It is this that makes them potent, not anything inherent in their design. Yaya describes in detail how an offering – twenty cola nuts and a cockerel of a specific colour depending on the year – is made to the tree before it is cut down, and this invocation is made:

Spirit of the tree, I wish to offer to you this [buck, goat or cock].
Permit me to cut the wood and to bring out all of its potential,
To find what is inside. Forgive me, because it is not mine to take.
You are the creator of the wood. I wish to carve the wood.

Yaya has found a unique place as both a blacksmith/maker and performer, balancing the sculptural and the performing arts. What we see in rehearsals is a very practical man of the theatre with a wealth of experience in very many fields. His enthusiasm means he often steps up to participate – offering to drum, for example, with the line: 'I am a musician.' By the end of the process we have a good list of what Yaya is, and he offers it to me in one bundle: 'I am a writer. I am a director. I am a choreographer. I am a musician. I am a puppeteer. I am a dancer. I am a historian. And I represent Malian culture here.'

The giraffe is Futurist. The giraffe is the grandeur of a civilisation and of a people, but at the same time it is a symbol of telling the future. The eyes of the giraffe have lots of sensitivity, and with the height of the giraffe they see so far. The giraffe is a symbol of vigilance, therefore, and also of great wisdom.

Yaya Coulibaly

What does the giraffe represent? As an African man, I can tell you it's a big animal that lives in the savannah. I've seen them many times; and it's an animal that is not dangerous, if you don't attack him. And it's a beautiful animal, with his *particularités*, with the long... *cou*, and his legs, and his colours. For me it is an animal.

Koffi Kôkô

Sandile Matsheni with the giraffe (2005 production)
Photograph by Damien Schumann

Handspring, of course, are also makers, performers and directors. And they don't have the benefit of the same traditional sculptural foundations from which to experiment, so the decisions they've made about what their puppets look like and are made from have been based on their own untethered aesthetic. As Adrian observes, 'I've sort of become fairly settled in what I like as the type of puppet.' But this process has been a gradual one, and its development can be traced from their first work for children, through their first adult piece, *Episodes of an Easter Rising*, with string puppets, and then the succeeding adult productions, until the decisive rediscovery of wooden figures as a principal medium in the collaboration with William Kentridge, *Woyzeck on the Highveld*. Asked about his memories of Handspring's work, Marthinus Basson remembers that particular production with a fondness bordering on reverence: 'One of the best pieces of theatre ever to come out of this country was the *Woyzeck on the Highveld*... very small, very tiny, and riveting beyond measure. It moved me no end. I found it beautiful and compelling.'

As we've seen, the type of puppet that Kohler has settled upon is a near life-size figure controlled from the waist by two puppeteers. Usually the arms are controlled from behind the elbow with a rod that runs the length of the forearm into the hand; sometimes the hands are controlled with a slim metal rod from below, which swivels in line with the palm of the hand. This type of figure, working alongside actors, has been at the heart of a remarkable sequence of shows: the *Woyzeck*, *Faustus in Africa!*, *Ubu and the Truth Commission*, the opera *Il Ritorno d'Ulisse*, and *The Chimp Project*. And Kohler has explored similar and related mechanisms, populating these productions with mechanically intricate animal puppets which have an astonishing subtlety and variety of movement. The Hyena in *Faustus*, the vulture, crocodile and dogs of *Ubu*, and the complex chimps made for *The Chimp Project* are now joined by a pair of baby giraffes, each about the size of a large dog and operated by two or three puppeteers. A substantial engineering challenge, they are not finished in time for the first week of rehearsal. Consequently, they travel back and forth between Handspring's base in Kalk Bay and the theatre in Stellenbosch for additions and adjustments. Adrian's freedom in working without the responsibility to a tradition, and the natural curiosity that Yaya and he seem to share (perhaps it's endemic to puppet makers) encourage him to alter his designs. So there are many variants on the basic type here: the Fashion Designer is a full-body version (with legs and feet), further distinguished by some experimentally-articulated hips; Clothilde has swinging hips that send movement right down to the beautifully made hem of her full skirt; the King's Minister has a pogo-stick where his legs should be; Drovetti's long, elegant legs nearly steal the show as they lope around the stage in pursuit of their torso. And of course there is the full-size giraffe.

It's a fair question to ask what has brought these two African companies together, and the answer is America. Handspring and Sogolon had both toured to Washington DC's Kennedy Center, where they had been programmed by Alicia Adams, Director of International Programming. It was she who suggested that these two African companies should collaborate and who supervised Handspring's first visit to Mali to meet Yaya.

Basil Jones remembers the initial approach: 'The original idea, I think, was simply to get us and Sogolon together, which normally wouldn't be something that would be interesting, because…working with another puppet company… [is] a skill that we already have. But because it was Mali and the tradition that I'm afraid I always call Bambara but should be calling Bamana, it was certainly very interesting.' Characteristically Yaya invokes something much grander: 'The connection through the Kennedy Center, today, is like a cosmic sign. I say that because, look – we have an equilateral triangle. A, B and C [Mali, South Africa and America]. In the cosmic sense. If you have an equilateral triangle, it's positive for the full moon. And that is the meeting of many connections.'

It was Alicia Adams who, in the way that American producers construct artistic teams, found Handspring, Sogolon and Koffi Kôkô, and put it to them that they could make something together that could be larger than anything they had made before. Reflecting on the combination, she says: 'Yaya's stories are colourful and linear, and Handspring have a very distinct style and discipline; they're knowledgeable about the theatre world. My motive is to bring artists together. As globalisation continues to happen, to be able to put together some of the best people who are out there is a good thing from my vantage point.' The idea that she put to them, and the pleasure they took in their first meetings, has taken them all through five years of planning and playing, and finally to rehearsal in South Africa. And it was also Alicia Adams who provided the story of the giraffe. Jones remembers: 'And that too, because it was something that was unachievable without puppets on stage, appealed to me.'

The story runs like this: In 1826, the Pasha Mehmet Ali was Viceroy of Egypt under the Ottoman Empire and began assisting his Sultan in crushing the Greek nationalists in their War of Independence. This had raised concerns in Britain and

The Queen of France on a small *castelet* for her first entrance

France, who were threatening to intervene on the side of the Greeks. A grand diplomatic gesture was called for, so Mehmet Ali conferred with the French Consul-General in Egypt, an Italian dealer in Egyptian antiquities called Bernardino Drovetti, who informed him that the French King, Charles X, was a great lover of animals: his particular passion was rebuilding the royal menagerie.

Ali determined to send to each of the British and French courts a living giraffe. *Tall Horse* follows the journey of the French giraffe, which was organised by Drovetti. Live giraffes had not been seen in Europe since the time of the Romans, and the transportation of the animal posed a number of problems. Not least of these was the capture. Adult giraffes will die if removed from their accustomed habitat, and mother giraffes will fight to the death to protect their calves – the kick of a giraffe can kill a lion. In Khephra Burns's script, Drovetti sends Atir, one of his most trusted slaves, to supervise the hunting and capture of the giraffes in the Sudan and to conduct the two calves up the Nile by boat. The healthier of the two giraffes forms an attachment to Atir and refuses to be fed by anyone else. And so Atir is forced to accompany the giraffe from Alexandria across to Marseilles, and beyond into the heart of France. The real Atir stayed in Paris until he died.

Tall Horse roots the story in the present, in a museum in Mali, where an arrogant young black Frenchman has come to research his ancestor, Atir. As the scientist Dr Konate begins to show him exhibits that tell the giraffe's history, the student, Jean-Michel, is dragged into the story in place of Atir. The African sculptures and artefacts of the museum are animated by the museum's assistants to create the characters of the story – so the whole story is played out within the museum. King Charles and his Queen Marie-Thérèse, for example, are presented by traditional Malian royalty puppets – the king as a hunter (Charles did spend a lot of his time hunting) and the Queen as an enormous, towering figure as tall as the giraffe, carried on the back of a cow *castelet*. Only four characters are played by actors: Jean-Michel and Atir (by the same actor), and, in a similar pairing, the actor playing Dr Konate reappears as the eminent French naturalist Étienne Geoffroy St-Hilaire. It was St-Hilaire who was entrusted with conducting the giraffe from Marseilles to Paris. He and Atir evolve a mutually distrustful relationship along the journey that eventually develops into respect as they approach Paris and the end of the journey.

The finale is the presentation of the animal to the King. Atir has learnt to love the giraffe, which had previously seemed to him to be a burden, and despite his enormous financial reward, he chooses to stay in France.

The giraffe was a popular sensation all over France, the more so for its epic walk from coast to capital, and the script (and the collaborators) see it as the beginning of an influx of African culture into Europe. 'The negrophilia that gripped Paris in the first three decades of the twentieth century,' says Basil Jones, 'saw Africa and things African as an essential element in the development of Modernism. Africa, through Jazz, Cubism and dance (influenced by traditional African steps), became synonymous in the minds of many leading artists with sophistication, sexuality and liberation…we've had decades and decades of Africa being the basket-case of the world. And it's entirely justified in some senses. But this seemed something very positive, and yet not didactic; just a positive phenomenon, something coming out of Africa. And also the idea of a diplomatic initiative coming out of Africa.' There is a story that the young Gustave Eiffel saw the giraffe as a child and was inspired by it to create his four-legged, long-necked, grid-patterned tower.

For Koffi Kôkô, the scientific and political culture of the time is as important as the artistic culture: 'Now, the story is a relationship between human beings around an animal. And at this time, this was something very incredible, because it's as if today, they tell you that in the forest of Amazonia they have found one man who is totally green and is living in the rainforest – and people try to capture him, and to bring him to New York or to London, or Paris, to show. To show him as a specimen of [a type of] human being that we have never known before.' The giraffe is a gift; the giraffe is an African; the giraffe is an animal; the giraffe is a curiosity; the giraffe is a character.

Part of the attraction to Handspring, of course, was that the story revolves around this character. What other company could make a giraffe that could stand over the stage with such elegance and express such subtle thoughts? It's also an African story. And it's a more ambitious project than any Handspring have undertaken before. The company have been acclaimed across the world for the quality of their work, and this project offers an opportunity, not only to connect with a fundamental exponent of their practice in Yaya, but to do so in a grand spectacle capable of reaching an even wider audience. For Sogolon this collaboration seems to offer a wider platform to show Yaya's skills and the potency of the traditional Bamana style of puppet. Yaya often speaks of how important the cultural contact is, and is wryly conscious of the relativism of values: here in South Africa he is mainly happy to be led; but it's easy to see that he often feels that the way things are done here, in this more 'Western' theatre structure, is simply an alternative to, and not necessarily an improvement on, the way he would organise a rehearsal and performance in Bamako. He sees that this could be the beginning of a series of collaborations.

At times Yaya seems to have a *laissez-faire* approach, possibly rooted in his focus on the potential for development over future collaborations, that can infuriate his collaborators. Marthinus tells me at the very beginning of the rehearsal process how pleased he is to have Yaya there, a responsible, articulate spokesperson for the culture and heritage he's brought to the collaboration. Basson is modest about his own abilities and background: he sees his strengths in the making of theatre, and it seems occasionally as if he considers his status as a white South African directing a story about 'African-ness' as leaving him in an awkward position. He said to me that he hoped Yaya would keep an eye on this and on how the Malian traditional work was treated in the show.

Yaya is clearly proud of his company, their achievements and the tradition. So it's surprising sometimes that on most occasions that he's asked, 'Is it OK if we do this?' his response is a beneficent shrug and a *'Oui, pas de problème'*. Perhaps it really is OK. Perhaps he wants to see how big a mess the non-Malians can get into before offering to dig them out. It's possible that he is approaching this collaboration with a completely open spirit – 'This is the tradition and material I bring: but what happens to it here isn't sacred.' And since Yaya tends to keep his counsel and loves to keep people guessing, no one can ever get a straight answer out of him

Yaya Coulibaly with King Charles X; Téhibou Bagayoko and Yacouba Magassouba as hyenas

about this. I tried to press the question on him before I left: he would do no more than say he had a few things he was looking forward to discussing with Marthinus after the last performance. I bet he hasn't had that discussion yet.

Alicia Adams's intention seems to have been to bring together exponents of the best in African performance: one company that speaks about an Africa in touch with the art that has existed on the continent for centuries, and one which shows an Africa absorbing and adapting cultures and traditions from across the world, and then exporting them in a mode that is also African art. And for both, this collaboration implies a departure from their usual style. For Sogolon, the physical objects (masks, puppets, *castelets*) will be used in a completely different performance context. Handspring's shows have got progressively larger since the focused, studio theatre-sized *Woyzeck on the Highveld – The Chimp Project* and *Confessions of Zeno* played in quite large auditoria – but *Tall Horse* suggests a different sort of relationship with the audience even from those – a more spectacular piece. Perhaps the inclusion of the Malian puppets will require the performance to be more in tune with the energetic outdoor festivities through which this style has developed. Adrian and Basil are also excited about the prospect of working with Koffi Kôkô. Kôkô is many things: an animist priest in Benin, an actor in Paris, the artistic director of the prestigious In Transit festival in Berlin, a dancer and choreographer known across the world. His work is wordless and fundamental dance, distant from the narrative tradition of Handspring's puppet theatre. He deals in a physical and visual language of breaths, slowness, internal rhythms and extraordinary feats of muscular control. Videos of his work that we see feature dancers climbing up and balancing on the top of three-metre, vertical bamboo poles with absolute precision; toned, tight bodies held in what seem to be impossible conjunctions; and at the centre of them Kôkô himself, every muscle held in balance as he moves with incredibly precise, utterly compelling movements. It's the kind of performance whose meaning or content can't be easily summarised, but which is so detailed and sure that it sends the mind firing off with associations and thoughts. Can this be compatible with a story? Kôkô seems enthused by the possibility of working with puppets in the abstract, but although he is one of the originators of the project, there are no clues in the script as to where his contribution will come in. More troublingly, a prior commitment in Europe means that he will miss three weeks of the rehearsals. His first visit will last just under a week, and he will return later in the process to pick up and continue.

Theatre companies are like most teams: however good a certain combination might look on paper, success relies on a free connection of trust and enthusiasm between the people within them. Whenever people are asked to work together for the first time, there's a bit of guesswork involved. As they did here, the new team might engage in a workshop together, exchanging ideas and showing each other the way they work to see if they're compatible. In this case, the stakes were high for both of the main companies. And if the Kennedy Center was to invest heavily in this project – a project which involved bringing together companies from different parts of another continent and organising for them to create a new language capable of playing to audiences all around the world – then the team had to be right. Over the first couple of years of the project's development, this team changed. Initially, the creative team that Alicia Adams drew up included an American composer and designer, and a South African writer and director. Personnel dropped in and out. Many were US-based since this was where the production was expected to take place. Others were Africans based in various countries around the world. Some suggested artists weren't going to work well with the existing team. Others, initially interested, found that they didn't engage with the material strongly enough to make it the right project for them. And even when the team did seem right, it wasn't a simple matter to get together to do some work, as Basil Jones recalls: 'When we had both a writer and a composer sitting in New York, and a costume designer sitting in Cameroon in jail, and the possibility of a writer based in London…it all seemed like trying to control something with five thousand long prosthetic arms.'

But somehow, development of the ideas and story did take place, and as the team evolved, so did the ideas, scale and focus of the story. At the core throughout were Basil and Adrian, Yaya and Koffi Kôkô. A defining moment in the development was one of Adrian and Basil's trips to Mali. Adrian Kohler recalls how they were just getting to know Yaya. 'He became our host on this journey round Mali and it was just fabulous, he was introducing the country to us. He hardly ever gets angry, you know? He's very refined as an individual, he keeps his emotions in check, and protocol and diplomacy are very much part of his demeanour. When I walked around Bamako, I know he is a person of some stature there, and that's a role he fits very well.'

But Kohler saw another side of Yaya during the trip too. 'On this trip, this first trip, the South Africans didn't have his sense of humour then, but he was saying that he was… The Kennedy Center people had paid for this whole trip, and halfway through he was saying he was awfully sorry, but the next day he had to catch a plane to Zimbabwe. [Laughs.] Terribly sorry, but he had to be leaving. And quite a number of people took him seriously and couldn't understand, what…is…this…? And we would be in the middle of the Niger river, somewhere… [Laughs.]' In rehearsals too, all of the Malians were big fans of the running joke. It offers great value when interacting in a foreign language: you only have to learn the one joke, and it works every day. So Yaya's trips to Zimbabwe kept coming. 'Are you coming for lunch, Yaya?' 'No, I cannot. And I will not be at rehearsal tomorrow. I have an appointment, a plane, to go and see my good friend Robert Mugabe.' And he would be totally straight-faced for a moment, and then chuckle. Somehow, even when you knew what was coming, it was always funny. Yaya is a big-hearted man who likes to smile, and make other people smile, and his company follow him in this. The trip to Mali gave Adrian and Basil a chance to see both sides of Yaya on his own territory, as an approachable humorist and as the custodian of an extraordinary puppet collection.

By the time *Tall Horse* reaches rehearsal it has a composer and director, Warrick Sony and Marthinus Basson, from South Africa, and the writer is from America – Khephra Burns. Burns hasn't been the only writer on the project and his script includes images, moments and whole scenes and sequences that were conceived by others. One of the major questions of the process will be whether it all coheres.

Perhaps the single most important event in the history of *Tall Horse* happened long before I arrived to take notes. *Tall Horse* lost Alicia Adams and the Kennedy Center.

Basil Jones and Adrian Kohler
Photograph by Enrico Wey

The game of arts funding is a guessing game: it's not so much whether you can jump through the hoops, but whether you've chosen the right hoop for the year, who else is jumping through the same or other hoops, and whether you're told afterwards that although your hoop-jumping was second-to-none, hoop-jumping is not after all the principal criterion for selection. And so, despite years of preparatory work, including international visits and workshops, creative discussions and work locating secondary sponsors (the South African mining company AngloGold Ashanti), Alicia Adams's application on behalf of the giraffe project didn't receive the funding that would allow it to fulfil her vision.

Basil Jones describes the arrival of the news. On tour in Europe, in the winter of 2002, it was the most dispiriting news possible. All their work and planning; all the excitement and enthusiasm; all the emotional investment in meeting and dreaming with Yaya Coulibaly and Koffi Kôkô, two of the great creative men of West Africa; all the ongoing challenge of finding just the right team – all of it, it seemed, had hung on this one single decision. And somehow, the funding had gone elsewhere. They realised that this project might never happen. It's the darkest of the dark times that Basil looks back on.

'We were very low,' he says. So low that he couldn't bring himself to make the calls to the supporting sponsors he had brokered at AngloGold Ashanti. Alicia Adams recalls the meeting that had secured the support from AngloGold Ashanti – a presentation at Basil and Adrian's house to Bobby Godsell and Steve Lenahan: 'They were exuberant about the work.' And so it was that Basil, in Belgium, got a call from them. '"We hear you lost your funding," they said. "But you are still going to do the show?" And I said: "Well, I don't think we can do the show."' And so it came about that AngloGold Ashanti agreed to become the principal sponsors and supporters of *Tall Horse*. It meant scaling back. No longer would it be a Broadway-sized undertaking with a huge cast of actors, dancers and puppeteers. Now the

We've been through very hard times with this project. And very dark times when it seemed totally impossible. I feel now that it's much more within the bounds of possibility. Now, it's much more... you know, it's easier to control. But it's still terribly difficult. We've got fourteen different types of puppet, and people that are not used to them. And a director that likes [stage] business... It seems like a thousand layers. But we have to get there.

Basil Jones

cast size would be more like twelve; the scenery would have to be one flexible set rather than a three-ring circus of spectacular transformations; an aesthetic closer to Handspring's previous work. Crucially, the change meant that Basil Jones would be producing the whole show himself from Handspring's office in Kalk Bay. But most importantly, it meant that the idea survived.

Tall Horse is a good thing for AngloGold Ashanti. The company is a huge multi-national, but is based in South Africa and has mines in Mali (as well as many other countries). It was this international link that first and most enthused them. For AngloGold Ashanti, the meeting of these cultures on an equal footing apparently symbolises some of what they hope to advance with their social development work. Basil is consistently full of praise for the way AngloGold have worked with Handspring to create the show. As the producer, it's often his job to reflect on those who have made it possible, and he always refers to how they have been 'the ideal funders': they have left the company complete creative control. From time to time executives and representatives from AngloGold Ashanti come to visit the rehearsals – and part of the purpose of the February workshop was to show them the progress. They are always curious, fascinated, supportive, and considerate. Some come from a different world from the performers they're watching; millionaires looking at artists who live very modestly indeed. But if there's resentment between the camps, I never see any of it. The mining magnates are always full of respect for the performers and artists. And without the sponsor, this opportunity wouldn't exist.

With a new, smaller *Tall Horse* in prospect, Jones set about contacting the collaborators to find out if they were still interested. All of them were. Khephra Burns scorns the idea that he would have been put off by the scaling back of the budget. Something of the commitment to the idea exhibited by the collaborators at this moment has served to bind them closer together for the preparations and work that followed. Yaya speaks fondly of his discussions with Khephra on the script and about the authenticity of the West African flavours: 'He asked me many questions. I think that definitely gave Khephra a clear route. But I didn't sit down and write anything; I responded to his questions. Khephra was the researcher… and I was the museum.'

Marthinus Basson has been involved with the collaboration for about eighteen months when we start rehearsals. He's a big figure in South African theatre. 'Marthinus has a kind of reputation, as a sort of, in his younger days, an *enfant terrible* of Cape Town theatre,' Basil explains to me. 'It was…buckets of blood on stage and a good deal of, well, sexuality. And, ja, he's always been someone who's interested us.' From others I find out that Basson's reputation is built on exquisitely judged new work and on classics staged with verve, wit and immediacy. Buckets of blood may well have been involved – he is certainly ready with anecdotes that relish an impressive *coup de théâtre*.

But what does it mean, this collaboration? The question hangs over the making of the show. What is the aim? To make a show that sells tickets? To effect cultural exchange between Handspring, Sogolon and Koffi Kôkô? Is the intention to create something unique that draws on both styles, or is it to serve and preserve both styles within one portmanteau project? There are certain aspects of puppet manipulation that Adrian Kohler and Basil Jones regard as points of principle: will these principles be open to adaptation, as Yaya's traditional style is? A question is asked several times in rehearsals: are we trying to create something authentically African? Are we trying to avoid or to embrace 'heritage theatre'? And will this adaptation compromise and dilute the strength of the individual, successful techniques?

I suspect that each of the main collaborators has a slightly different idea of the answers to the key questions. It might be impossible for them all to agree. The starting point for a lot of these discussions is the inescapable fact that the puppets, basically, look different. 'When the collaboration was proposed, between Sogolon and Handspring, I thought, well, how do we mix our styles?' says Kohler. 'What I've been making are fairly naturalistic, carved figures, and Yaya's are not.

A drawing by Adrian Kohler of puppets in Yaya Coulibaly's collection

They're very stylised, and they're very within the African canon of sculpture. Of traditional sculpture, not modern.'

For Adrian and Yaya, this question was fundamental. They had to decide who would make which character, and what they would look like. Adrian still has his initial character sketch for the Queen of France. She couldn't look more different from the Queen of France that Yaya eventually made. Adrian's drawing is a caricature of a spoilt European monarch – a pampered, fat white woman in a powder-puff dress. With this puppet, the political force of Marie-Thérèse would have been an iron fist in a lace pouffe. Coulibaly's puppet of the Queen, taken from the Malian tradition, is an arresting prospect for her pure, commanding power. She's a giant figure that dominates the stage, almost as tall as the giraffe itself, with a terrifying face that looms down: shotgun-barrel eyes either side of a nose like an axe. The difference in styles seems to make the choice of carver in each instance a crucial dramatic decision. The story contains African characters and European characters: would it make sense to make each group in a different style? Adrian went back to Mali to decide this with Yaya.

'Adrian came to Bamako, to look at the puppets,' recalls Yaya. 'Adrian photographed the puppets. He did drawings of them, to find which puppets might have reflections in the production. The idea of these puppets is from Mali, but [made with] the techniques of Adrian. I have traditional puppets, that's important, I have a traditional way of making them, and he has his own too.' At this stage the project was still being run through Washington DC. Adrian identified heads of puppets in Yaya's collection that could serve as inspiration for his own carving work or for new puppets to be made by Yaya. This visit proved to be crucial to the creative relationship between the two men, as Adrian's account confirms:

> Whenever I had anxieties about perhaps if I was going to make Clothilde a full-on Handspring-type *bunraku* figure... how is that going to mesh? And how did he [Yaya] feel about it...? I remember sitting in Bamako on my second visit there, e-mailing America every day, trying to get an answer about how I negotiate this thing. And they weren't reading the e-mail, or they were out of town, or something, and so eventually I just spoke with Yaya. Which seems to be the obvious thing to do in retrospect, but I was incredibly anxious about the nature of the collaboration. I didn't think it was his call whether to accept or not, I felt that I wanted to have a clear picture of what the Americans had in mind in terms of the collaboration. But when I spoke with Yaya, he wasn't anxious about that at all.

They reflected on the discussions about how the story might be framed, as told by an African company with the puppets they have. 'To begin by designing the European characters in the story as seen from Africa, that helped a lot...with bringing the two styles together. Imagining that they could function together.' Adrian found Yaya wasn't possessive or territorial about which puppet was made in which style. For him it already was a mixture of the two styles. Adrian had been speculating about the most appropriate puppet design for each character: if Clothilde will have to fall in love with Atir, wouldn't it be useful for her to be able to turn her head and soften her wrists? But Yaya had a confidence that all of the puppet types could be able to take on all of the roles, and so the division could be more or less arbitrary. Which is what Adrian resolved to do. 'And so what I did with the cast list, I didn't do a complete random split, but I went down the list and I said, "OK, you, me, you, me, you, me..." and the King and the Queen came out like that, as Sogolon. And I didn't know how they were going to be visualised.' Adrian and Yaya are such fast friends by the time I arrive, and both men are so open and approachable, that it's difficult to imagine the apprehensive Adrian who found it hard to speak to Yaya in Bamako. But at that point Adrian's French was very limited. For these two men to communicate at all was difficult; and while it's pleasantly romantic to imagine, like Yaya's father, that these two artists would instinctively find some way of understanding each other, it was necessary for them to make some key artistic choices that would have a decisive impact on the development of the piece.

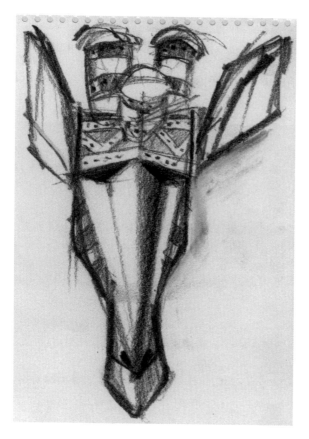

Sketch by Adrian Kohler for the head of the giraffe puppet

Even after the character roster had been split up between the two puppet makers, there was the question of how the designs would look together. Adrian offered up a series of his sketches, including a contemporary portrait of Drovetti showing his full whiskers and a sketch of an old woman in the crowd in Marseilles, based on one of Yaya's puppets. Kohler's sketches are just that – sketches – not hugely detailed, but a guide to or a sense of what the puppet's face will be defined by. But Yaya Coulibaly doesn't draw his designs at all. He simply sits, with a set of adzes and a knife, and carves the figure from the wood, stroking slivers off the timber until the face stands out. I suppose he has a picture of the character in his head, and I suppose it alters if the adze uncovers a rotten seam in the timber. It might explain why there is such a freedom to his carving and why, although the two male Soirée guests might at first glance seem to be taken from exactly the same design, they can soon be distinguished quite easily. Adrian's puppets are made from wood, but Yaya's are cut from a tree.

Looking at one of Kohler's pieces from Handspring's previous work, you're struck by how complex the play of shadows across the face is – his signature style leaves you in no doubt that these faces have been made with a chisel – but what's marvellous is how soft and rounded the figure feels, despite the many hundreds of tiny facets and gouges that actually make it up. Yaya's puppets are much smoother, with fewer but more decisive details in the design – a strong brow and a sharp, defined nose. While Kohler's puppets might get their effect from a bulging cheek, an irregularity in the line of the brow or a twist in the smile, the Malian puppets manage to be more decisive about the character – one might have a very definitely jutting chin – but still retain an ambiguity.

As the Malian puppets are explored in the workshops, we see the power of the carving. It's very clear how the simplicity of design, the smoothness of the faces and the neutral expressions are the fruit of so many years of development of design; an elegant and effective piece of abstraction. Even though it's a principle of manipulating Kohler's puppets not to let them 'die' by stopping the breath, these *merens*, held in tension, command the viewer's focus without the puppet moving.

The fierce queen seems at first an exception to the carefully ambiguous neutrality that helps to give these faces their power. But despite her probing eyes, she too is smiling. The more you look, the more subtle signals they give out – and the more fascinating they become.

It is a circumstance unique to puppet theatre that the characters are created in advance of rehearsals. And while an actor's face is flexible, the expression on a puppet's face is fixed. If it doesn't seem right for the character in rehearsals, the puppet either has to be remade – not always possible – or the character acquires a new quality and dimension. 'And that was the scariest part, I guess, of the thing,' remembers Kohler. 'Because he went away and did them, that was the end of last year [2003]. And I wasn't at all sure that…the kind of briefing session, the discussion session, had been mutually understood.' Kohler couldn't really be sure what Yaya would come back with from the other end of the continent for the February workshop. Under ordinary circumstances, he would have worked with other carvers in the same workshop. Meanwhile, Coulibaly would have been wondering how his sculptures would be received.

Adrian has been very keen to engage further with the sculptural legacy of West Africa in this piece. In racially-charged South Africa, one of the most wonderful features of his unpainted wooden puppets was that there was no question about the colour of their skin. Kohler has found a way of carving a face that makes its racial characteristics indeterminate, or at least secondary to its basic human character. The level of abstraction that the Bamana sculptors have achieved has a similar effect. These faces simply evoke the essence of a human; and after sketching and analysing so many of them in his research trips to Mali, Kohler invites their influence into the characters he will make. Some of his puppets are explicitly based on heads in Yaya's collection. Others use a particular Bamana way of shaping a beard or an eyeline, and Adrian allows himself to expand the character outwards from there.

As he indicates whenever he discusses the engineering inside his figures, Kohler has a jackdaw's eye for inspirations, and when leafing through Handspring's extensive collection of books on African sculpture, he lights upon other faces that he wants to incorporate. The Prefect of Marseilles, renamed Count Grandeville de Largemont in case he has any litigious descendants, has a wide-eyed, curious face that is not only ideal for his status as a cuckolded bureaucrat, but is also based on a Nok figure – one of the continent's most ancient styles. Taking these influences from West Africa and specifically from the Coulibaly collection has opened up Kohler's style, and many of the puppets for *Tall Horse* are noticeably more stylised than those for other Handspring productions.

There's an enormous cast list. Kohler's imagination always suggests another puppet as a solution to each new character, and consequently he has ended up with many, many figures to make, some of which will have only the briefest of appearances. What's more, he has his eyes on new challenges. Some of these figures will involve untried variations on his normal design – and it's hard to schedule time for the unknown. 'You can't know exactly how long it's going to take. I don't know how long a giraffe neck takes to make when I plan it,' he puzzles. All that can be accepted is that he will work morning, noon and night until everything is finished – and even as rehearsals are under way, there is still work to do. Yaya hasn't been given this opportunity – he's far away from his workshop. But while he has the ability to do so, Adrian will continue to improve, tweak and develop his designs.

Notes

1. I am indebted in this section to the research of Janni Donald, who worked with Yaya to select and document puppets, masks and ritual figures from his collection for Patrimony, an exhibition which accompanied *Tall Horse* at museums in Stellenbosch, Cape Town and Johannesburg before a longer stay in AngloGold Ashanti's 'Gold of Africa Museum' in Cape Town in 2005.

2. Georges Balandier, Jacques Maquet (eds) *Dictionary of Black African Civilization* (Leon Amiel, 1974).

3. Mary Jo Arnoldi *Playing With Time: Art and Performance in Central Mali* (University of Indiana Press, 1995).

4. Janni Donald 'Sogo: Puppets and Ritual Objects in Bamana Culture', in the brochure for the Patrimony exhibition.

5. Arnoldi, p.149.

6. Arnoldi, p.134.

THE COMPANY HAS FIVE AND A HALF
weeks' rehearsal before there will be an opportunity to
show some of what has been made to a public audience
here – with a final week to rework it before the première
in the larger Baxter Theatre in Cape Town.

Koffi Kôkô's time is limited. The choreographer from
Benin has been involved with *Tall Horse* from the beginning,
but other commitments mean he will leave rehearsals after the first week and not
return till week four. Worse still, flight irregularities mean he doesn't arrive in
Stellenbosch until Wednesday afternoon. So his work with the company now has
acquired an extra significance. It will also constitute the greatest leap of technique
for most of the performers. Few have experience as dancers, and few dancers have
the sort of experience that would prepare them for Kôkô's focused asceticism.
Not only is the rehearsal script narrative-heavy, but Khephra Burns's style is full of
rapid-fire verbal arabesques. The text is a world away from what happens when
Koffi moves. As if there wasn't enough of a challenge marrying the two styles of
puppets, there's also this potential mismatch of theatrical languages.

A bit later in the rehearsals we all watched a video of some of Koffi's work. The
movement stunned the company with a mood and rhythm independent of the
music and drumming. In fact, it wasn't clear whether the music was intended to
work with the dance or independently of it. I asked him whether the music or the
dance came first, or whether they came in combination or developed alongside
each other. He smiled. 'The dance comes first. Always.' This wouldn't be a system
based on marking time.

'We need to go with the music or go in paradox with the music,' suggests
Koffi on hearing Warrick Sony's pieces for the first time when he arrives. 'If we
go with it, I think it will not be very interesting. But if we go in opposition to the
music, then I think it can be quite shocking. People will hear the music and also
see what we are doing.' He proposes a shorthand structure for how he will relate
to the music: 'I remember three colours: the Savannah; the tension between the
giraffe and Atir; and Versailles. From there we can start something.' Throughout
rehearsals, Kôkô pursued and retained this simple structure. While the text was
throwing up complex associations and demanding a range of rhythms, the dance
was able to balance these three fundamental elements: the openness and wildness

of Africa, the grandeur of Paris, and the relationship that is our constant in the journey between them. In a story that often became wildly confusing, Basson and Burns would have loved to be able to reduce their considerations to something this clear.

But the relationship between the music and text is far in the future as Koffi begins to work with the company for the first time. Like Adrian and Yaya introducing the puppets, he needs to start with the mechanics of his system. He reiterates some principles he had introduced at the first workshop. The vertical axis of the body runs directly upwards from the ground, between the legs. The energy that the body uses in dance is drawn up from the earth with every in-breath and returned to it with every exhalation. Kôkô works very slowly. Patience and calm control from the performer is of great importance, even when they are performing quick, sudden and dynamic movement. The group, excitable about engaging with him, need to be calmed and centred. So he asks that they stand. 'Listen for the silence inside you. Listen, as if no one is around you.' So they stand, and breathe. For quite a long time.

'This is the first stage.'

Kôkô's work is in fact very technical, and perhaps it's because of this, or perhaps it's because of his other life as an animist priest, that his approach to it – and his rhetoric – is spiritual and psychological. He does invite the performer to build a personality cult around Koffi Kôkô, and the vocabulary and rhythm of his training tend towards the semi-mystical. It rankles slightly with those from the modern, Western way of theatre-making, which has had to work hard to justify itself as a profession and a craft, rather than as a way of life or a spiritual quest. That tradition has fed into the South Africans' training and attitudes via the influence of and contact with Europe and America. The South Africans aren't necessarily any more technical than the West Africans in the company, but they don't always feel as comfortable with this approach to learning technique. I think Koffi is used to working with people from different backgrounds like this. He makes sure that he is clear about the purpose of each movement and exercise, and precise about which parts of the body are keeping still (usually most of them) and which are moving (often with great slowness). He works through more principles. The performers bring up the energy from the earth with a movement of the arms and return it with another, downward one. Koffi introduces the concept of a 'circle of potential' around the body – the places that the body can reach. Slowly, slowly. Slowly enough that you can hear the sceptical tongues being bitten. And then, suddenly, he wins over the impatient students by showing a startling conversion of his tension and slowness into speed and precision. As quick as breathing, and with no apparent effort, he drops to the floor, landing on his toes and fingers, perfectly parallel with the ground and only inches from it. Just as quickly, he flips to land on his back, and then seems somehow to have moved smoothly to standing, without any awkward 'getting up' stage intervening. It's a showman's technique but there's a perceptible gasp from the company.

What Koffi's presence offers is the hope that the company can pick this up: the ability to shift between levels of energy. From pregnant, held tension, to swift, fluid muscularity, while retaining a constant poise and rhythm. It's part of what makes Koffi so watchable and so magnetic in a room. He knows from experience how dynamic this restrained poise is. It's not how he moves, but how aware you are as an observer that he has the potential to do anything. Koffi goes through the fast movement for the group to follow: 'You don't make a noise. Silence. You decide. The body does not fall down. The body goes with the hands and feet to trap the earth.'

Standing again, he reflects. 'Never let the energy go…if you are in *répose*, you are asleep.'

As the actors attempt the sequence, he knows where the first mistake will come – not retaining energy and tension on the first drop to the horizontal position. 'The thing is, when you arrive like this,' he says, dropping but this time letting his belly sag to the ground, 'you can do nothing.' He lifts his full body into tension, touching the floor only with fingertips and toes. 'But when you arrive like *this*…' …and he flips almost casually onto his back.

This exercise instantly releases some of the tension of the younger actors and builds a bridge between the groups: Téhibou, the youngster from Mali, and Fezile, the celebrity from SA, are equally keen to be the first to match this movement – and they don't need language to enjoy each other's progress.

This little dynamic demonstration was a well-timed intervention, and the company are ready to take in more first principles. Kôkô wants to talk about walking. His approach aims to underpin everything that the performers do on stage. Again the energy is carried in the torso, between the hips and the chest; the power at the solar plexus. Koffi demonstrates that with the energy carried at this centre of gravity, he is harder to overbalance – the company try walking and then being stopped. The exercise develops into one where two performers are moving towards one another when one leaps and is caught by the other – with no loss of balance. It's another moment of release as apprehensive performers find themselves surprised by their own stability.

'You carry your weight with you. Don't think it's your feet that are going to do something. It's your centre that is *agile*. You walk with your *densité*.' Koffi's

Koffi Kôkô, leading his 'expanding arms' exercise

teaching comes right from the very basics and it leads the performers into an area where they are exploring a new vocabulary for their expressiveness on stage. It's an introduction to a style of performance which would take a long time to understand completely. I sense that not all of the company are comfortable. They might have expected a little choreographic warm-up, but this seems a long way removed from the task in hand of rehearsing the epic. The little scepticism from before the dramatic dropping move early in the day returns; this set of basic exercises seems endless.

The next is about expressiveness. The actor begins at the back of the stage with his hands together at the solar plexus. As (s)he walks slowly forward towards the audience, the arms open very slowly until, just as they are about to fall off the front of the stage, the body is completely open, energised and aimed at the audience. Like the puppetry exercises, it seems like nothing at first; and it's only with repetition and the personal engagement of the performers that it comes to fruition. At the back of the stage, hands clenched, they are anonymous. As their arms open and their chest and body open with them, they demand more space, more attention. By the time they are open, if they've really 'opened up', they are impossible to ignore. The exercise teaches the performer to control how dominant they are on stage. But some of the performers are reluctant to commit to it. It's only after many repetitions, with Kôkô always watching for falseness or self-consciousness, that the exercise expands to include the face – from a neutral expression upstage, to an extraordinary exaggerated grimace at the end of the walk. 'Do not prepare,' says Koffi when he sees that the actors are deciding in advance what emotion or expression their face will take. 'Remember the silence inside. Let the thing be born inside.'

Many of the group commit fully to the exercises and are surprised by what they find in themselves. No one refuses to do anything, but there's a cursoriness to some of their attempts, and an edge of mockery to some others. Sometimes Yaya contrives to sit out of an exercise or miss his turn; but there is a trust in, or respect for, Koffi. At first Marthinus watches, but he decides to let Koffi have the space to do his work and leaves to do his own privately – although it's surprising that he doesn't want to see how Koffi's develops.

While Koffi is redefining their presence on stage, the puppeteers must also get used to the puppets. Kohler later observes that puppetry skill is part instinct, part practice: 'Yaya and us, we can pick up any [one], his puppets or our puppets, and once he's got round the difference in technique, he knows what to do with a puppet.' But initially it takes some concentration to get one's hand used to the control inside a Handspring puppet. The thumb and one finger (usually the index) are being used to rotate the head rod; a second finger is slipped through a ring, attached to a string control that adjusts the angle of the head for nodding or looking up or down; and the remaining two fingers grip the handle that supports the weight of the body. These puppets work with two operators. Because one hand is occupied with working the head and the body, the primary puppeteer can only operate one of the puppet's arms. The secondary puppeteer manipulates just one arm – whichever is spare. It demands a lot of restraint and sensitivity to pick up on the first puppeteer's rhythms and intentions. For most of the time they are on stage, the secondary manipulator will work hard to achieve the impression of doing almost nothing.

With the Malian puppets, the first challenge is to find a way to support their weight. All of the puppeteer's body is involved in giving expression to the puppet from where he holds it at its waist. The relationship between the arms and the body offers greater variation. The Malian rod controls are big, chunky, and unapologetically present – a stout length of timber lashed to the wrist of the puppet, with varying degrees of tightness. The basic system, one hand at the waist and the free hand working the arms, is the same as the Handspring design. In fact, some of Kohler's puppets for *Tall Horse* have similar arm controls to the Malian puppets. With his, though, the puppeteers are handling slim metal rods, with a loop at one end bolted loosely (and free to swivel) against the palm of the puppet's hand; at the other end is a short piece of knurled wooden dowel. Typically, the manipulator of the Handspring variant would hold both rods in one hand, flexing them across each other to create a range of attitudes. The difference in design leads to a difference in performance style: with a Handspring puppet, only very occasionally would one rod be dropped. With the larger rods on the Malian puppet, you'd need big hands to hold both rods at once. When one of the Sogolon puppeteers handles one of the puppets, the style of performance is direct, the gestures of the hands representative rather than closely-observed imitation. Very often only one rod is held.

The puppeteers are fairly free to find their own style of expression with their puppets. They will need to keep searching for better ways of expressing each moment with the puppet and of developing more skill with the unique controls of each figure until the final performance. Occasionally someone does teach one of these old puppets a new trick, but in the main, the puppeteers learn to find the strengths of the different designs. It's not always an elegant process, and of course there's puppetry happening in rehearsals that no one would be happy to see on stage. But Adrian knows that this is the way that people must learn, tiring though it is. You can see how frustrating it is for him, knowing the puppets so well, to watch his performers struggle with them. 'The first week,' he says, 'was full of anxiety of getting puppets actually up and running, trying to make sense of where it all is on the stage, and it felt like a junkheap out of which we had to make something.'

But finding out what to do with a puppet takes time, and like Kôkô, Kohler has to start with the basics. 'Explore what it means for your figure to walk,' says Adrian. Each puppet, even those made by the same maker, is different. So, between the four Soirée guests that Yaya has made, there is variation: in their face of course, but also in the relative length of neck to body, the angle of their eyes, the way their elbows are tied, the way the control rods are attached to the wrists. To bring out the most of these qualities, the puppets need to be manipulated differently. But they also need to create a unity of logic on stage, a coherence about how they are worked. The simpler the joints of the puppet, the greater its range of movement (in the right hands). And even though the figure has no mechanical flexibility – these puppets are a single upright stick from waist to head – the movement of the puppet can still be gentle or fluid. Yaya is asked to instruct on the techniques. It's immediately apparent that Adrian and Yaya's teaching technique is similar: they invite the performers to try things, and they watch.

Just as each puppet has its own specific needs, each puppeteer has their own natural energy, which can coincide with, or stretch, the puppet's potential. So the movements and energy of the four similar Soirée guest puppets can range from arch camp – in the case of the scene-stealing lady operated by Craig Leo – to cartoonish buoyancy in the hands of Fourie Nyamande, or a more delicate, brooding crispness of movement in the hands of Busi Zokufa. These three South African puppeteers are faced with the challenge of finding a way of operating a type of puppet they've never experienced before, and all have expressed doubts about their ability to make these characters really breathe. Most of the manipulation training sessions consist of a simple request followed by experiment on the part of the operator, with guidance coming from the 'teacher'. Often, the puppet maker sees qualities displayed that he hadn't expected. Yaya is also keen to defer to Adrian as the main teacher of puppetry, perhaps because he knows that the eventual style of performance will be closer to Adrian's, perhaps because he wants to see what Adrian makes of his puppets. Adrian's sessions usually don't demand that the puppeteers handle only one type of puppet. They are treated as interchangeable: the beginning of the quest to, in Koffi's words, 'find the way where both styles of the puppets cannot be different.'

The Soirée puppets

In an exercise to develop pacing and clarity of movement, the puppets stand in a long line. At one end, a puppet whispers into the ear of the next. The 'Chinese whisper' is passed down the line. Each puppet needs to move and 'speak' (none of these faces have moving mouths), but the real key lies in the changes of rhythm, the stops, pauses and shifts of pace, that register with the watcher as a character hears something, responds, moves to the next puppet, whispers to it, and watches for its reaction. Each moment in the sequence is crucial if an audience is to understand the thought processes of the character, and each moment is interpreted differently by each combination of puppeteer and puppet.

The exercises are built around the execution of simple moves. 'Look up. Look down. Move one hand behind the puppet's back. Now breathe in that position.' The puppets process in a circle, twisting and turning, finding breaks in rhythm and different ways of walking; emphasizing the steps of the walk, or the movement of the hips, even where the puppets have neither legs nor hips to roll; turning, reaching out to each other and, finally, touching.

From all around the stage come a series of muted clunks as wooden hands make tentative contact with the wooden faces. Adrian doesn't like it. 'In my experience it's better not to touch. It doesn't have the same power. When the wood goes clunk, the magic goes.' Basil will express the same sentiment on a number of occasions. They talk about a zone near the surface of the puppet: the tenderness of touching the air around the other puppet is as sensitive as fingertips on skin. It's only in rare moments like this one that you find Basil and Adrian talking about 'magic' or being unable to explain practically how it is that the principles they use for manipulation actually work. Their puppets are deep-gouged with chisels in a style that emphasizes the wood as it shapes the contours of the face. Their manipulators are visible and unhooded. There are very few concessions

below and following pages: Some of thirteen pages of ideas for puppet systems proposed by Adrian Kohler during the development of *Tall Horse* in 2002

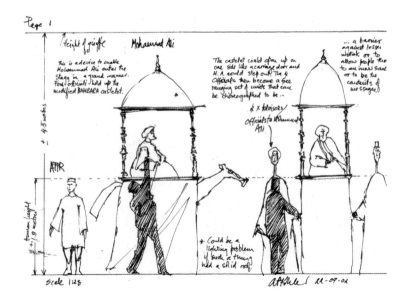

to illusion in the Handspring aesthetic, and its founders are usually pragmatic and sometimes even prosaic about their figures. There's no suggestion that the figures have any ritual or spiritual significance, and they function as tools of performance. But it seems that they guard this moment – of touching – defiantly. Their puppets do address moments of deeply felt, subtly expressed emotion, and these are often the times when the puppets 'touch'. The physical discipline of not touching might be what brings taut energy to the moment of contact.

In contrast, the Malian puppeteers have few qualms about the moment of contact. Perhaps it's because their style of story-telling doesn't emphasize these tiny moments of gentleness. But, as in the European glove puppet traditions, there's a thrill in the 'moment of clunk' – when the figure that you have started to believe has its own life reminds you audibly that it's wooden. In some ways, the double nature of the puppet (as simultaneously alive and dead) is necessarily more obvious in these elongated, abstracted Malian figures. The Handspring puppets, proportioned more accurately to the human figure, tease and invite the audience to filter out the manipulator. Some Malian figures, like the *meren habitable* and the *castelet*, almost completely hide the manipulator in the puppet, offering a similar invitation. But with these *marionnettes à tige* (rod puppets), the manipulator and the artificiality of the figure are essential parts of the stage image. And from what I've seen of the Malian puppeteers playing and laughing with the puppets, it seems natural to them to switch fluidly between the serious and the comical.

When Koffi Kôkô turns his attention to the puppets, his approach is different. First, each performer studies a puppet in detail as Koffi asks: 'What is the character of your puppet?' Looking occasionally at the prone, inanimate puppet, the performers begin to explore the character in their own bodies, and spend almost ten minutes performing to the puppet itself. There are lots of moments when the puppeteers will marvel at the simplicity, complexity or carving of one of the puppets, but this is the only time they are invited to meditate on the character in the carving. Perhaps it's because Adrian and Yaya are the sculptors of these characters that they don't ask the performers to study them in this way, either because of their modesty or their own familiarity with them.

The following afternoon sees the puppets moving around alongside actors. I'm struck by how liberating it is that most of them have no legs. The actors look earthbound next to the effortless progress of these torsos through the air. This might partially explain the success of Handspring's combination of actors and puppets: in good hands, the puppets manage to be at once more solid than the actors they work alongside, and also more mobile around the space. Many Malian puppets simply don't look like they should have legs; because they are already so stylised, there's no sense that something is missing. Koffi finds the movement without legs most interesting, but is aware that he might be covering ground that's well-known to the puppeteers – and he appeals to Yaya and Adrian for guidance. Both puppetry directors are curious to see Koffi's experiments continue, but where Koffi is so taken by the puppets' capacity for dynamic movement, Adrian

and Yaya gently demonstrate their power when stationary. This too is something of a surprise. Typically one would try to keep a puppet 'alive'. What these strongly-carved figures demonstrate is that often a puppet can remain 'alive' simply by being held with energy and tension.

Kôkô's perspective becomes a little clearer the next day when he talks to students at the University about his interest in the project. 'The basis of my work is that the energy comes from inside. When I start to dance, it is no longer me. I like to make [an] abnegation of the personality of Koffi Kôkô, and become the energy of the dance. Perhaps,' he speculates, 'the puppeteers do the same thing – the puppet completes what they want to say, and makes it more intense… Working with a puppet company excites me – I have never choreographed a puppet company. And now that we have started to work, I have seen dance in a different way. I started to dance like a puppet.' I don't know what he means, but it sounds good.

One thing that he has been exploring is the puppet's height off the ground. When working opposite humans on stage, a decision needs to be made as to where the puppets' 'floor level' is. Usually these puppets would be worked slightly above human height: a more comfortable position for the puppeteer, with better sightlines for the audience. But some of the puppets do have legs and work on the ground, or have skirts cut to a naturalistic length.

With Fezile and Bheki playing human characters with them, the base height will have to be close to a realistic 'human' level. Clothilde has settled on a fairly

natural height, only slightly off the ground – although it can vary, and Koffi sees early on a wonderful opportunity to break out of realism as Atir lifts her with a gentle finger right off the ground and into the air. It's the kind of move a dancer would love to be able to do – to become lighter than air with a thought – and that a puppet can do without difficulty. And it's an example of what this process is like at its best: the eye of the man who dreams the movement of people, applied to the movement of puppets, and vice versa.

Kôkô's approaches and inquiries open up inviting avenues but are rarely applied to the actual material. Marthinus Basson is wondering how to incorporate these ideas into his rehearsal schedule. Is it right to ask Koffi to start with a scene from the script so that progress can be made? 'How do you, in actual fact, without treading on toes,' he says, 'start incorporating all kinds of different elements in a very simple linear story that you're now trying to move from point A to point Z?' Perhaps the hardest part of Basson's job will be to avoid treading on toes. While Handspring are on home territory, and speak the same language as him, Sogolon and Koffi Kôkô both have a language barrier to conquer (Kôkô's English is workable but French is still his preferred language of expression), and all he knows of their work is what they are able to show him during this process. He hopes to bridge the gap between Koffi's relatively abstract dance and Khephra Burns's urbane script-writing by emphasizing what he calls 'the poetry' in the transitions. This, fortunately, is the area that puppets work in.

An example is the transition from Burns's scene between Mehmet Ali, Pasha of Egypt, and Bernardino Drovetti, the French Consul-General there, into the African savannah – a complete change of scene from palatial splendour to natural wildness. Marthinus and Adrian Kohler have been inspired by an image in one of Ali's speeches of a dung-beetle rolling a dung-ball, which the Pasha uses as a cynical metaphor for the activity of colonial administrations – making life from waste. They have contrived to design a giant Mehmet Ali, whose stomach is a large ball, which can be detached from the rest of the body. Marthinus edits the scene so that the speech about the dung-beetle comes at its end, and as he speaks it, a puppeteer rolls the ball from the stomach. The 'reality' of the scene is immediately fractured. As Mehmet Ali recedes into the distance, still speaking, the dung-ball (or is it the globe?) begins to roll about the stage, pursuing Drovetti, who flees, before engaging in a dance that Koffi Kôkô creates between the ball and a lion of the savannah. It's one of the most successful transitions in the show, and both Burns and Kôkô are happy to alter their original plans to allow for the fluent handover. It's a happy combination of the resources at Basson's disposal, although the connections are not always as comfortable as this.

A series of sessions is scheduled for work on the Savannah/Hunt sequence: an evocation of the sub-Saharan grasslands, punctured by the arrival of Atir and the hunters who have come to kill the mother giraffes and kidnap their calves. Koffi is expected to work from the structure that evolved in the workshop, but instead he rearranges all of the elements, forcing them into different – and sometimes counter-intuitive – relationships.

On the one hand, each element of the dance is exposed and held up for examination. On the other, a long time is spent developing a choreography that doesn't obviously express the story of the scene. As the week continues, more time is freed up for Koffi to work on the scene, to see how this process will resolve itself into a staging. And each time, Kôkô starts again from scratch, thoughtfully reorganising the passage of events, or spending time developing a moment of detail. He seems oblivious to the practical considerations of how long it might take the performers to get off stage in a Malian *castelet* and return on stilts, or whether the lions' presence should affect the behaviour of the *castelets* (which represent antelope and cattle). He likes the way that Craig Leo operates a *castelet* and keeps him in it, despite Leo's specialism as a stilt-walker, putting others on stilts instead. His immediate goal seems to be to find the most effective uses of each of the shapes and to construct a sequence involving them that makes visual sense, regardless, initially, of narrative sense. The shapes are an extraordinary paintbox. The broad forms of the *castelets* contrast strongly with the tall elegance of the stilt-dancer giraffes and the shaggy length of the traditional Malian lion costumes; and inamongst them, the unadorned human forms of the hunters and Atir.

This is a frustrating process for the performers, keen to make progress, and for Marthinus, worried about how much time he needs to schedule for Koffi over the course of rehearsals. No one wants to unsettle Koffi's process. Marthinus often leaves Kôkô to work without the presence of a director looking over his shoulder, while he goes through text with Bheki and Fezile. Yaya Coulibaly expresses a concern that Marthinus may not have as much influence on Koffi's work as he needs. But what would be the point of bringing this celebrated international choreographer across the hemispheres only to restrict the way he makes his work? Basil, Adrian and Marthinus all want to get the most out of Koffi, so they express their enthusiasm and remain patient.

The first time the hunt is staged, Basil and Adrian are in *castelets*. Bheki Vilakazi does some work in one too, despite the fact that his role had not been envisaged as including any puppetry. 'I'd love to be a *castelet*,' he says. 'In normal plays all I do is just stand and talk, talk, talk…it would be great to just…' There isn't a simple word for what the *castelet* operators do. They're exhausting to carry, a cage of stout roots lashed together, covered with cloth and grasslike fringing, and with a heavy wooden head sticking out of the front end. The puppeteer finds some way to grip the inside of the cage; there is a pad which sits on his head to take some of the weight. The operator is required effectively to dance while carrying the *castelet* on top of him. It's a puppet with no moving parts whatsoever (later we find control strings to wiggle ears and open and close mouths on some of them, but this is ornamentation compared to the ordinary action). What is extraordinary, the more we see the *castelets* in action, is how effective and expressive the human spine and legs can be in varying the movement of this rigid object.

Koffi's three weeks away from rehearsals mean that the priority in this week is to set down some basic shape for the few movement set-pieces: the Savannah and Hunt; the processional Marchdown when the giraffe is presented to the King at the show's climax; a surreal scene in which French scientists sing while puzzling over how to assemble a giraffe skeleton; and, most delicate, the Stable scene where Atir (an actor) and Clothilde (a puppet) consummate their love affair. Basson is also interested in Kôkô's input on the revelation of the full-size giraffe puppet, and the development of Atir's physical relationship with the giraffe.

On the Saturday of the first week, Basson and Kôkô start to look at the Scientists scene together. Koffi watches as Marthinus begins to define it. He wants this scene to do two things: establish the character of the French zoologist St-Hilaire, showing the link between him and Dr Konate (the archaeologist in the framing device), and to visually echo or parody a moment at the beginning of the play, when Konate is leading the examination of a human mummy. It's inconvenient that this moment itself hasn't yet been staged.

Basson has already worked with composer Warrick Sony and video designer Jaco Bouwer on this sequence, and there is a soundtrack for the performers to sing along to. The song has a verse/chorus structure, and Basson would like to incorporate into it a series of events: the entrance of the museum attendants, their transformation into French scientists, the entrance of Konate, and his transformation into St-Hilaire. Meanwhile, the performers can refer to a witty animated sequence, which will be running on the projection screen behind them. Kôkô stands and watches as Basson begins to let the actors know which events should come where in the song. The Malians in the scene, Téhibou and Yacouba, are puzzled; without effective translation, Basson often has to repeat himself or demonstrate. Repetition doesn't always put across what he means. The English-speakers help to guide them through the sequences. Koffi Kôkô looks on. By the time Marthinus has finished laying out his events, the rehearsal is over and Kôkô has only watched. In any case, there seems precious little space for the sort of

The Soirée: St-Hilaire (Bheki Vilakazi) and the guests inspect the
Foot with Seven Toes (held by Yaya Coulibaly) Photograph by Damien Schumann

movement that Koffi seems to specialise in. What's needed here is dance steps
to formalise the performers' movements as they sing – steps that come with the
beat. This looks like it could be a problem: as we know, with Koffi, the dance
comes first. Always.

In amongst all this the practical preparations continue. Here in the first week
the giraffe puppet needs to be measured for its raincoat. The puppet costume
designer, Hazel Maree, is blending period pattern-cutting with brightly-printed
modern and contemporary West African fabrics. In this case, the length and fall of
a plastic fabric needs to be measured against the puppet's body – impossible up
until now without Téhibou and Yacouba to stand inside it. She and Adrian discuss
the placing of seams and how to blend the design more successfully with the rest
of the costumes and the overall visuals of the show. They decide to add a long
fringe to the coat. It will echo the long cascades of grass-like bark that hang from
the Malian animals – the *castelets* and lion costumes – and add movement to the
giraffe's walk.

Across these first weeks, questions are asked about what needs to be sourced
or made. Students from the University of Stellenbosch will help with making props
and shadow puppets. We know what the set will be, but what dressing will be
needed? How many cardboard boxes will it take to fill these shelves – and how

will everything be transported? Handspring have flight cases from their previous shows, but none large enough to take either the body or the neck of the giraffe – and so dedicated cases will have to be custom-made. Alongside the optimistic artistic collaboration, there is still a tight and ambitious schedule being made for the production of the play in three venues across South Africa over the coming months. Wesley France, Handspring's experienced production manager, is in charge of ensuring that everything is done in time, and his is the most important voice in the production meetings.

At the first workshop in February Koffi Kôkô had memorably said that he was looking forward to working with Handspring because, 'the puppets dance, but they [the puppeteers] don't dance'. An interest in the whole picture of puppeteer and puppet is essential when working alongside the Malian puppets. When watching Yaya Coulibaly operate the King, one's eye is as much on him as on the figure, which sits, relatively passive, in a belt socket. The bird puppets are a good example. Both Yaya and Adrian have made bird puppets that sit on rods with strings hanging down to flap their wings. Each also have their refinements and elaborations on the basic design: some of Yaya's have loose heads that nod with a very natural movement as the bird flies; one of Adrian's, set up to be shot by the King, is spring-loaded to break in half with the removal of a pin. But everyone is agreed that 'we don't just watch the bird, we watch the whole body'. Both Zandile Msutswana and Nana Kouma, South African and Malian, find ways of moving their own legs, and of carrying their own bodies, that add to rather than distract from the small puppet, which is the focal point of the large image. Kôkô referred to this connection when, after the play had opened, he said, 'Another way I worked with the actors, the puppet-players, was to insist that [they] give their movement from inside. This gives a big space for the puppet, and takes care about the relationship between the puppet and the human being. Because the challenge of this play is outside the text; the puppet says 'na na na', but outside this…[we must] find when the puppet and the human beings are communicating: [when] we can, for one moment, forget who is the human being and who is the puppet.' Koffi's engagement with the challenge is one that involves examining the very fundamentals of puppeteering.

Puppet manipulation classes continue alongside Kôkô's sessions. Adrian has been setting up improvisations of conflict between the Malian puppets, leading up to a blow or a slap being given. After the detailed series of thoughts in the 'Chinese whispers' exercise, some of the violence is over-embroidered. The discovery: 'An aggressive movement doesn't need a story. You make a movement. The puppets are very strongly sculpted. The audience have an imagination. When we look at

I discovered that this relationship can happen: the puppet, and the human being. It can happen, and with enough space, it can create a different level of understanding, because it's so beautiful, the puppet. I discovered the puppet can simply move, without saying anything, and we think we can understand what he's saying.

Koffi Kôkô

The Fashion Designer. Adrian Kohler on his feet and Basil Jones operating his left arm

the puppet in a moment of stillness, we have time to take in the thought.' For all the close observation and the naturalistically rooted acting at the heart of a performance using these puppets, there needs to be a filter between them and the audience which reminds us of their status as sculpture. The trick here is not to show the thought, but to hold the stillness long enough for the audience to imagine it. These moments of stillness – frozen images in the sequence of thought and movement – are what a puppeteer's scene are built around.

When Koffi sets up a session to develop some stylised movements for male and female puppets, some surprising discoveries are made. Burns has scripted Count Grandeville de Largemont, the prefect of Marseilles, as a cognac-soaked old cuckold, spluttering reactionary platitudes about Europe's dominance over Africa. Basil Jones is the puppeteer and the instinct is to make the characterisation of the puppet appropriately stooped and weak. But something in these movement studies – asking the puppet to represent masculinity – reveals a genuine strength in the puppet that Adrian Kohler has made. There's a teasing glimpse of a proud, embittered character that brings the puppet to more vivid life. Could this quality be included in the play? Khephra Burns is not here, and script rewrites aren't practical without him. Since he can't see what he would be responding to, and his changes would have to be retranslated into French, opportunities which would need textual alterations usually have to be let go.

Koffi's exercises offer tantalising glimpses of what a scriptless collaboration between Kôkô and puppets could be like. Adrian and Basil are both very enthused about such a prospect and Adrian says more than once that he'd like to abandon the project and just do a six-week workshop on puppet movement with Koffi. 'But we are rehearsing a play, and we have to do that first.' What chimes very well between Kôkô's approach and the puppetry is an enforced restriction. For example, Koffi generates three movements for the male puppets and three for the females. He has the puppeteers walk and carry out the movements themselves first. 'Do not travesty the movement of a woman,' he says. 'Do not imitate the movement of a woman... Feel this movement inside you.' Once the shapes have been learnt, they are like the physical restrictions of the puppets – tools for expression of feeling. With just three positions to move between, the puppeteer only has to decide which one of them to move to. This allows them to concentrate on the movement itself.

Koffi's slowness and calmness are suggestive of a long-term strategy – something which will be difficult to implement when he is away from the company. His daily reworking of material results in a flexibility in the performer, and a greater understanding of what they can actually do with these puppets as they are required to reorganise a sequence of movements. But it's the opposite method which Basson prefers: to fix a structure early on, which can then develop and take alteration as details and moments within it change their length and weight. The following weeks will show weaknesses with both systems, as the puppeteers on stage struggle to reconcile their director and choreographer.

I'm sure the anxiety about their working relationship affects both men. Kôkô tends not to let it show. Basson is at once conciliatory and slightly defensive: 'People actually want to understand each other. And usually do,' he says about the occasional mix-ups and crossed wires between himself and Kôkô. But he won't put it down to linguistics. 'I find it very interesting that misunderstandings arise, not out of language; it's very often a cultural-personal, you know, or debating a sense of style. I think that is a very difficult one for me. If a group of people don't know each other, and they come from very different backgrounds, and come from very valuable artistic fields: how on God's earth do they, you know, negotiate that into one pie? I think that is a tough one.' He's talking not just about Koffi Kôkô, but also Yaya Coulibaly, the puppeteers, and sometimes Handspring too. He will be chewing on this question throughout the process.

During Koffi's six-day burst of work, Marthinus has put text work, exploration of the story, and basic structuring of scenes on the back burner. But at the end of the week, even though Koffi has been discussing the music with Warrick Sony, we don't know enough about the length and structure of the sequences for Sony to usefully prepare something to accompany the dance.

On the evening that Koffi leaves for Germany, there's a production meeting with Wesley, Yaya, Basil and Adrian (in their roles as producer and designer as well as representing Handspring), Marthinus, and stage manager Leigh Colombick. Among the issues discussed is how work will proceed on the key movement sequences without him. We should be practising and developing these sequences – but Koffi has left the Hunt especially in a state of some confusion. Assistant choreographer Philani Mbana is capable, but Koffi's approach is as new to him as to anyone else and he won't be able to develop the process. When Koffi returns, there won't be time to rediscover these sequences from scratch. To these results-oriented theatre-makers, this is a terrifying prospect.

Marthinus is also interested in some other images in the Hunt. The giraffes in this sequence are represented by stilt-dancers wearing tall Malian backpack/head-dresses crowned with giraffe heads. Adrian has had two tiny giraffes made, small enough to be held by the dancers, to represent the babies that will be captured during the sequence. Marthinus wants to see if smaller stilt-dancers on shorter stilts might work as the baby giraffes instead. This would mean that the sequence involves the rolling ball, the three lions, who will also play hunters, three *castelets* to represent grazing animals, and four giraffes. The performers would still need to be switching from one role to another, and the stilts take time to attach securely. Everyone has an opinion on how the Hunt could be structured, but Koffi's explorations have successfully outlined the possibilities offered by the puppets, without leaving them in a particular sequence. And for each change made to the Hunt in the coming weeks, further energy will be expended on wondering what Koffi will think of them.

Shadow puppetry has long been part of Handspring's repertoire, and it formed the basis of their most recent collaboration with William Kentridge, *The Confessions of Zeno*. Here and in their 2000 show *The Chimp Project*, Handspring have worked to good effect mixing projected video or animation with live shadow puppetry. It's been suggested as a solution to a number of tricky transitions in *Tall Horse*, and some of it may be pre-recorded. Jaco Bouwer, a South African animator, actor and director, is creating video animation sequences to run behind the action. He will be able to combine his work with recordings of shadow puppetry, as well as setting up areas of light on the screen that live puppeteers can use to play shadows across.

The next morning, we hear that Koffi has been experiencing difficulty boarding his intercontinental flight in Johannesburg. The South African passport control and Air France officials think they have found irregularities in his passport. Basil has had a rather fraught telephone discussion with an Air France representative, and unsuccessful efforts continue throughout the day to call Koffi on his mobile phone and to contact his wife. Rehearsals have to continue of course, and attention turns to the scene where the two young giraffes are transported up the Nile to Alexandria. The giraffes are new puppets, as yet unfinished, designed by Adrian based on previous four-legged animals in Handspring productions: the rhino in *Woyzeck on the Highveldt*; a bush-pig in *The Chimp Project* and, memorably, the Mephistopheles hyena familiar in *Faustus in Africa!* The animals are operated from the side and so present only one profile to the audience – meaning that they cannot change direction. The legs are very complex mechanisms that, with considerable practice, offer beautifully naturalistic movement. They're made out of sheets of plywood, with the middles cut away, so that the effect is of an intricate skeleton of slim ribs. It's compellingly artificial – and yet, because the shapes are

Téhibou Bagayoko and Nana Kouma with one of the partially-finished young giraffe puppets

those of a curved body and the component sheets are cut according to the logic of anatomy, the lines (and of course the joints) suggest life.

Until now Marthinus has not had a chance to take on a scene with puppets, and his method soon becomes clear. He plays. Marthinus is delighted by the animals and tries to find the best poses or movements for them. From these he begins to map his scene. Two or three moments in the script are given very precise detail, leaving plenty of space in between where things will emerge and find their setting later in rehearsals. Adrian enjoys this attitude – Marthinus seems genuinely concerned that the puppets are fully exploited – but points out that there is more to come and apologises that they're not ready. They will both have swishing tails (there's a wooden stub where one should be), and the larger of the two will also have moving ears. These – the ears and tail – are the key expressive tools of the large giraffe puppet (the one which has been dubbed Sogo Jan, after the Bambara for 'giraffe'). Adrian wants to establish the character's language of ear wiggles and tail flicks in this smaller puppet so that the audience can find a consistency of characterisation with the grown-up version.

Marthinus's enthusiasm is utterly charming, and here, with Basil, Adrian, Busi Zokufa, Fourie Nyamande and Fezile Mpela playing Atir, he is able to work in English. It becomes clear at once that Marthinus is used to working fast with articulate and intelligent actors. He talks energetically, forming his ideas in his mouth as they spill out, refining them in the space between himself and the actors. He's constantly trying ideas out on the performers and re-explaining or developing the thoughts he's just had. He wants, and loves, to see things happen, and for them to be entertaining, crisp and detailed. His zeal fills the room, and the main conduit for it is his language. The obstacle is the puppetry. It soon emerges that three puppeteers will work on the healthy giraffe (Sogo Jan), and only one on the weak giraffe. Slumped down in the boat, it will never stand or move its legs; head, neck, torso and tail can all be handled with two hands. So Basson's main focus is the healthy creature, which can stand, kick, walk, look all around, nudge Atir, and so on. Co-ordinating three puppeteers isn't always straightforward, and for them to execute one of the moves he suggests often means they have to stop and work out what each would do, and in what order; co-ordinating the head, ears, feet and tail. By the time we stop working on the scene it's clear that some of the moments that Marthinus considers plotted haven't yet been worked out by the puppeteers.

Puppetry can be time-intensive like this, and it acts as a brake on Marthinus's rhythm and flow. But what comes out of this scene is already very promising: gentle, intelligent, nuanced and subtle, it allows Khephra Burns's speeches to work in parallel with the purely physical relationship that is building up between actor and puppet.

More often it is the need for translation that slows Basson. There has been talk of students from the university coming to help with the translation, but the few who do visit infrequently. The French vocabulary of Adrian, Basil and myself is relatively poor, and lots of what has been going on in the rehearsal room isn't being translated. So when Marthinus has been speaking to the group, potted summaries have been conveyed haltingly to the Malians, who are doing a terrific job of keeping up. This means that when translators are in the room, Marthinus often forgets that he has to speak in bite-sized chunks and wait for it to be translated.

Adrian observes the difficulty for the Malians. 'The international collaboration has always been an exciting prospect, but it does throw up the translation difficulties. And one often feels for the Malians, that they're having to just remain in a kind of, in a less informed space. And sometimes in the excitement of a moment, translation gets completely glossed over.' Every moment that's creative is an exciting one for Marthinus. And with the Malians performing in French, he's also unable to respond to their interpretations of the lines.

The intention of these early weeks for Marthinus is to 'rough out' the scenes with some key moves, positioning and character relationships. He wants the performers to be familiar with their material: 'I like to provide a structure. And once the structure's there, you will see what fits in it and what does not. But you have to backtrack.' So it's surprising and sometimes perplexing how he can work for a long time on a tiny moment taken completely out of context, and not always one that would seem to be crucial. It's up to the company to trust that his idea of the rest of the scene will build around this moment. But often these moments seem arbitrary: beautiful, brilliant ideas plucked from the movement of a puppet or an energy on stage, that don't seem immediately to relate to the action in the script. He'll also often give a line-reading: a suggestion of how to stress and pace a given line. I'm used to seeing this frowned upon, and resisted by performers. But these puppeteers, especially those who are working in their second language, appear to appreciate and accept this sort of influence from the director.

The differences between the Handspring and Malian puppets, spotted in the first workshop, have become a great asset in controlling the size and style of the scenes. When the enormous Queen of France enters, twelve feet tall, she carves through the stage space metres above the earthbound characters.

There's a range of abilities among the performers. Of the Malians, only Yaya seems to have a facility for inflecting language in a naturalistic way. Téhibou and Yacouba aren't familiar with using language expressively. They tend to bark their lines and it's a long hard road to find the gentle inflections. Nana is a dancer; she has her work cut out to master either puppetry or dialogue. In fact, we have found that she is almost unable to read, and she navigates the show by memory. Yaya indicates that a typical rehearsal process for Sogolon favours individualism (and the story-telling is usually wordless). He explains that he would watch a scene and pick out what's good, emphasize these points and improve it gradually. Of course he will also decree certain movements (some are traditional) as the company rehearse over a number of weeks. The South Africans are trained in a European-influenced theatre process. Bheki Vilakazi has considerable theatre experience, and although Fezile Mpela has mainly been working in TV and film since he left drama school, all of the South Africans have a shared training which involves making notes in their scripts and a quiet deference to their director. The Malians are also respectful, but their responses to the moves that Marthinus decides on are noticeably more flexible and playful.

As Marthinus 'roughs out' the scenes, discoveries are made with the manipulation, offering him material. The Soirée guests have developed a game where their natural height, just off the ground, varies according to mood. It makes their rhythm dynamically visible, as the male guests bob up and down, or as an elegant lady slumps impossibly low to the ground to sulk. The pictures that begin to be made around Bheki as St-Hilaire, and the surreal dance around him, move the scene into another dimension from the simply real. Basson engages warmly with visual story-telling, and the added possibilities of the puppets often sees him delightedly constructing almost carnivalesque sequences. He has to be strict about how much or little the puppeteers give – too much and the focus is pulled right away from the centre of the scene; too little and the movements or pictures lose their shape.

Basson has a vision for the transition between the Scientists' scene and Marseilles. In the first scene, the scientists of the Academy in Paris anticipate the arrival of the giraffe. It introduces us to Etienne Geoffroy St-Hilaire, the eminent French naturalist who supervised the giraffe's journey through France. The aim is to show their ignorance of the animal comically. Bouwer's video sequence shows bones being misassembled in their attempts to understand the anatomy of a giraffe, much as dinosaur bones were mistakenly arranged into the form of a unicorn. This is soundtracked by a rewritten version of the spiritual 'Dem Bones': 'the head and the neck bone join together…', in a reference to the influence of African musical culture on the West. The second scene balances this. It shows the people of Marseilles – the 'rabble' – whispering superstitious rumours about the giraffe ('It's a devil…a leopard…it has wings!'). Khephra Burns has interspersed this with the Prefect of Marseilles's administrative work on the transportation of the animal from Alexandria to Marseilles. He sits in his office, stamping documents. 'Invoice for shipping from Alexandria, 4500 francs…quarantine documentation…per diems for animal handler…' In Burns's original draft, the realism of the prefect's work gets infected by the surreally escalating gossip: as the hysteria peaks with 'It's a flying horse!', the prefect responds dryly with: 'Equine flight manuals – thirty francs.'

Basson has decided to show the madness of the mob by making the rabble's sequence more rhythmic, instead of whispering building into chaos. Can the Prefect's stamping of documents take place on a drum to keep rhythm? He wants to build repetition of the rumours so that each line works its way around the stage as the next one overlaps, generating a pulsing energy from the very start. So instead of one actor saying, 'It's a devil', and the next saying, 'It's a monster', the sequence goes: 'It's a devil!', 'A devil!', 'A devil!', 'A monster!', 'A devil!', 'A monster!', 'A devil!', 'A monster!', 'A devil!', 'From Turkey!', and so on, with each rumour echoing and hanging between the townspeople. His attempts to explain this to the company don't go well – it's nothing like what's in the script – but

Yacouba Magassouba

eventually they manage to master the idea, by leaving out all of the Prefect's lines. ('We'll work them in later,' says Marthinus.) Working through the idea helps to build a bond across language lines.

The process depends on Basson's eye. At this stage the performers are enacting his ideas and aren't sure whether they're being invited to influence or discuss the progress of the scenes. Basson's system is not always obvious – in some cases he sets the key moment of the scene, in others he builds around an idea that doesn't appear in the script at all. None of the performers here have worked with Marthinus Basson before. The South Africans are all aware of his reputation as one of the country's best directors, both for his edgy, inventive and irreverent re-versions of classic texts, and for his tight, sensitive direction of new plays by some of the country's best playwrights. He's held in great esteem. But his methods here are difficult to read, especially set in contrast with Koffi Kôkô's far-reaching system. Basson's rhythm is continually broken by the need for (often halting) translation. And simultaneously the company are taking training from Adrian Kohler and sometimes Yaya Coulibaly too on their manipulation techniques, which will themselves have an effect on the flow and quality of the scenes. Basson has the unenviable task of guiding the company through this bewildering crossfire of voices. His voice needs to be the dominant one and the one that people trust. It's not yet clear whether it will be.

Especially for the Malians, operating in their English-less space, Marthinus and Koffi can come across as negative and prescriptive. One day, Yaya suggests to me that their styles contrast with the way he likes to work, via encouragement. In English, Marthinus conveys considerable encouragement and enthusiasm: perhaps not enough of it is reaching the Malians, who are many miles from home, entirely dependent on their hosts for even the basics of living and accommodation. Their rehearsal days are long, and the evenings offer no diversions from the company, who are billeted together in a Stellenbosch guest house (except the few who live in Cape Town, who commute in every morning). Certainly, Basson and Kôkô, searching for structures to build on, express frustration when something that has been arranged is forgotten. Everyone can sense how difficult it is for the French-speakers, but there are no easy solutions, and it's the Francophones themselves who are the first to deny there's a significant difficulty.

The different theatrical languages that need to be balanced are also coming to the fore as we look again at the Nile sequence with the young giraffes. It's a series of short, reflective monologues by Atir spread across the passage of several days, with the subtle giraffes providing a mute counterpoint to his musings. Marthinus wants to add in another layer, of things the boat passes. To preserve the quietness of the scene while giving it punctuation, he adds in puppeteers passing behind it, carrying small traditionally carved (Malian) boats and traditional Malian birds flapping past.

Marthinus has asked for slaves passing the boat on the Nile to sing a traditional Malian song. Yaya has been teaching the company one – 'Jonnya Mani', which is the lament of slaves as they contemplate their separation from home, family and nation. It's a valuable opportunity in the mélange of English and French for the Malians to express in their first language, Bambara.

Ah! Jonnya mani,	*Ah! Slavery is terrible,*
Né sirana donnya de nye.	*I fear becoming a slave.*
Jonnya mani, mmmmmmmm.	*Slavery is terrible, mmmmmmmm.*
Né sirana donnya de nye:	*I fear becoming a slave:*
Balima jugu la,	*The subjugation of my nation and family,*
Jonnya mani.	*Slavery is terrible.*
Né sirana donnya de nye:	*I fear becoming a slave:*
T-aden jugu la,	*The enslavement of my parents,*
Jonnya mani.	*Slavery is terrible.*
Né sirana donnya de nye:	*I fear becoming a slave:*
Sigi nyo njon la,	*The segregation of my race,*
Jonnya mani.	*Slavery is terrible.*
Né sirana donnya de nye:	*I fear becoming a slave:*
Jaamana fi la la,	*Between two countries,*
Jonnya mani.	*Slavery is terrible.*
Ah! Badenu yo:	*Ah! The voices of my people cry to all the world:*
Né sirana donnya de nye.	*I fear becoming a slave.*

Yaya's singing is extraordinary and powerful, though not in the Western sense tuneful. It's the potency of his gifts as an actor, projected through verse. It's almost impossible to learn or set a tune from what he sings, but the emotional content of the song is nakedly present. The South Africans, however, struggle to find what might more ordinarily be seen as a melody that they can learn, and work hard to lend the unfamiliar words meaning.

The disjunction of the exaggerated stylisation of the Malian birds and the more precise construction of the young giraffe puppets is immediately apparent, and even more so when the birds are animated. The bird sits on top of a rod with a string hanging down that flaps the wings. The whole thing is made from wood. As Téhibou comes through with his bird, it flaps like crazy, the wooden wings clattering against the body. It moves with terrific energy but not much precision. It threatens to destroy the delicate action which is the main focus of the scene, but if Basson is concerned, he doesn't show it. He leaps onto stage to co-ordinate the movement of the puppets, perhaps reasoning that a language of gesticulation will connect with the French-speakers. He seems to have planned the sequence of birds and boats (and the procession of slaves singing 'Jonnya Mani') to co-ordinate with specific lines in the script, even before he'd really seen what their movement looks like. I can only guess whether this is what he was expecting. But Basson isn't afraid of letting the chaos find its own resolution. He sets all available elements spinning. When he sees Téhibou experimenting with his bird swooping down to 'catch a fish' in the river, he seizes on it and plots it into the scene. If he spots a possibility, he allows it a chance to stake a claim on the stage. The scenes lose control a little. One assumes he plans to rein them in.

The delightfully crazed quality of Basson's engagement with the work (and perhaps the occasional confusion of the company) is emphasized by the fact that different scenes elicit different approaches from him. Whereas, at the Marseilles docks, Basson had a rhythmic plan to develop the text into something he felt would be more powerful ('I find,' he says later, discussing it, 'that using rhythm like this speaks about the mob mentality. The voices cease to have individuality, they become like a machine, following each other, without their own thought.'), in the following scene, the 'Soirée de la Girafe', he starts with the puppets.

He has to, because Khephra Burns's script allows for up to eight guests, whereas there are only four guest puppets. In the initial read-through, Basson redistributed the lines and introduced another cheeky reference to the framing device of the Museum. In the Museum, Yaya Coulibaly's character, the security guard (or 'Monsieur la Securité' as Adrian comes to translate it) is the protector of the collection, and Coulibaly's physical presence on stage gives a looming authority. Already, in an attempt to make the chanting at Marseilles easier, M la Securité has been given a line and drafted in to drum along with the Marseillaise rabble – as if one of the characters from the story-telling has been caught up in the story alongside the puppets. Basson invites Yaya into the Soirée too, as an over-assiduous (human) security guard in the (puppet) Count's château. It adds another level to the interplay between the different styles of puppets: in this scene (and others), Handspring puppets, Sogolon puppets and actors work together, unconcerned by the difference between them.

Basson begins to work through the scene line by line, but his focus is on the puppets. No matter how minor the character, Basson builds up their relationships to a high pitch. This is completely different to the approach to the Marseilles chanting, and there is even less emphasis on the script than in the roughing out of the Nile and other scenes. The director plunges into the details of invented relationships, moment by moment, encouraging a story to come out of physical reactions and responses. Basson has seen that these puppets respond best to dynamic movement – and that this will have to come from high emotion.

Khephra Burns hadn't seen the puppets when he wrote the scene as a lengthy piece of social satire. The eminent naturalist St-Hilaire arrives in Marseilles to inspect the giraffe, during a society event being held by the Prefect of Marseilles, Count Grandeville de Largemont. The Count and all his guests are collectors of antiquities, which they keep in their *cabinets de curiosités* – and it is here that the social one-upmanship will end with the revelation of the giraffe. Burns's scene sets out to ridicule the European bourgeoisie and set up St-Hilaire as their intellectual superior, so he's poured on the irony, inviting a well-educated, sophisticated audience to see through the foolish guests. The guests repeatedly applaud St-Hilaire's erudition, oblivious to the fact that his obscurely worded pronouncements are actually insults. The insults become progressively less veiled, making the guests appear progressively more stupid. It's a long scene full of diplomatic *faux pas*, urbane sophistication and verbal dexterity. 'I love language,' says Burns, 'and I play with a lot of language, and *double-entendre*. The sexual innuendo and stuff like that comes out of the blues tradition, where things always have another meaning, below what you hear on the surface. I had fun doing the Soirée scene, because of the repartee and that sort of thing, and it was a chance to kind of, you know, develop and add a little humour to the piece.'

Basson starts to use the puppets' movement to make the petty rivalries between the guests dynamic. Instead of behaving with self-composed nobility, the puppets whirl around the stage in extravagant over-reaction to the slightest perceived insult or rivalry. The social subtext of their crisply-worded dialogue is made vividly clear. Moment by moment, what Basson starts to construct is not at all about the main characters of the scene – St-Hilaire, the Count and the Count's young wife Clothilde – but about the guests and their bickering. And these characters are not even straightforwardly the ones written by Burns, since Basson has combined and reallocated the lines from eight characters to four. Minor characters' crises dictate the movements around the stage and become defining moments in the scene. It's hectic chaos. After the first session on this scene, it's hard to see how it will perform its dramatic function. Is Basson's enthusiasm for playing with the showmanship of the Malian puppets going to compromise the meaning of the script?

If the Soirée scene is initially built too much around the puppets for its own good, the Marseilles gossip scene seems not to be built around the puppets at all. There are five puppets of the Marseilles characters: three wide-eyed or suspicious men, a mother and her little child. When Marthinus converted the text into chanting, it was done purely with voice, without involving the figures. On revisiting the scene, feeling that the rhythm is starting to catch, Marthinus tries to integrate the words and the puppets. It's a terrible mess, with the puppeteers struggling to pay attention to their puppet while still keeping rhythm. 'We've got a lot of focus to develop with the puppets,' says Basson, rallying the cast, adding optimistically, 'but we will first get used to the speed, and then add in the detail.'

The head of one of the Marseilles rabble in the vice
in Adrian Kohler's workshop in Kalk Bay

But there's a new difficulty. In order to pick up from the previous scene, the puppeteers must start the words before they have the puppets in their hands. The sequence begins as words flying around, building a rhythm and an atmosphere that is gradually inhabited by the puppets. The puppeteers take an opportunity to grab the puppets, find the right place for their hands and finally bring the figures on to contribute to the visual impact of the scene – revealing that they are the characters who are speaking. It comes out as a pretty effective device, except that by the time all of the puppets are on, the word sequence is nearly over. So the visual effect is of several rather nice puppets roaring onto stage, arriving and then leaving immediately – ultimately an unsatisfying one. And the speed of the words around the stage is too fast for the puppets anyway. These puppets need to be carefully controlled and at this pace they are jiggling about like dolls.

Basson can see the difficulty, and he turns it into an opportunity to develop the rhythmic flow, work in some of the Prefect's material ('import tax: forty francs') and give the puppets a moment to establish themselves authoritatively. He restructures the end of the sequence, creating a break in the hysteria once all of the puppets have arrived, and then having a second build-up of muttering which will allow the puppets to find their own irregular, distinctive rhythm. It looks like it will work – if the puppeteers can master the rhythmic chanting and their characterisations at the same time.

In the Marseilles docks sequence, as elsewhere, the French-speakers have been invited to perform their lines in French. Here they choose to go for a sort of combination, opting for the interlingual 'un devil', for example, instead of 'un diable'. Marthinus seems reluctant to ask the French-speakers to speak English: conscious, presumably, that to learn lines phonetically will be impractical. Oddly, the subject is never directly or publicly discussed. Away from rehearsals, it's something that Basil Jones of Handspring is concerned about. What will an audience make of a multilingual show? In much of Handspring's previous work this might not have been a problem: in productions with less text, created for smaller auditoria, where the clarity and careful control of the puppets' movements would be the dominant mode of communication, a layer of foreign words and sounds wouldn't be a problem. But this is a bigger prospect, scheduled to play in the 650-seat Baxter Theatre to a mass audience. For many South Africans, English will not be their first language, and French will be completely unknown. It's also an exceedingly complex story. Although the central relationships between Atir, St-Hilaire, the giraffe and Clothilde have enough stage time to be shown visually, the political subtext is hard to follow, often turning on a single line, sometimes not even explicitly stated. With the King (played by Yaya) suddenly chirping up in French, will anyone be able to understand this? But on the other hand, how can the production be described as a collaboration if the Malians are forced to work in a foreign language?

The surtitling solution is not an enticing prospect for Wesley France, the lighting designer and production manager. The production will already have video projection from behind a large screen. Surtitles would mean a second projector, hung in the auditorium, throwing onto a second small screen. Adrian is keen that the screen be integrated into the set – but this doesn't seem practical. It can't be on the shelves, because as the shelves move, the screen will roll out of the projector's beam. So it needs to be above them. The potential difficulties are noted. This will require a proper discussion with Marthinus.

Over the rest of these early weeks, as more of the scenes are roughed out, the dominant energy is of Marthinus Basson's delight at working with the puppets. Adrian Kohler will co-supervise a session when a new type of puppet is to be used for the first time. His direction has a much more moderate feel than the brio of Basson's inspiring calls-to-arms. Fezile Mpela occasionally has enough time on stage for us to take a quick look at his character – but mostly, attention is taken up by the novelty of the puppets. Mpela is crisp and efficient, certainly aware of the pressure of time, keen to show that he can work with the team – but he must have been expecting more attention to be paid to his character development.

Meanwhile Basson is seizing every opportunity to bring outrageous set-pieces to life: the flamboyant fashion designer; the giant bulk of Mehmet Ali set against the vertical and brittle Drovetti; the huge and stately giraffe. Each provides him with a whole different vocabulary of movement, and he grabs every one with both hands. In fact, he's bubbling with enthusiasm for his new range of expression. 'What puppets are capable of. That for me is very new and very nice. And I like the fact that they open up all kinds of…with all the limitations, they open up extraordinary possibilities. And they inspire you to think in a way that you would never be able to think with actors, I think. And that I find truly, truly exciting.' People often comment on how childlike Marthinus Basson's genuine engagement with theatre-making is. 'I think that Marthinus is possessed by a theatrical knowledge that's very essential. He absolutely loves the theatre, and he loves to play in the theatre. He's got a very good eye for what works and what doesn't work,' offers Basil's vote of confidence shortly after the first week. 'And already, things have come from nowhere into being something quite OK. So it's a matter of whether he can keep the faith of everyone in the project, and not only keep it, but build it, so that people think: *this is going to be amazing*.' Will he be able to combine all of these inspirations? Will he able to control and settle them into one show?

No one expected things to be going this slowly as rehearsals move into the third week. Working relationships between Marthinus Basson and his collaborators are starting to build, but none of the collaborators are in their best environment – and it shows. Koffi Kôkô is absent, his time compromised by other commitments in Europe. Yaya Coulibaly is a long way from home and attempting to work in a foreign language. Adrian Kohler and Basil Jones are combining their roles in the production with their other Handspring responsibilities. Jones, supported by his administrator Estelle Randall, is producing Handspring's most ambitious ever show (and learning his lines in the car); Kohler journeys home each night to a workshop with a seemingly endless list of puppets that need to be finished, fixed, adapted or altered. Basson might seem best placed to take control of the project. He is, after all, in his home town; he sleeps in his own bed each night. But he has distractions too – although he has time off from teaching, the faculty is still very close, and its work impinges on his concentration to some extent. And he doesn't feel free to shape the piece. Not only does he have the contributions and status of Yaya and the absent Koffi and Khephra to consider, but as he says, 'ultimately for me in my head, it's not my project, it's Basil and Adrian's project'.

As rehearsals began Marthinus commented that he 'found it very difficult to come in because they [Handspring] are people with a particular vision, and the project had been going for a very long time: there was a writer on board already, so one was sort of tagging in at the end of it.' Part of Basson's difficulty might be that he doesn't feel ownership of the piece. With the script already written when he came on board, he might reasonably have assumed that it would make allowance for the combination of different puppeteers, their skills and languages. But in the same open, pioneer spirit that characterised the division of puppet carving and the choice of story, the plan seems to have been to make no apologies for these potential pitfalls, and instead simply to approach the story with the puppets and...collaborate. A new play written for actors here in South Africa might expect to rehearse for three weeks. A larger, more technical production – a musical, say – might expect two or three weeks longer. Seven weeks, as have been scheduled for this rehearsal period, seems at first glance luxurious. Basil Jones has worked hard to offer this much time. But the days are ticking by, and by the time

Koffi returns there will be only one week to go before the company presents 'open rehearsals' to the students and public in Stellenbosch – the intention being to present the show and gauge audiences' responses to what has been made.

In the February development workshop Marthinus's high mental metabolism manifested itself in short, focused sessions on different aspects of the production. He generated a hungry, questing energy that swept the company along with it, allowing them to just feel the click of engagement or progress on an aspect of the work before whisking them away to the next one. Coming up against the day-to-day reality of a multilingual rehearsal room full of puppets seems to have impeded that forward motion. Basson's schedules still bear his mark: usually just an hour on any given scene, enough to make some progress before tackling the next one. But the desire to have made some progress is stronger than the desire to move on – and where it takes longer to achieve something, longer is taken. It's a rare day when everything that was scheduled is covered.

Is Basson genuinely rattled by this? Of course, he professes not to be. Schedules are there to be aspired to and there's nothing unusual in diverging from the day's plan. Undoubtedly, his extraordinary enthusiasm for the moment of connection between the performer and the play remains undimmed. He's not a man to lose his temper – there can't be more than a couple of moments in the whole process when he so much as hardens his voice when addressing the company – and on these occasions it's usually an exhortation to remember work that has been done. But, equally, it must be the case that if he's making less progress every day than he normally does, and the number of days available is not increasing, then he's going to run out of time. And his ebullience and drive to keep the room working, while terrifically motivational, especially for the English-speakers, can also be bewildering. The cascade of ideas and words – falling on a detail in the scene where you least expect it, expanding a moment of pure puppetry or a tiny look between actors into the key moment – can seem to have broken free from the logic of structuring the scene. To the French-speakers, the torrents of words are certainly disorientating, and the struggle to convey some of it in French must seem desperate. Sometimes the atmosphere verges on the hysterical, and it's through sheer force of personality that Basson makes his desires understood. Increasingly this mode will be one of the key tools: gesticulation combined with vision. The young Malians take it in very good humour. Once the story has shifted to France, both Téhibou and Yacouba are in the giraffe. Their movements are necessarily very simple – two men on stilts harnessed together have a good turning circle but they move slowly – and it doesn't take them long to pick up a basic English vocabulary of where to stand. Yaya's English comprehension is better than his

Téhibou Bagayoko, Yacouba Magassouba and Yaya Coulibaly,
with Marthinus Basson a blur between them

English speaking, and he can usually follow the gist of the direction. Nana Kouma,
the Malian dancer, has the worst of it. She's neither a regular member of Sogolon
nor an experienced puppeteer. French is her second language and she's less secure
in it than the others – she usually communicates in Bambara. And throughout
the piece she has various roles with different demands, so the variety of French
vocabulary used in talking to her is wider than hers, despite the limited skills of
the makeshift translators. Giving direction to her is not only slow, it's also not
always clear whether it's been successfully communicated. The student translators
do still visit occasionally, but with Nana their fuller vocabulary is not necessarily
an advantage (although their fluency and speed in conveying meaning are very
useful). They also use accurate grammar, something which can be a considerable
challenge for Adrian and myself, both struggling to conjugate in the future or
conditional tenses.

When the translators are present, the pace of the impeded rehearsals does
increase. Marthinus Basson gets close to fulfilling his schedule more often
than before. But his vitality still allows little opportunity for a full and reasoned
translation – and the students don't feel they have the authority to stop him in

mid-flow to make sure every thought is conveyed. If Basson has a quick specific note to give to Zandile Msutswana and Adrian Kohler, the English-speakers manipulating Clothilde, for example, does it need to be translated for everyone? At least a summary of the progress would be useful, but without a separate full-time translator next to each French-speaker it would be impractical. So even the presence of the translators doesn't make it a lot easier for the Francophones in their 'less informed space', or change the progress of the company as a whole.

But progress is made. Basil Jones prefers to look on the bright side. 'People are making huge strides in learning each other's language,' he says. 'I, at one point, felt in absolutely no doubt that we should can all the French and only speak English. Now I'm feeling actually, I don't think it's that important that we hear or don't hear the bits of French that are there; I think that the story is actually coming across very well.'

Marthinus has been working with Warrick Sony to create structure for the dance sequences, and to find what music he can use in other parts of the piece. Basson is very sensitive to rhythm and enjoys using music. For as long as he is in the room with the show, he will be tinkering, in conference with Simon Mahoney, Handspring's sound designer and technician, in order to improve the underscoring, or change levels and timing. He's very conscious of the support a well-timed underscore can lend to a single moment or to the building of emotion in a scene. He also engages particularly with Fourie Nyamande's role as 'Newspaperman' – in which Fourie gives a commentary on the political and salacious aspects of the story. This role is to be accompanied by a live drummer, and Basson works on these sections to develop syncopation and cross-rhythms which support Fourie's lines. But whenever he gives a structure to Warrick, he is also suggesting one for Koffi Kôkô's return.

Puppets eat time. Every movement needs, at some point, to be choreographed. To see even if a moment will succeed, some degree of technical work has to be done. Often this will involve several puppeteers working together to co-ordinate their puppet limbs. Consequently, even a couple of weeks in to the process, Fezile Mpela and Bheki Vilakazi, the actors taking the lead roles, have barely yet been the focus of attention on stage. Instead they have had private sessions dedicated to text work with the director.

One of their key scenes follows the chaos at Lyon during which Atir and St-Hilaire, the African and the European who both feel responsible for the animal, have been separated from the giraffe, Sogo Jan. Burns's original script has Atir alone in a forest, where the giraffe finds him sitting, reciting a prayer and thinking of her. Action then shifts back to the 'special stable' where St-Hilaire and Atir address the giraffe. They've realised something about their relationship with and affection for the creature, and in this sequence, some of their rivalry and antagonism fades away. Khephra Burns later describes this scene and the other occasions when the characters address the giraffe: 'The giraffe is the Zen Master…or the psychoanalyst. So, you know, they ask the giraffe questions, the giraffe doesn't answer, they answer for the giraffe – but they're really bringing the answers up out of themselves, both he and St-Hilaire.' Basson doesn't see a need for the two scenes to be separate and has both Atir and St-Hilaire in the forest, each looking for the giraffe but unaware of each other. In fact, to build the dynamic and show their agitation, he prefaces the scene with each man running through the space in desperation. Only then does he show Atir's desolation and the key moment when he gives up looking for his animal and begins to fall back on his ancient prayer. Later, St-Hilaire happens upon the reunion of the giraffe and its handler. The scene has, effectively, no puppetry. There will be some later – the entrance of the giraffe will have to be plotted, as well as what it will do with its neck, head, ears and tail, where it will face, who it will watch – but there's no doubt that the engine of this scene is the two actors. By now Basson has a good idea of what the giraffe can do, and for this moment he doesn't ask it to bring something eye-catching into the scene, preferring the audience's focus to rest on the human scale. Basson has prepared the actors a little during text sessions away from the stage, and both men enjoy finding their range on the stage without the circus of puppetry around them. The first stage session goes smoothly and quickly: here Basson doesn't get held up in detail – a shape is found for the movements and rhythm, and work moves on.

The contrast is strong between this and the following session, which is on the giant puppet of Mehmet Ali. The making process has not allowed Adrian a chance to see the puppet in one piece. Although his workshop is theoretically large enough, the puppet takes three people to operate (or even just to hold it up to look at), and the distance from its position on stage to even the front row is larger than he's been able to simulate at home. Kohler has had to trust that his instincts, plans and measurements have been right in creating the proportions. Each time the puppet is assembled, Kohler is assessing how it works. It comes in several parts. The head is detachable from the neck; the neck, shoulders and spine form the main part, from which the arms can be detached; the shoulders/chest sits on top of a large ball (the 'dung-ball'), which rests between the legs. All of this sits on top of a base of two flight cases, and it is covered with two large pieces of fabric. The huge arms are solid foam, and the hands and head have been carved from polystyrene, covered with laminated paper and painted. The combined shape

I think the most interesting part for me, in the early days, was conceiving the puppets. Somebody like Drovetti was conceived to be a puppet, a single-bodied puppet. But when I saw the legs, they were so compelling I thought it would be insane to attach them. OK, so maybe that's also a cheap trick. But that's the kind of thing that a puppet can do and an actor can never do. And it opens up possibilities. So I loved that.

Marthinus Basson

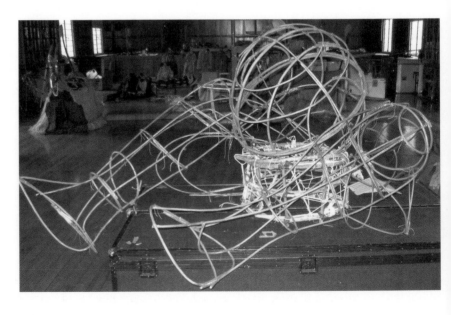

The legs and belly of Mehmet Ali under the fabric

Mehmet Ali squashes the head of Téhibou Bagayoko under his hand.
Adrian Kohler and Fourie Nyamande operating Drovetti;
Yacouba Magassouba, Basil Jones and Téhibou operating Mehmet Ali

of the legs, belly-ball and shoulders is made from bent cane for lightness – it's only when the fabric is laid over them that Mehmet appears weighty and solid.

Even to begin looking at this scene means that flight cases need to be manoeuvred into position. The dedicated flight cases for *Tall Horse* are being custom-made and will not arrive for another week or so. They will have castors so that they can be whizzed around the stage, and some thought has gone into finding a way to lock them together in the various necessary configurations. Each is an identical rectangle: in one arrangement they make a square base for resting this puppet on; in the Nile scene, laid end to end, they make a long raised strip which suggests the felucca boat on which the young giraffes are transported. But even once the puppet is put up, work can't quite start. Why is it that he looks taller than yesterday? The mechanics of his assembly need to be inspected. Is his chest sitting on a different part of the belly? Is the belly sitting differently between the legs? As rehearsals continue, so do adjustments to this puppet. The legs need to be strengthened and the join between them made more sturdy. The ball needs to rest in a 'nest' so that it doesn't roll and displace the legs. This nest raises the height of the chest and shifts the angle of manipulation. The arms are currently tied onto the shoulders with thick cord. This is eventually replaced with a system of clips and rings to allow for swifter attachment. The puppet is far too large to transport in one piece, and these practical considerations offer an opportunity. With the ball emerging from his body at the end of the scene, it makes sense that the rest of the puppet should dismember itself too. And so, the exit of Mehmet Ali sees his head lift from his neck, his arms and shoulders move off in one direction and his legs float away in another. The head finds its way up onto one of the shelves on the set, and the two flight cases wheel off into the wings.

The scene is between Mehmet Ali and Drovetti. Ali's vast, massy bulk makes Drovetti's skinny body look incredibly fragile. Basson exploits the possibilities with relish. Again, it feels as if he's pushing against the text to make the most of what's available visually, but he makes wonderful pictures. He brings Drovetti in close, to accentuate his vulnerability. He has Mehmet Ali lay a hand casually on Drovetti's shoulder, with the effect that the smaller puppet is forced to its knees. He wonders if Drovetti can end up sitting in the Pasha's lap – but there's no room. The manipulator of Drovetti's left arm ends up sitting there instead, with Drovetti squeezed up tight to the giant. And then Basson sees the potential of Ali's huge voice when it comes up against the potential separation of Drovetti's legs and body. With one bellow, Ali's breath explodes Drovetti, sending his body and legs spinning crazily around the room. Marthinus is ecstatic, roaring with laughter. At moments like this, all of the inconvenience of the puppets vanishes from his mind. 'God, I love puppets!' he cries. 'You can never do that with actors! Spin them apart!' Basil Jones peers over the shoulder of Mehmet Ali to offer the next step. 'The bits could come together the wrong way round,' he suggests. The sequence will prove to be a favourite with audiences, and the visual impact of this scene is perhaps more powerful than any other part of the production. It's a great thing to have early on in the show.

But this playing takes a long time, and all is not well. Basil Jones is operating the head and body of Mehmet Ali, and Téhibou Bagayoko and Yacouba Magassouba, the young Malians, are manipulating one arm each. Even though it's made from a framework of light cane and foam, and spread between the three of them, it's hard work just to support the weight of the figure. In fact, the contribution of the arm-operators can pose further problems: when one arm moves, it pulls on the shoulders, and can pull Jones, holding the hefty 'spine' rod, off-balance. Delicate co-ordination isn't an option when so many new moves are being explored so quickly. Kohler is brought across to assess the possibilities for lightening his partner's load. Of course, with practice and familiarity, everything will become easier. And the length of time the puppet will need to be worked in performance is much less than the sustained sessions of work that come up in rehearsal. But there may be mechanical remedies too. The support rod carrying the puppet's weight is currently resting on the flight cases, from where Jones wrestles it into the correct position, while maintaining control over the head's rotation and angle. Three possible engineering solutions are proposed. One is to mount a socket on top of the flight cases, which will allow a more easily controlled swivelling of the main rod (in anatomical terms this would be like a joint at the base of the spine). The second is to support the main rod in a belt (like a flagpole bracket). This would mean that when he pulls the figure off the vertical (which is most of the time), some of the weight is taken down into his legs, lessening the load on his arms and lower back. This principle of spreading the weight should help to keep the strain on any one part of the puppeteer's anatomy within reasonable limits. The third suggestion is that some of the weight be transferred to Basil's shoulders via a harness, connected by cord to the upper part of the control rod.

Where there is a technical improvement like this to make, Adrian will assess it on the spot and then return to the subject at lunchtime or at the end of the day, to chew over the implications, strengths and weaknesses of each suggestion. He'd been expecting to have to introduce a belt, and also begins to explore the possibility of a swivelling socket. But at the end of the scene it has been envisaged that the component parts of Mehmet Ali would fly apart; and the socket would have to be supported on a broad plate or fixed permanently to the flight-cases. It is now crucial that removing the puppet remains as simple and as easy as possible – and preparations are made for a supporting belt and a shoulder harness. The mechanical and physical problems are the immediate focus of attention: but what lasts is the power of the figure. 'The other thing that surprises me constantly,' marvels Basson, 'is how something that is dead, even surrounded by four people, Mehmet Ali, still holds its own. And it's not his size. It's not that; there's something incredibly compelling about a creature like that.' It's true. Ali has an extraordinarily potent life.

The Savannah and Hunt sequence has been undergoing slow but radical change. A session allowing Craig Leo to work on stilts has exposed immediately the idea that anyone else should play the principal mother giraffe. Leo is a very experienced performer in the experimental circus/theatre/spectacular circuit, and certainly one

Craig Leo and Fourie Nyamande

of South Africa's best stilt-walkers and trainers of stilt-walkers. Where Nana and Zandile are just beginning to find an elegant gait, Craig can do this effortlessly, and can shift into kicking, running and falling. The latest structure involves all three of them playing mother giraffes, but time for Nana and Zandile to practise their stilt-walking is hard to find, and it's a concern for the team that their movements continue to lack confidence and control. When this reallocation of Craig was first proposed it seemed to throw the whole section of *castelets* into jeopardy – and Adrian was very concerned about this threat. But with Basson's assurance that the *castelets* will survive, and a moment's anxiety over Koffi's response, work continues.

Meanwhile, the Nile scene has settled down quickly as one of the most reliable and involving in the show. It's just one man talking to the two baby giraffes, and it has been staged with a sensitive eye for the puppets. Busi Zokufa and Fourie Nyamande are becoming quietly expressive as the heads of the two giraffes, and are getting better each time. Its potential for difficulty is its length – it's four short monologues spoken by Atir across four days. They're separated (we imagine) by the lights fading to black and coming up again. Basson seems itchy as we revisit it, though, and starts to increase the activity supporting the main action – another bird here, another boat there. By the time the scene is coming to its end, the secondary action has built up to the extent that we are expecting the scene to open into something more busy – which it does, into a scene at the port of Alexandria. Piling on the action like this initially appears to risk smothering the subtleties of the text and performance with extraneous activity. But it's a lovely illustration of Basson's experience in using the depth of the stage to build rhythms that lead the audience into anticipating the next scene.

The slave song in the Nile scene, 'Jonnya Mani', has developed. A student from the university has come in, listened to Yaya's singing and made a notation in musical form that the non-Malian singers can learn from the piano. The slow march of the slaves behind the Nile boats now has some real vocal power to go behind it. It forms an awkward hiatus in the scene as Atir stops to watch the slaves go past before continuing with his speech – and sometimes in rehearsal this awkwardness seems utterly right. For all the reflections on the slavers that Khephra Burns has scripted, the simplicity of the song can be more moving. But it's necessarily a slow movement, and despite their tune, the singers aren't getting inside the song like Yaya did when he taught it to them. For reasons he won't explain, Yaya is reluctant to join the line of slaves and sing with them. The solution that's eventually found is effective: the slaves don't sing, but Yaya sings powerfully from backstage, alone. Eventually, his shadow is included, thrown across the screen. All of the rawness, potency and unpredictability of his singing is restored to the moment – it makes the passage of the slaves, so crucial thematically, genuinely arresting and uncomfortable.

Work also continues on the most disorientating scene in the piece: the scientists' song. It seems in a different world from the rest of the play. Is it a remnant of a Broadway imagining of *Tall Horse*? This is the only sequence in which characters break into song 'theatrically', and the style of the music is utterly different from the textures and pieces that Warrick Sony is creating elsewhere. The surreal shifting of levels, with the scientists of the Academy in Paris morphing into rapping dancers, is puzzling. Although the music, based on the old spiritual 'Dem Bones', has a connection to the themes of slavery and migration, it's not clear how this is an appropriate point to use this song. Does having these French intellectuals express themselves through the music of an enslaved people add to the 'African perspective' that the play promises? Does it even make sense? One can see where the idea came from – they are assembling the bones of a giraffe, and, as the song goes, 'the knee bone's connected to the thigh bone', and so on. In fact, Warrick Sony has adapted the words of the song to provide a wry commentary on the march of science during the Enlightenment. This adds some edge to the concept, and Basson's idea of using the song to show the transformation of Dr Konate into St-Hilaire gives it some dramatic function other than as enjoyable decoration. In a strange way, Basson's enthusiasm for pushing each of the other scenes in different directions – from the oppressive rhythms of the Marseilles docks to the camp Soirée – make this only one of a series of departures from the flow of the piece. But this is the first, the most jarring and the least understandable. Plus, some of the singers are still having trouble keeping time.

The dramatic climax of the story comes when the convoy reaches Lyon. Here (in real life) the giraffe, hemmed in by the crowds, sparked a riot by breaking loose from its handler and kicking out. Khephra Burns has seen the opportunity to pull a number of his themes together. The momentary loss of control over the giraffe will become a complete separation from its handlers in our version: the end of the scene sees St-Hilaire and Atir alone and the animal lost. Burns's script suggests that the growing tension between them has brought on this disaster. He ties in Atir's amorous adventures as a contributing factor: with Atir distracted by a beautiful lady, St-Hilaire is unable to control the animal. He has also used this scene to highlight French anti-monarchism: the Mayor of Lyon sees the giraffe as a symbol of the King to whom it's being sent, and wants to destroy it, using that most iconic of French revolutionary methods, the guillotine (given added relevance by the giraffe's magnificent neck). The episode at Lyon offers an opportunity for all these threads to come together, disastrously for the expedition. The scene has clearly excited enthusiasm from the collaborators in plotting the script, and there are lots of witty details. It opens with the sight of the beautiful lady, and two young children, who catch and decapitate a cat using a small guillotine. When Sogo Jan arrives a carnival is in progress, the crowds led by a headless man. A blind doctor breaks off from the procession to accost Atir, speaking in Bambara and ordering him to return home. In the midst of all this, Atir and St-Hilaire are separated from the giraffe. As the headless man breaks into song, they struggle to get back to the giraffe, but, surrounded by crowds, they are too late – she is already in the custody of the bloodthirsty Mayor.

Well, that's how it goes in the script. It's one of the most focused sequences in the piece. The two children catching the cat is a gem of a sketch – puppetry as visual story-telling. The beautiful lady and the blind doctor/prophet are archetypal characters, and when we see Atir caught between them, we seem to have entered a world that's constructed on a more essential level than that of the social satire we see elsewhere. Lyon has an otherworldly feel, as if the two men and their giraffe have wandered into a Hieronymus Bosch painting. Its fantastical quality makes perfect sense of the two men surrounded by puppets. The headless man and his song have already been cut in preparations – this might have worked in a more musical version of the piece, but here there's no need for the interruption to the action. This aside, the scene is not over-written, as is sometimes the case elsewhere. Dialogue is brief and to the point, except for the Mayor's speech – and even that flows rhythmically, building up the macabre carnival mood. As for the carnival itself, that too is a little surplus to the scale of this piece. But the structure of the scene is strong: each section overlaps and hands on to the next, working up from the scene with the cat (which takes place on and around a single flight case), via the intimate liaison with the beautiful lady and the doctor calling across the stage, until the crowd (only four puppets, but given the sense of a larger

The Lyon crowd puppets

crowd by their operators) begin to swamp the space and hem in the giraffe. By now there's very little difficulty with seeing the two styles of puppet together. The little children are Handspring puppets, but they are more like little imps. Their design is based on one Adrian Kohler made for a young chimpanzee in *The Chimp Project,* and once you've seen them moving you might recognise the connection. The rest of the puppets are Sogolon's. Kohler's and Coulibaly's imaginations have been in accord: the distortions and abstractions of the human form in these figures complement each other. The Beautiful Lady is a *meren habitable* – a rod puppet like Sogolon's hand-held designs, but worn on the body, attached to a backpack/head-dress construction. The adaptation of this system used for the stilt-walking mother giraffes had a lace veil hanging over the puppeteer's upper body.

Yaya Coulibaly (with one of Polito's big hands) in discussion with translator Luke Younge

Here, in its more traditional form, the puppet's clothing completely envelops the puppeteer, hanging down to the ground. A long neck emerges from this dress, and on top of it, a delicate, haunting face. The Mayor, Polito, is a mask character in the Malian tradition. Yaya performs him in French, beautifully and terrifyingly, with oversized wooden hands, a big wooden mask and a comical laugh. The character is threatening, funny and majestic all at once.

But, just like every other sequence, there are mechanical problems to contend with. This sort of mask is not designed to accommodate intelligible speech, and Polito's speeches are long. It's a full mask which covers the mouth. Yaya has carved it with teeth, between which there are spaces, but his voice still resonates enough inside the mask to blur the articulation of the words. The other main cause for concern is the guillotine itself. This sequence should be a real show-stopper, and Kohler has prepared for it as such. The giant guillotine, complete with a dropping blade, is actually a section of the four-metre high shelving units which form the set. The wooden blade, set into a heavy box, is held up with a metal cable, which can be released from the other end of the shelf unit, allowing it to plunge downwards. The proximity of the heavy blade and the fragile giraffe neck promotes anxiety. In the story, the blade jams, failing to cut the giraffe's neck – which in turn leads to accusations of witchcraft and further rioting. It's decided that a fixed height will be found, below which the falling blade will not go – a sudden stop just above the animal's neck. There are two ways of stopping the blade as it falls: to put a block in the way of the blade itself, or to put a stop in the cable itself. Putting a stop in the cable seems the most sensible solution. The weight of the blade and box could probably smash aside most things that stood in their way, but if the stop comes in the cable, its natural elasticity should help to absorb the shock. Even so, there is general apprehension whenever the blade falls.

There is a sense of progress now that most scenes have been covered lightly, and the cast are starting to pull together. The work outside of the regular rehearsal schedule is continuing, especially between the Malians. Each morning, Yaya takes the members of his company aside and gives them notes on all of the previous day's work. Indeed he's rarely without his yellow notepad, and has his own position at the side of the stage, silently observing all of the work that goes on, even when he's not involved. The other performers might loll in the stalls or sit upstairs with a cup of tea; Coulibaly is always on hand, observing silently. But he isn't offering advice to Basson. When Adrian Kohler is in this position he's able to get the ear of the director, and the two often confer on ideas for staging. It's not as easy for Basson and Coulibaly to confer without breaking the fluidity of the rehearsal. But although Yaya is not always able to feed his influence through Basson, he does make his contribution by giving detailed direction to his performers. As the leader of Sogolon, Coulibaly is also an experienced director of puppeteers and dancers. Sogolon works with many young performers – Téhibou and Yacouba are both nephews of Yaya – and Yaya sees his role as partly one of a guardian and teachers as well and employer as director. He often points out what an important opportunity this is for his performers to work alongside a major South African director and in the large theatres that *Tall Horse* will play. Equally often, he looks forward to the company's visit to Mali, where, it's implied, the South Africans will learn a thing or two themselves.

The adaptation of the Malian puppets to accommodate the restrictions of venue and convention continues. Yaya explained at the first workshop how the Queen puppet in traditional Malian performance always rides on a cow. There is an enormous and majestic *castelet* for this purpose, with a huge cow's head, lolling tongue and great crescent horns. There's room for three or four people in this great cage, although once Téhibou has demonstrated that it can be moved by one person alone, it is operated like this – one person carrying the *castelet*, and one carrying the Queen who rises out of it on her long pole.

But while the Queen puppet's fearsome, severe beauty is very appropriate to the character of Marie-Thérèse in the play, the way the scenes are constructed is different. Khephra Burns is a writer who is steeped in TV and film as much as in theatre and variety, and the fluidity of intercutting scenes requires the Queen to come on and off stage frequently and quickly. The mass of the full Queen and *castelet* rig is hugely effective, but quick it isn't. And so experiments have been ongoing to explore how the Queen can be, if not nimble, at least more mobile.

Essentially the Queen puppet is the simplest design imaginable: a very long pole with a head on top. The pole runs through a block of wood which supports a set of shoulders (stylized as a cylinder lying on its side) and her breasts. The Queen, huger and more majestic than the other women, has a longer neck covered with even more gold. The same is true with regard to the tradition of bared breasts: hers project from the chest like torpedoes. It's an effect accentuated further when she's been painted red. Hanging over the

Adrian Kohler prepares the Queen for a publicity photo shoot

shoulders of the Queen is an enormous sheet of light fabric in blue and white, decorated with burgundy, blue and gold fleurs-de-lis, which hangs all the way to the ground when she is at her full height of four metres or so. One of the first experiments is to take her off the *castelet* and see if shapes can be made with the fabric – giving the effect of an extraordinary pyramid tapering to the shoulders and head. It looks great, with several people crouching inside it to pull the corners tight to the ground. But not when it's required to move. Instead of the crisp tension of diagonal lines, its mechanical interior is exposed as the lines are broken up by the hunched bodies under the cloth, scuttling to keep up with the person carrying the pole. This clearly won't work. The next variation is to try poles. Two bamboo rods are attached to the bottom front corners. This should allow the puppeteers holding these corners to position themselves further back, so they can nestle more discreetly under the 'tent' they are making with the fabric. There's an exciting and frustrating work session exploring these possibilities; and what's most interesting is that when it comes to improvising solutions, the key collaborators fall into equal status. Marthinus Basson has the eye for the picture, and both Adrian Kohler and Yaya Coulibaly have the expertise and ingenuity to come up with potential solutions. Even though on this occasion it's one of his puppets which is being experimented with, Coulibaly keeps his counsel, observing, smiling, nodding, offering little more than the occasional '*Ça va*' or '*Oui, c'est bien*'. It's a contrast to Basson's more demonstrative drive towards a decision. Now, as often, he seems to defer the day-to-day decisions to Adrian and Marthinus, preferring to observe and offer comment only if asked to. The absence is felt by Kohler and Jones, who are keen to benefit from the engagement with Sogolon. But in the moment, when a decision has to be made and when Yaya chooses not to express an opinion, a decision still has to be made. Kohler is in his usual mode: moving between the auditorium (to confer with Basson), the stage (to adjust or demonstrate) and the toolbox (to effect some alteration to the system). As the most natural puppeteer in the company, he's quickest to grasp how a new idea or variation might best be expressed physically, so it's hard to keep him next to the director so that they can discuss the ideas. The sticks are held by people in front of the pole-carrier – but again, in motion, the sagging cloth settles on their heads, and with the operators bunched up near the central pole, it's impossible to move the figure smoothly. They try standing behind the pole-carrier. But the figure seems lopsided. The poles are difficult to control precisely, and the two puppeteers are holding them at awkward angles, while trying to co-ordinate their movements with the main pole-operator and someone else's speech. And as soon as they try to move the figure, the three trip on the fabric which hangs down around them. Finally, someone tries holding both of the poles, with the third operator working as an attendant to gather and arrange the fabric behind them. It's awkward, but it works for a time.

Much of our progress is as halting and technical as these problems with the Queen. It sets back Basson's schedule even further. The Queen's scenes are rarely rehearsed in detail because so much time is spent on trying alternative manipulation systems. Busi Zokufa, who plays her voice but does not manipulate the large puppet, waits patiently to offer her lines in French, which she has been learning and practising phonetically – but she's rarely able to get involved. It suggests that more could have been done in advance to determine how the figure should be operated – but when and by whom? The spirit of discovery and collaboration that engendered both Handspring's and Sogolon's engagement with this project demands that these problems be encountered and solved here as part of the process – and yet how different this period has been from what anyone expected. Even with seven weeks to create the piece, everyone is feeling the pressure. As we head towards the work-in-progress showings in the sixth week of rehearsal, Basson will have expected to know the flow of the piece, and be able to edit and alter parts of it. Instead, he might not even have a full show ready to present.

Basil Jones has identified one of the difficulties, which comes from the different training of various members of the company. The South Africans are used to a tradition based on extensive note-taking, and (usually) end each rehearsal session by writing down the new moves and changes that have been explored or fixed on. Of course this is done less scrupulously by some, but they're all aware of the system. The young Malians don't make notes and seem bemused by the practice. Yaya, on the other hand, makes notes all the time, both of what he's doing and what others are doing. One of Basson's great frustrations is when performers return to a scene and can't remember the changes that took place in its previous rehearsal, several days or up to a week ago. Although Téhibou, Yacouba and Nana are encouraged to take notes (and on occasion, the boys do it assiduously), they don't keep it up. But with Nana's poor reading and writing, she doesn't relate to the script in the same way that Yaya and the others do. Yacouba likes to refer to the script, and Téhibou is always enthusiastic to learn the way things are done here. But as time goes on, and more and more of Téhibou's and Yacouba's scenes are in the giraffe, their movements and cues are minimal and simple, and they have no problem remembering them. The same isn't true for Nana, who has a complex involvement in various scenes, and is still overwhelmed with the supportive babble of English advice and direction. Yaya, meanwhile, keeps his position by the front of the stage, diligently noting everything that happens. While I'm taking notes for this book, I often wonder what would be in Yaya's version.

Some scenes aren't as taxing to deal with as the Queen's dress. The romantic liaison between Atir (Fezile Mpela) and Clothilde (a puppet) requires almost no mechanical adjustments. It's built around two scenes. The first is a seduction in the stable at Marseilles, where Clothilde's husband the Prefect is housing the giraffe. The second is a consummation of their relationship, with Clothilde pursuing the giraffe's caravan and meeting Atir in another stable en route. With the giraffe in the background, the stage is almost clear, and a quiet scene with few distractions is a welcome thing. Yaya, Basil and Marthinus (Adrian is one of the two puppeteers on Clothilde) can focus on the intimacy of the scene. Things certainly progress more quickly the less puppetry there is, and these moments are crucial to Basson regaining control over his material. It's a scene where Koffi Kôkô's influence is definitely missed. The company haven't forgotten what he has to offer. 'What I saw [Koffi] doing with the wordless development made me realise…I've always instinctually felt that the dance way of developing time on the stage is closely related to puppets – to what puppets do. A lot of dialogue is in the way, we all know that,' reflects Kohler. Koffi's work with Fezile could help him develop a physicality to chime with the minimalist gestural style of the Clothilde puppet. Basson concurs in his more pragmatic tone: 'This needs to turn into a sort of dance. Because otherwise we'll never sell any of it.'

But this smoothness is an exception. The chanting in Marseilles ('it's a devil') remains hard work. Marthinus had hoped that fixing a tight rhythm would give him an effective aural set-piece that could then be shaped visually. He's used similar techniques in the past, and the effect has always come across very well, he says. But this group of performers can't seem to keep the rhythm between them. Of course they remember the sequence, but keeping three or four chants going around seems too much. There are several failed attempts before they pick up puppets. As soon as one eye is on the manipulation of the Marseilles puppets, things collapse. Meanwhile, Marthinus needs to bring in the Prefect, and asks one of the chanters, Yacouba, to operate his second arm as he stamps the administrative documents. The Prefect is to be positioned above the action, framed in the 'window' of a high shelf, with a radio microphone to raise his catalogue of documents above the welter of chanting. Basil Jones, who plays the Prefect, will already be wearing one to amplify his voice as Mehmet Ali. But both stamping and chanting (in different rhythms) while halfway up a ladder throws Yacouba, and if it isn't him, it's a late entrance by someone else, or someone mishearing the previous chanter. It should be possible for one performer's missed cue not to affect the continued flow, but here, the slightest mistake seems to throw the rest of the sequence into collapse. Of course the language barrier doesn't help, and even when it works, the furious rhythm remains stubbornly ill-suited to the puppets. Mechanical movement in an actor can be surprising, sinister or comical; in a puppet, it more often just looks soulless. Here it's a real struggle for the performers to hit the clockwork beat of their chant while keeping their puppets alive and natural.

Marthinus Basson is becoming frustrated. To help them keep rhythm, he asks Yaya to beat time with them. Perhaps Yaya interprets this as an invitation to take over the teaching of the rhythm, but, for whatever reason, the invitation to work together ends up exposing a surprising tension between the two men. Yaya sees a different route to helping the group master the sequence. Everyone has been finding this difficult, and I don't think anyone is sure why. Yaya varies the djembe's rhythm elastically to accommodate the chanters' indecision. Presumably he wants the pattern to get more secure before it is pulled into tight time. All Basson hears is Yaya not keeping time, and, anxious about the lack of progress, he halts the session and shouts at him: 'No no no!' Getting the pulse of the time is crucial to

Adrian Kohler's design sketches for Clothilde and the Prefect

him; but Coulibaly clearly disagrees, and each time the sequence is tried again, the drum just accompanies the sloppy rhythm of the actors. Basson picks Coulibaly up on it again, and this time more explicitly. He's losing his temper, and undercutting Yaya in front of everyone, as Adrian says later, 'including his guys'.

Disagreement and conflict is inevitable in a pressured collaboration. I don't think that communication between Basson and Coulibaly outside of the rehearsal session could have avoided this, and it's out of character for Basson to criticise Yaya openly. Later the same day Yaya discreetly raises reservations about the protocol of the collaboration and his status within it. Both Coulibaly and Basson avoid conflict. The Handspring directors are more likely to bring an issue to the surface and discuss it, but Marthinus and Yaya seem to prefer to find a way around confrontation. Consequently, it's very difficult to find out how either of them really feels the collaboration is proceeding, or what they think of each other. I sense that both would like to connect. When I ask Yaya, he is diplomatic to a fault, as courteous as always. He speaks about what a pleasure it is to be working here. What he said earlier, he explains, was not important, because in the wider context this is how making work happens. If he is feeling undervalued or underutilised, he won't let on. Later I manage to get this out of him: 'Marthinus is a very very good director. I've worked with great directors all over the world. I knew that Marthinus is a classical director. And also a university director. So it's a genuine pleasure for me to work with him. But I should also have a contribution, because it's a meeting of two cultures. And [I have] a different vision from an academic system.'

Basson, too, brushes aside suggestions that there is a problem. But if you talk to Basil or Adrian, they are in equal parts concerned that the Malians are getting a rough ride (and that Yaya in particular is not taking as central a role as he might have expected) and frustrated that Yaya won't admit there's a difficulty or speak up for himself. At this stage they're not critical of Basson's handling of the relationship, but there's cause for concern.

The next day the company attempt to run the first half of the play in one go. We're into the fourth week of rehearsals now. It could easily turn into a disaster, with so much to forget and so much consistently forgotten – but instead turns out to be, for the most part, a tonic. The run cements a lot of the recent work, and gives the performers a better grip on the sequence of the scenes. There are a couple of errors of positioning, and the Hunt sequence is walked through slowly rather than taken at pace. Marseilles, of course, is where it grinds to a halt, with the frustration showing on Basson as the performers struggle to remember details that had been worked on that same morning. But the disappointing end doesn't disguise the definite progress.

Runs like this make a big difference to how the performers locate themselves in the sequence of directions they have been given. Because Basson's style is relatively visual, and so often born of an idea he's had on the spot, the movements of the puppets and characters have rarely come from the performers. Rather, they've been given a set of moves which it's their job to inhabit. Many directors work in this way, and others prefer to let the actors make suggestions, shaping and altering them. Basson uses a combination of these approaches, but when the performers are also operating puppets, they don't seem to mind some decisions being taken away from them. So in these early runs the staging sometimes appears stiff and forced. But it's by putting them in context that they can find a way to make these movements their own.

The technical team continue to plan ahead. Leigh Colombick, the stage manager, has seen how the staging is progressing, how many puppets there are and how they will have to be moved around. She asks for two backstage crew to keep things running smoothly behind the scenes. It's not a lot on a production this big, and while most of the puppeteers, well used to working on smaller-scale shows, will be familiar with organising themselves backstage, it will be almost impossible for them to navigate all the puppets, stilts, *castelets* and props without support. No allowance has been made for backstage crew. Colombick herself will be running the technical aspects of the piece, calling the lighting, sound and video cues. Basil Jones had hoped that with this many performers, there would be enough people offstage at any given time to keep things working, but arrangements will have to be made. Enrico Wey is visiting the rehearsals as an intern; he's a student of puppetry and dance in New York. He's already been invaluable in helping Adrian with puppet making and has been working well with the company. Can he be persuaded to join the show in this essential but far from glamorous role?

The translation/note-taking problems are feeding into themselves in a vicious circle. The more often Basson arrives at a scene to find that lots of rehearsed detail hasn't been retained, the more he relies on his ebullience and enthusiasm to get it moving again, brimming with descriptions and directions, and the less time there is to translate and interpret them. So, the more chaotic it gets, the more chaotic it gets. Whatever language you speak, the sheer quantity of direction is hard to take in and organise. Nana seems more estranged, while Téhibou and Yacouba are making great strides with the rest of the company, learning English words and phrases incredibly quickly. They are now much more fluent in English than Nana and sometimes even more so than Yaya, who understands quite a lot of English but doesn't like to speak it. Perhaps it's because of Yaya's status in the company that he doesn't want to speak clumsily. The boys enjoy the responses they receive when they get it right, and those they receive when they get it wrong too.

As the date of Koffi Kôkô's return nears, Marthinus Basson wants to make sure he's looked over the whole show properly so that Kôkô will have something coherent to respond to. And so the beginning of this fifth week sees a frenetic rush through the scenes. It's a difficult atmosphere for everyone. Basson needs to foster a sense of achievement, but for the company, each week is a continuation of the same uphill struggle. A piece this ambitious couldn't have been made any quicker, but these seven weeks seem endless. The windowless theatre doesn't change from day to day or week to week, and sometimes it's as if no progress is being made on the scenes either. There's nearly another explosion as Basson takes on the presentation scene, where the giraffe is finally presented to the King and Queen after her long journey. As the culmination of a story which has seen a lot of alteration since Koffi Kôkô's early examination, it needs to be completely overhauled. Everyone is on stage, which always seems to mean that some of them don't hear what Marthinus says. Basil Jones has had some large parasols made for a photo shoot, dressed with colourful Malian fabrics. He's keen to include them in the show, and feels that this scene needs as much colour as it can get. Marthinus accepts them and works them into his plan – but he has a lot to put across. His energy gets soaked up in confusion, attention continues to wander, and large things are moving slowly – the huge and unwieldy Queen *castelet* and the giraffe on stilts. This is not the nimble, inspiring pace of work that Basson thrives on, and as he gets more and more tense he is reduced to crisis resolution mode: he's directing the scene like directing traffic, with brief, terse instructions. There's no

The *Tall Horse* company in July 2004: back row: Busi Zokufa, Adrian Kohler, Zandile Msutswana, Yacouba Magassouba, Nana Kouma, Basil Jones, Craig Leo, Fezile Mpela; front row: Téhibou Bagayoko, Bheki Vilakazi, Fourie Nyamande, Yaya Coulibaly

translation at this pace, so it's anyone's guess what Nana Kouma will be able to retain. The director is desperate to get some progress out of the scene, but from the outside it's one man barking at the stage – not a mode that guarantees cohesion or confidence in the company, and certainly one that exacerbates the Malians' linguistic disadvantage.

So it's a pleasant surprise that support for the determined director comes from Yaya Coulibaly, who takes the opportunity of a pause to agree publicly with one of Basson's more surprising choices (to have the Queen exit dramatically before the scene is over) and to adjust the movement. Coulibaly speaks calmly, quietly, in French, in what's perhaps a conscious contrast with the tightness of Basson's voice today. He takes his time and lets Adrian handle the translation. Although a small event in the day, it's a crucial influence on the way the company respond to Marthinus's staging of the scene. That the words of Coulibaly come through Kohler's translation also gives a sense of the two men coming together to support the decisions of their director.

But only later that day when the company are working on Lyon, the cracks begin to appear again. Basson is unhappy with the scene. What had seemed such a beautiful sequence of moments creating something larger, now isn't. 'There's no flow, there's no focus and there's no situation,' he laments. 'There's no scene.' He sets about altering the flow, allowing the distinct moments to feed into each other and overlap more. The scene grinds into even slower progress when Mayor

Polito enters to give his speech. Yaya is almost incomprehensible speaking through the holes in the wood. The rhythmic flow that he creates is generated by pauses and details; it's a character solo rather than the swift, efficient, supporting build that the director is hoping for. Basson needs the scene to grab the audience and carry them until the moment the guillotine falls on the neck of the giraffe. But in Yaya's conception of the scene and character, the Mayor has a more complex role in defining the location and developing the nature of the threat to St-Hilaire. The director challenges Yaya about his reluctance to deliver the speech with more fluency. Coulibaly's response is just as calm and thoughtful as earlier on, but its thoroughness surprises everyone.

Where Marthinus's interpretation of the character was developed out of dramaturgical necessity – a sense of 'I need a quick, dynamic character here' – Yaya's is based on a close study of the text. Any preconceptions that the Malian way of looking at characterisation might be less rigorous are destroyed this afternoon. Yaya's characterisation of Polito is psychologically watertight in the spirit of Stanislavsky. Yaya is undoubtedly a showman, and on stage he has a charisma and magnetism that are so immediate and vital, you assume a level of improvisation is present. The characterisation of Polito has always seemed to be a comic turn, a slightly self-indulgent riff on a favourite persona. And of course he has carved this mask himself: his vision of this character may pre-date the script he's working from. But here he explains, with reference to the lines, the development of Polito's thought, and how these moments of pause, of manic laughter, the looks askance and the movements of the big wooden hands, are part of a detailed interpretation of the text. With this knowledge, it's easy to see how the same applies to all of the roles he plays. It underlines what a thorough actor Coulibaly is, and how seriously he takes his craft: his preparation is more rigorous than any other actor or puppeteer on stage. He's also the teacher and director of Téhibou and Yacouba, and this provokes a reassessment of how they might be relating to the material. And it also reveals his modesty. None of the others would have known about this preparation unless Basson had questioned Yaya's clowning.

The contrast puts a perspective on Yaya's behaviour in opting out of artistic, directorial and conceptual discussions about the way the piece should be staged: his characteristic shrug, poker face and 'c'est bien' may have been calculated to remove himself from this realm so that he can concentrate on his work on stage. His choice not to demand a vocal role, collaborating directly with the director – which I interpret as a decision not to interrupt and cause obstacles to the direction – has led to him becoming, for the most part, one of the company: an actor and puppeteer without special status. Most of the time it seems a role he's happy with, and he is able to commit to his work more single-mindedly than Basil or Adrian, with the multiple demands on their time.

Both Adrian and Basil immerse themselves in every aspect of the production, almost obsessively accepting a share of the anxieties felt by each member of the company, from the director to the interns. They are always ready to lend a hand or a supportive shoulder, but feel most keenly the pressure of their own extra roles as designer/puppet maker and as producer. If there is an engineering problem with one of the puppets, it will occupy Kohler until it is solved. Every producing crisis is an urgent one for Jones. The consequence can be that they don't have the same time to spend on preparation for their rehearsals that they expect of the others. It's not rare to see them arriving for work in the morning learning their lines in the car, and the strain of juggling so many roles does show on them.

Kohler explains how it feels: 'I am switching as the needs come. Sometimes Wesley [France, production manager] really needs me to discuss something about the set, and my head isn't there at all. But I've got to make a switch and pull me out of the rehearsals, out of the constructing of the piece space. And that is a wrench. The puppets themselves are designed now. On a show of this size there should be a designated puppet constructor, working now on those pieces that aren't ready. To reach the beginning of rehearsals was terrifying for me because of that. Because I knew that suddenly, my days would be gone. And where do you find the time, to actually finish the stuff that isn't finished yet? I mean, the reason why I'm all of those roles is a financial one, but also to design a set for puppets, you need to know their requirements.' It's clear that he feels responsibility to each of his roles, and has the appetite to keep doing them all. But the scale of this has daunted and surprised even him. He finishes, slightly disbelieving: 'It's absurd. That I've done all these roles. It is absurd.'

It's the eighteenth of August, the middle of the fifth week of rehearsals, when Koffi Kôkô is welcomed back to the company with a run of the whole show in order.

Koffi had said when he left that on his return he would be looking for 'the space to dance' in the piece. Marthinus's constant desire in shaping the overall rhythms, has been to keep the play flowing, to keep the energy passing from performer to performer in order to create and sustain story, and to eradicate spare 'space'. Oddly, one of the sections where Marthinus thinks Koffi might work is the Marseilles rabble scene – the epically difficult choral section. It seems barely credible that the performers will be able to take on choreography as well, and the fact that Kôkô doesn't work to music means that he may not instinctively connect with this piece of almost pure rhythm.

Philani Mbana has also been working on the scientists' dance – but there is concern that Kôkô might not like it. The two had very little time to consult on this scene, and the style that Marthinus Basson is expecting is much closer to the sort of hip-hop dance work that Philani is familiar with than to the work that Koffi usually produces. But he should be more comfortable in the stable scene, where Basson hopes to continue Kôkô's work on expressive movement as a metaphor for Atir and Clothilde's sex. And Kôkô has also to see the changes that have been made to the two big movement set-pieces: the Hunt and the Presentation. These grand moments should have the stamp of the choreographer and although Basson has tried not to pre-empt his colleague, he's had to make changes. With tension between Basson and Coulibaly simmering, Kôkô's return may throw up another conflict.

The strain of competing for time with the puppetry, combined with the general chaos, is starting to show on Fezile Mpela. *Tall Horse* is a unique prospect and not a gentle reintroduction to stage work. His successful career in TV and radio must seem a world away from what is happening here. For weeks he has waited patiently and professionally for his moments, and has increasingly been a good-humoured and helpful companion to Téhibou and Yacouba, helping them strap into their stilts and put on the bulky giraffe body over their heads. One of the most frequent sights on the rehearsal stage is Fezile standing with the giraffe's neck resting on his shoulder as Téhibou takes a rest from holding it upright. But being valet to a Malian stilt-walker can't be what he expected when he was invited to play the leading role in a Handspring Puppet Company show directed by Marthinus Basson. Fezile is a modern South African. He's well-educated, articulate, confident, optimistic and flexible. If he feels either more or less at ease in different company, he doesn't show it. He's charming and professional, skills which will have helped him make his way so far in his successful career, and which are being tested here. The first signs of frustration on his part came very late (much later than the point at which most of the other members of the company exhibited dissatisfaction). In the run of Act One in the fourth week, his first real chance to string his story together, his acting was mannered to the point of bizarre. There was an enormous shift in his style of performance, away from the crisp, detailed work we'd seen in the rehearsing of individual scenes. Suddenly, Jean-Michel was

Fezile Mpela and Bheki Vilakazi

played as cheesy situation comedy, and Atir was melodramatic and overdone. It wasn't like Basson's vision of the character, and neither did it seem to tally with Fezile's own view of the character and scene. At the time I put it down to the actor flexing his muscles, using this platform to request a little more attention and rehearsal time. But because that Act One run ended with Basson invading the stage to remedy a collapse at Marseilles, Fezile didn't get his time. Once again the focus went to the continually misfiring rabble-chant.

With his leading actor starting to lose focus, and most of the company banging their ever-tiring heads against the brick wall of the Marseilles chanting, is it fair to say that Marthinus Basson is out of control? His response to an ever less secure relationship with his company seems to be to withdraw, discussing less and barraging them with his own faith in his ideas. It's easy to see how his trademark enthusiasm is both a motivational tool and a genuine feeling, and I don't think the company doubt his ability to conceive this piece. But the bursts of energy aren't always focused. Session after session centres on another disjointed piece of stage business, and there's almost never discussion of the performer's own ideas and responses. Is this impish playfulness really supported by a loyalty to and understanding of the text? And if it is, why is discussion on the rehearsal room floor mainly about the technicalities of staging? Perhaps Basson's eye is off the ball of the story, distracted by the joy of making something brilliant happen whether it's the right thing or not, trusting that he'll be forgiven by an audience equally delighted by the dazzle of the visual humour and charm. There's no doubt that he has a direct line to an audience's delight, but the work isn't making the storytelling feel more secure. All the company can do is trust him. His track record would suggest he knows what he's doing.

The morning of the 18th sees Fezile apparently dispirited and bored. Everyone's tired, and the pressure of work is starting to show on Adrian, who just looks bewildered. Koffi watches as the company launch into Act One – but it's a plodding, downbeat effort. Marthinus Basson looks on grimly, munching his beard as he does when he's under stress. He takes his notes and scrupulously avoids looking at Kôkô. As it gets going, some of the performers start to find their energy in the piece. There are sequences that already have their shape – the embarkation at Alexandria, for example. This time Basson isn't drawn up onto the stage to intervene, but what he sees on stage isn't what he'd rehearsed. The reasonable tone of his comments on the run draws a positive response from the performers, who are always pleased to run the show in order, and seem a little invigorated, both by having done it and, especially, by not being showered with brickbats afterwards. At lunch, Koffi Kôkô keeps his counsel.

The mood in the afternoon is different: positive and productive. A company this big, this tired, with this many disparate types of training, will always be prone to distraction, but the afternoon's activity will be to run the whole piece again, and everyone has an appetite for it. Those of us watching are disappointed to see how many notes remain forgotten, but again Basson ensures that it's the successes that are recognised. It's clear how difficult it is to perform this show. The puppeteers are running on and off stage, grabbing puppets in split-second changes and returning in a different frame of mind as a different character. Often they are returning as an arm of another character – and must sacrifice their own 'backstage journey' to be part of someone else's for a time. They're moving the scenery as the huge shelves trundle backwards and forwards to alter the proportions of the stage-image. And sometimes they're even remembering the moves that Basson has worked with them on.

The day ends with a creative meeting to discuss the runs with Koffi. Marthinus, Basil, Adrian and Koffi gather around a table at the bar opposite the rehearsal theatre. Marthinus seems apprehensive, but you know he will take whatever arrives in his stride. Basil and Adrian invite Koffi to make the running. All three are keen to hear a voice that has been removed from the situation give a response to how the piece is shaping up. 'I am not criticising,' begins Koffi. 'I am just saying…what I see. I am completely involved artistically with this production, so I must say what I think.' Always diplomatic. Marthinus readies himself for criticism.

Koffi's first suggestion is that the piece is too illustrative. You do not need to hold a big bucket up to the giraffe's head to show that it is drinking – you can mime the bucket. His point isn't that mime is inherently better than the real prop, but rather that the point of the action is not the bucket itself, but the offering of the drink, and the drinking of the drink. The question asked is whether the large metal bucket distracts from showing this relationship. I don't think anyone was expecting Koffi's thoughts to be this fundamental. It's a world away from the day-to-day concerns of performers remembering moves or organising backstage puppet-placement, or the trouble of hauling some of the more elusive scenes into a comprehensible shape. There's a moment of almost-panic as Basson tries to take this perspective shift in. His response is to look to practicalities. If we mime the bucket, then we should mime everything, from St-Hilaire's walking-stick up. The piece would become about the movement of bodies and puppets in relation to each other. He opens it to the group. It's a bolder, more avant-garde conception of the piece – exactly the sort of influence that Kôkô is supposed to be bringing. It poses particular problems when you start to look at it in detail. In a play where the framing device is a museum and most of the characters are represented by objects from that museum, the status of a prop is not straightforward. In principle, all puppets, as physical objects handled by actors, are in some sense a prop. In this new idea, a distinction would have to be made between the objects that are only objects that shape a relationship, and objects that are characters, that are shaped specifically to be people. It seems an easy one, but here, where there is a nod to the status of puppets as exhibits and as fetishes for the cultural historian or anthropologist, the props (presumably also belonging to the museum) should also have some charge.

The discussion goes on to how Koffi will work. Once again, he'll need a lot of rehearsal time, and Marthinus engages to work more closely with him. Koffi asks, as he promised to when he left three weeks ago, how much 'space' there is to explore in. Marthinus responds that he wants Koffi to be able to explore fully and transform all of the scenes – although he inevitably picks out the visual set-pieces. Maybe he's conscious that, if Koffi works in the same way that he did before, he won't have time to apply his eye to the other scenes. The meeting develops into a warm chat, talking about some of the difficulties of staging that have been encountered, and the continuing obstacle of the language barrier. They talk about what work has been done on the movement sequences, how Craig's stilt-walking is too good to leave out of the Hunt, and how the love scene has been roughly plotted out. And Adrian points out that Basson's preparations, by leading up to the two runs the company made today, have left the company ready for a new eye and some fresh input.

Two hundred years ago… it was something impossible. It's something very important, and something almost impossible to do. But they arrive.

Koffi Kôkô

The starting point was an extraordinary animal going north. Something that people have not yet seen. So you have the familiar, from our point of view, travelling into the unfamiliar.

Marthinus Basson

Yaya Coulibaly manipulating the King with two whirling *castelets*
Photograph by Damien Schumann

I like the play because of the fact that it was an African man going into Europe, and sort of discovering Europe.

Basil Jones

I think it's very good, for this initial exploration between us, that it takes place in Egypt and goes to France. That, in a strange way, is much better than doing a great Mali legend, or a South African historical story.

Adrian Kohler

Bheki Vilakazi and Sandile Matsheni with the giraffe (2005 production)
Photograph by Damien Schumann

6

WITH KOFFI KÔKÔ BACK IN THE REHEARSAL room, the energy of the company shifts. As they build up to the work-in-progress shows, the company will be reconciling the different approaches of Kôkô and Basson. But this time they have a stronger context to do it in – they know their way through the story. The other collaborators have settled into their roles now. Basil's producing commitments set him a little apart from the other performers; when not on stage he is likely to be working on a spreadsheet in the auditorium or fielding calls in the theatre foyer. The necessity for him to get back home to do office work in the evening means that he and Adrian are rarely in the bar after rehearsals – where Koffi, Yaya and Marthinus can usually be relied on for a visit. Adrian's simple love for performing endears him to the company. His experience and skill as a teacher of puppetry means that they want to turn to him for advice on technique; and this is rewarded with a demeanour that's at its happiest when he is just being a puppeteer. His enthusiasm is undimmed by his extreme fatigue. Yaya retains more gravitas as the leader of his company offstage, but he too allows his exuberance and enjoyment free rein when he's on stage – there's no mistaking that these two men share common ground. Both are skilled makers, but completely at home on stage, giving life to their creations and generating the energy of the scene.

Yaya is still looking after his company, having quiet meetings before rehearsals start; while the South Africans are dragging themselves in and looking for coffee, Yaya is usually giving notes from his yellow legal notepad. The previous friction between Basson and Coulibaly has quietened down, but there's less trust between them. Yaya is continuing to avoid creative conversations with Marthinus; and a question is arising: what is this collaboration trying to produce? Koffi Kôkô says that when he saw Yaya on stage with a drum in the Marseilles sequence he was worried – that this was a cliché of 'African' theatre and not something he felt comfortable with. Wesley France's quiet response was that it's the truth of West Africa: if you visit, you'll see many black men playing drums. Sogolon perform with drums. Is it a cliché? Or is it the championing of African puppetry and performance? A similar question arises whenever a Sogolon puppet is used in a non-traditional way. Basil Jones is adamant that this should not be 'heritage theatre'. Sogolon's Bamana tradition is a live one, and here or in Mali the company are making their shows for today's audiences, not recreating old spectacles. But Yaya's indulgent acceptance of Handspring's almost completely free engagement with the Bamana puppets is concerning: surely someone should be encouraging the inclusion of distinctly Malian qualities? Handspring would be mortified if this became an appropriation of Sogolon's visual style rather than a genuine collaboration. Almost as problematic is the director's professed distance from it. ('It's not my project, it's Basil and Adrian's project.') My impression is that they'd like a little bit of him to pull this piece together too. But despite his reputation as a conceptual auteur, his self-image is resolutely that of a worker: 'You look at what is possible, and what comes up and what happens on the floor, and you try and align that to the best possible effect for hopefully the entire production's benefit.' Adrian and Basil have both spoken about how Marthinus' love of the act of theatre doesn't leave room for an ego – but perhaps they need one to assert creative control.

The King and Queen scenes are recovering from the time spent on arranging poles. The poles themselves, holding out the Queen's costume, still aren't working. It had been hoped that familiarity with them would improve things, but the image isn't right. The next scheme is to try mounting the Queen on a *castelet* – not her enormous lumbering cow, but one of the smaller, more agile, antelope. The intention is to keep the large *castelet* back so that it has visual impact in the climactic presentation scene, but to retain some of the grandeur that the Queen has when she is riding. This works better, and allows the *castelet* operator (often Fourie Nyamande, who has an instinct and love for finding the crispest timing with his moves) a chance to really utilise the expressiveness of the moving ears and mouth in order to puncture the Queen's severe and upright rigidity. It's the ideal solution for the first scene, where the King and Queen invade the museum space; she looks wonderfully bizarre coming on. But being unwieldy, the *castelet* takes time to prepare, and when it comes on stage, there's no looking at anything else. So while it's right for moments when the Queen has a grand entrance or opens a scene, it doesn't work for some of the political scenes in the second half, where the Queen simply cuts into conversations between the King and his Minister. Marthinus asks if we might use a shadow of the Queen puppet for these appearances. Yaya shrugs and says, *'Oui, pas de problème.'* Experiments are made by throwing a silhouette of the Queen's head against the video projection screen (in the same way as Yaya's body is used in the Nile slave song), and Adrian is commissioned to prepare a Queen shadow puppet.

Basson proposes a speed run of the moves in Acts Three and Four to remind the performers of their blocking. The system is clear enough: the actors need only to move through the scene as quickly as they can, synchronising their moves with each other (and remembering them all). After a promising start, Basson

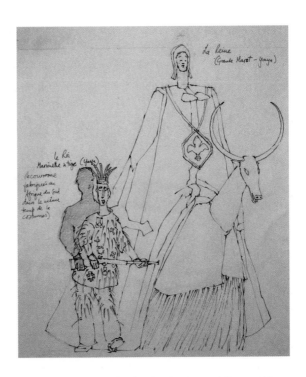

Adrian Kohler's design sketches for the King and Queen of France

finds himself beginning to prompt people. One of his reasons for suggesting this exercise is to see if the rhythms he has set out will work when they get up to a fluent pace. So keen is he to keep the rhythm going that, rather than waiting for the actor to remember it, he's happy to supply the forgotten move. Basson's voice is heard more and more, until he is dictating the moves to every performer in each scene. I'm not sure if it's helping the performers remember their moves better. But it does have a surprising effect. Basson's staging has often seemed whimsical, the fruit of a moment's over-enthusiasm. He chops and changes it frequently – hence the performers' occasional lapses in remembering which of the several moves they've been given is the 'right' one. But Basson gives a bravura performance here: he knows every move. The performers start to surrender themselves to his dictation. He creates an accelerated pacing of each scene with his delivery, and it reinforces the company's trust in him enormously. The changes aren't whimsical; he knows exactly where he has left each moment and movement. The exercise ends with everyone smiling and upbeat, more secure, if not necessarily in their moves, at least in their relationship with their director's authority.

The focus goes back to Koffi Kôkô as he takes control for a review of the Hunt. But to everyone's surprise (particularly the core creative team, after their meeting the previous evening), he begins to reconstruct the version of the scene that he was using before he left – with expert stilt-walker Craig Leo in a *castelet*. In contrast to Basson, Kôkô isn't completely sure how he left the scene, and as he reconstructs imperfectly he begins to create a variant. Leo himself is bemused, but goes along with what he's asked to do. Basson, Kohler and Jones all bite their tongues to see what will happen. Craig is also one of the best manipulators of a *castelet* – he's developed a skipping trot that's animal-like and very funny. Perhaps Kôkô does not realise that there will not be time for Leo to work a *castelet*, exit, strap himself into the stilts, head-dress and skirt, and then return in time for his mother giraffe's section of the sequence. Kôkô seems to be using the rehearsal session to reorient himself. There's a creeping feeling of unease as the performers remember the exploratory sessions Koffi led in the first weeks. Whereas then some of the company were intrigued and involved by the slow, generous rhythm of Kôkô's probing of the material and resources, by now everyone has one eye on the public showings next week.

Basson doesn't know quite how to respond. Kôkô isn't an idiot. He knows there is little time, so this must be a choice of his – a process. Basson desperately wants to understand, to contribute – but he can't see the system. And it means it will be almost impossible for him to offer notes on these sequences now they've been picked apart and left in pieces: 'How do you disturb a process before you know what it is, without killing something? I mean, you can see where the value lies in some of the smaller scenes, and the suggestions that have come up there I've found extremely good, and potent…superb. The larger sections, I'm not always sure what to do with it yet. How it works.' There seems no justification for doing exploratory work now, and although there's no outward resistance to the way Kôkô is working, some of the rallying achieved by Marthinus Basson's hectoring speed-run is being eroded by doubt. In the tea break there's a hurried conference between Kôkô and Basson, mediated by an eager Philani Mbana. For a young dancer and choreographer like Mbana, the chance to work with either Basson or Kôkô is an honour; he desperately wants to learn from Koffi at the same time as supplying Marthinus with what he needs. To be stuck between their apparently irreconcilable styles must be excruciating.

Fezile Mpela (Atir) is starting to find himself again; and it's the reappearance of Koffi that is helping him. Even though Fezile is one of the most resistant of the company to the quasi-mystical style that Kôkô sometimes affects, Koffi is most comfortable moving the human body on stage. In fact, Koffi approaches the play through the character of Atir and makes some of the most interesting points about how he might see the world. And, crucially, when he's put in charge of a scene like the seduction between Atir and Clothilde, he puts Atir at its centre. After one session of Kôkô's sessions on this scene, Basil Jones says to Mpela: 'It was the first time you really superceded Clothilde… We were absolutely watching you.' He means it as a simple compliment – it's hard for an actor to take focus from one of these figures. The history of the theatre is littered with complaints from actors who have been upstaged by puppets; Kôkô is helping Mpela find an economy and decisiveness in his movement that will allow him to compete. It is a useful feature of Kôkô's influence on the work that his instinct is to put more human figures in the scenes where he has the opportunity to do so. I'm not sure what his reasoning is – perhaps with limited time he finds it easier to improve a scene by bringing in Zandile Msutswana or Nana Kouma to dance (and, being bilingual, he is one of the few people who is able to communicate with both of them at once).

He takes on the chanting mob of Marseilles and finds a subtler structure within the stomping that the performers have been using to keep themselves in time. He also shifts the meaning of the mob mentality. Whereas Basson's initial conception was of a whisper that built into a hysteria, in Kôkô's mind the hysteria is a pre-existing absolute. The hysteria exists, and infects the townspeople before they are aware of it. It's come a long way from Khephra Burns's simple idea of a satirical inversion, where the superstitious natives are the French rather than the Africans. Kôkô's take on the sequence gives it a fresh life and a new structure, allowing the puppeteers (who have become a little jaded when taking on this moment) a new way of tackling it. He introduces decisive and bold choreography for Nana – as transformative as any of Basson's decisions to build scenes around visual jokes and tricks. The scene now culminates with the puppets fleeing, and Nana, alone, dancing as if completely unaware of the world around her. The hysteria of the people, held in the tension of the djembe (now, Philani is drumming), becomes abstracted again, trapped in her dance.

But if Kôkô is less inclined than Marthinus to be side-tracked by the novel possibilities of the puppetry, the director is also getting his focus back onto what's at the heart of any stage story – the relationships between the characters. He makes sure that the company take a rehearsal without the puppets and off the stage, in the theatre foyer. The light here is better, and the atmosphere more alert than in the dark, airless theatre. Free from the mechanical and visual distractions of manipulating the figures, some tough questions can be asked about the motivations and connections between the characters and their actions.

Three drawings (by Adrian Kohler) of the puppet from Yaya Coulibaly's
collection that was used as the model for the King of France

It's an essential rehearsal tool for anyone working with puppets; the operators can become so wrapped up in their precise manipulation that they forget completely what the reasons for the movements are. It's a wonderful relief to see the actors, even this late in the rehearsal process, finding the links between their thoughts and the movements that they have been given. It's another key step towards owning the movements for themselves.

Adrian Kohler has talked before (fondly) about a theory he's heard. In a week's workshop, the Thursday is 'Bloody Thursday': the day when each participant realises that not enough has been done, and blames the others. It's something to do with the participants feeling that they know each other well enough to make a criticism. It's the day when everyone pulls chunks out of each other and gets things off their chest. On *Tall Horse*, Bloody Thursday came on 21 August, a date which, even seven months later, I heard Yaya use almost proverbially: 'You know what happened on 21 August.'

Koffi Kôkô came out of a session reviving Marseilles with something to say. What followed was a general's speech of about twenty minutes. At first the company, expecting perhaps a few crisp notes, listened politely. Koffi is not always the briefest of speakers, and when he warms to a theme he can repeat himself in meandering circumlocution as much as Marthinus Basson does in his high-energy barrages of variations on a theme. But this was different: Kôkô had a lot to say about what he'd seen during his three or four days back.

'As we enter this final phase of rehearsal, we have to find the characters,' he begins. 'It's a question of finding the person in your own body, and feeling it through the puppet. We have very little time. Some people are just running through, and some are concentrating... Sometimes, it looks like the end-of-year school play. It's not good to have two levels of actors.' Kôkô is broaching something that not many people on the project have been happy to talk about. There's an atmosphere of goodwill in the collaboration, and of confrontation avoided. Exhortations have been made to the group as a whole, without picking out individuals' problems or specific performers' slowness in developing their work. In any production, all of the actors work in slightly different ways. One of the key skills of directors, choreographers and teachers is to find the right way to talk to each of the people. Whether the director chooses to use advice, encouragement, criticism or a professional distance, there are always actors who find their feet early in rehearsals, and others who don't find their rhythm until just before (or even just after) the audience become involved. It can be frustrating for the rest of the company and a worry for the directors and producers. The doubt begins when the actors (puppeteers are actors with good control over their hands) or directors don't know their colleagues well enough to be sure that they will come through.

And so the difference in cultural backgrounds between the Handspring, Sogolon and freelance performers has threatened to define the fault-lines in the group. Do the 'classically' trained South Africans perceive the young Malians as naïve and casual in their approach because they don't note their moves down in the script? The Malians themselves are being directed in a different style and structure from the way they are used to – do they find this perplexing? They've always said that they were happy up to this point – will this be the catalyst for them to speak up? We've seen how rigorous Yaya is in his character preparation, but he can have his lapses too. Fourie Nyamande's way of engaging with a scene is always to look for improvements and alterations, and playfully insert them, sometimes to the surprise of his co-performers – perhaps the Sogolon performers perceive this as irreverent or unprofessional.

The atmosphere as Koffi speaks is tense, but it's not threatening to boil over. I sense that the performers in the dim auditorium don't want the potential divisions to be pointed out. Until now, no one has had to discuss who is better or worse. 'We all understand,' says Craig Leo in response. 'It doesn't need to be talked about.' Lots of faces are turned downwards now. Marthinus Basson, out of Kôkô's eyeline, looks concerned: everything he's done to try to bond this group together might be blown apart by this hasty accusation.

But Kôkô is reasonable in trying to make the point. Optimism and openness of collaboration aside, no one involved wants the audiences to come away thinking that the performances were uneven. They don't want to reflect later and think that it could have been so much better if only everyone had pulled their weight. Anyone who's worked on the making of a piece of theatre can remember a director's speech that pulled the whole company together and sharpened the focus for the final push. Koffi's address stops short of targeting the accusation at any specific performers.

Yaya is the one who wants to respond. I think he's concerned that unless the implication is clarified, people will say it was his troupe who weren't working hard. He's wrong. Everyone here knows about Téhibou's commitment, and Yacouba's intelligence, and would agree that Nana, the least able to navigate the language barrier, is working as hard as she can. Most would acknowledge also that rehearsals that include both languages take longer and seem to be remembered less well. Yaya invites Koffi to explain more about the 'two levels'.

'Yaya perhaps is asking me to say something,' responds Koffi calmly. 'I do see that people who have more experience perform differently.' Koffi chooses not to offend Yaya – but by implying that Yaya (who is experienced) is on the upper level, his criticism falls on the other Sogolon company members, who are among the least experienced.

As the senior West Africans here, Koffi and Yaya have a special status in making this production. They are both used to being leaders, and while they both have respect for each other, they don't always feel that the other is correct. Yaya is conscious that Koffi has spent a long time in Europe, where he is very comfortably settled in Paris and runs a festival in Berlin. Between these commitments and the international work he does across the world, he sees Benin much less than Yaya does Mali. Both are impeccably courteous, and there's more going on between these men than is being discussed. Yaya isn't happy with this. He challenges Koffi's right to make the comment, explaining how difficult it is for the actors on the stage when they receive conflicting directions from Marthinus and Koffi. He delicately requests that Marthinus clarify how he is working with his choreographer. 'Who is the director and who is the choreographer?'

It's clear how little Marthinus Basson likes this sort of confrontation. The faces of Adrian Kohler and Basil Jones are also anxious as they try to think of ways to defuse it. To send the company away shattered and riven, mid-way through the Saturday afternoon of another tough week, with the first public showings days away, could be disastrous for morale. I suspect Koffi's initial speech was intended to be more of a rallying cry than an accusation. But while Koffi spoke in both English and French with occasional supplementary translation, Yaya's reply needs translation in full, and instead of a rapid air-clearing discussion, Adrian and I are stumbling to find the right diplomatic words to present the speaker most fairly. This is one of the moments when I appreciate how delicate a job being a professional translator must be.

Marthinus is unhappy to be called on to resolve this, but he is the director. He rejects Yaya's premise that there should be one dominant voice. He explains that he wants Koffi to have *carte blanche* to say whatever he wants, and that he and Kôkô are in constant discussion over how the show is shaping up. It's a bridge-building speech, intended to rally the company, which only partly succeeds – the energy is lost a little by the necessity to stop after each sentence for it to be rendered into French. This is one part of the direction that the French speakers are insistent on hearing every word of. But his most brilliant stroke to bond the group back together is not to let the day end like this, and in what seems a bit like a gamble, he takes the initiative and requests another crack at the troublesome Marseilles sequence. All of the actors – Sogolon, Handspring and freelance; experienced and youthful – get it exactly right. Including Koffi's new choreography.

And so the mood isn't as bad as might have been feared when the group begin the week of the work-in-progress performances. Enrico Wey has confirmed that he will accept the role of an ASM – an assistant stage manager – organising puppet movement backstage. His placement with the company extends for the full period of this run, and it's a good opportunity for him to be very close to all the stresses and strains of putting on a show like this one. He'll be able to get a feel for backstage as well as the production office, where he has also been supporting Basil. The company have asked Philani Mbana to take on the second ASM role. This will allow him to drum during the show, accompanying Fourie Nyamande's Newspaperman speeches and the Marseilles chanting, and means that he can continue to work closely with the company in his job as assistant choreographer, even after the show is open. This will be a great asset – or so it has seemed. There have been days recently when Philani has been absent, and it's rumoured that some private family difficulties have been disrupting his focus. Monday 23rd sees him missing again and Enrico begins to work out what he will do backstage if Philani is unable to come back.

The advantages of rehearsing with the full set start to become clear as the company run the show this last week. In another production of this size, a stage crew might be expected to operate the movement of the scenery. With practice, a good crew can do this with sensitivity and fit it right into the flow of the piece. But the crews and the sets aren't usually available during rehearsals, and so they have only a very short time to get the cues and movements right during the technical rehearsal. In a piece of theatre where the audience is being sensitised to the movement of objects, these rolling shelf units become an integral part of the show: not just pieces of furniture, when they move it's as if the environment of the performance is breathing and resettling in a different aspect. And so it's important for the puppeteers to move these units, and to be practised in doing so – and it's now, when the scenes are connected together, that you can really see how those movements have their own story through the show.

The more we've seen the scenes together, and how surprising the combinations of Basson's magpie imagination can be when their different styles collide, the more they seem to fit. Instead of being unified by the text or by a single overriding concept, what is emerging is something quite unique: as the exuberance of Basson's staging rubs up against the stylisation of Kôkô's movement, and as both men's approaches are applied to the technical brilliance of Kohler's and Coulibaly's puppets, the show creates its own logic of blended styles. There aren't many producers who would consider this jumble of disparate elements to constitute a strong backbone for a piece of work – but, despite all the miscommunication and lack of cohesion, it is a wonderful expression of the genuine spirit of the collaboration. Messy but honest, this production has always been strong on goodwill, dependent on trust and buoyed by enthusiasm. The hope is now for a band of performers demonstrating their fluidity between the styles, as well as the different performance conventions and techniques demanded by the puppets. And it's possible that Basson's energy, which has so often been a divisive and bewildering force in rehearsals, might be the very thing that pulls it all together.

Tension between Koffi and Marthinus is suppressed by Basson's policy of non-confrontation. And any complaints Yaya might have had about Koffi are silenced for the time being by Basson's pledge of support on the Saturday. There's no doubt that Yaya's question on 21 August raised a fundamental question about the show – he's identified the collision between Marthinus's and Koffi's different visions. Perhaps the most interesting thing about the way the collaboration is progressing is how the Handspring directors, Jones and Kohler, are disappearing into their performance roles, as Yaya had originally done, and spending less and less time in discussion with the director. Like him, they are hoping that the professional instincts of the collaborators will bypass their differences. Adrian's puppetry training is less necessary now (although there are still supplementary technical rehearsals), and both of these men need to focus on their onstage work.

Marthinus genuinely wants to include what he saw in the video of Koffi's work – that incredible focus, the tension of a ritual event, the expressiveness and physical poetry that Koffi can create. This is an opportunity for him too to learn from Kôkô. But as Adrian has said, 'Koffi's way through, of people learning an almost butoh-like stillness in the movement, is wonderful, but we would never achieve the end result in the time we have. Perhaps the actual play is in the way of the movement stuff. It's like a place I want to go to, but in this project, we are not really able to use what he can bring in the time that we have.' Basson's answer is to continue to offer Kôkô set pieces – the Procession, the Hunt, moments here and there – to get some of that flavour through strategically placed moments.

Perhaps understandably, Kôkô sees it differently. As he said in the meeting when he returned to Stellenbosch, he likes to be either completely involved in the piece or not at all. It's unfortunate that he has missed such a key period in rehearsals, but that should not prevent him from doing everything he can now. When Basson invites him to say which parts of the show he most wants to look at, he answers truthfully: he wants to look at it all, to work through it all, seeing where he can use his experience and perspective to influence it. Koffi is finding that the more he sees of the play, the less he feels he should be working on set pieces. 'I understand it's better for me to talk about, [how] with certain *gesturelle*, you can make certain metaphors – or certain *metamorphoses* – with what I bring...but also, now, when I make the plan, I think, this play doesn't need a pure dance. But all of the play needs to dance. It's different, you know?' This, at the precise time that the performers want to cement their knowledge of their material without too many changes.

Kôkô's new look at things is also positive for Marthinus, giving him the energy to implement his own developments. He's adding detail to all of the scenes, supporting them in the same way that the activity of boats and birds gave a richer rhythm to the long Nile sequence. Mehmet Ali now works with two attendant slave-girls fawning over him. They stand in the crook of his elbow, massaging and stroking his giant cheeks, shoulders and chest, and giving his majesty even greater impact. Marthinus's connection with his puppets is also shifting: 'You just forget that three people are attached to it. I think that's the only thing I need to constantly remind myself of. Because I've never felt that, "Oh, I'm looking at three people." There is just this one creature, and some of it works better than others – and that is in the same way that you work with actors, you know, an actor has the same problems: "that part of it doesn't work", or "give more attention to your voice", or whatever. So you tend to think of them as one creature.'

Marthinus's changes make the whole company feel that the show is finding itself. But a run on the Tuesday exposes how *Tall Horse* is teetering on the brink. It's awful. Scenes which have had input from both Koffi and Marthinus are pulled in two directions at once, serving neither man's talents. Much of Basson's artful stagecraft, performed perfunctorily, can just be hollow. Equally, Kôkô's search for essentials can come across as vague and unfulfilling when it's constrained by props, furniture and naturalism like this. But it's not just the directors who are to blame. Not one person on stage has a firm grasp on their character. The company stumble from scene to scene, mechanically enacting the moves and lines they've learned. Even the most experienced – Basil, Adrian, Yaya – seem to be blundering,

Bheki Vilakazi

looking to each other in vain for support. Fezile and Bheki, the anchor points for the puppeteers, don't look secure. Bheki seems bewildered and frustrated by the puppets, and his delivery becomes taut and forced. It's hard to tell whether Fezile is deliberately undercutting his performance or really panicking. He's overstating again; not at all the assured, nimble and subtle performer he can be at his best. Every shift of mood is clumsy and every note he hits seems both forced and false.

There are two performances at the heart of *Tall Horse*. One is the silent physicality of the giraffe puppet. The other is the honesty of Atir's responses in the face of the bizarre world around him. And honesty is what's missing from Mpela's acting today. The company complete the run but it's been a shambles. Everyone knows it, and the day ends with a crisis conference between the core creative team.

With forty-eight hours to go before a version of this piece is scheduled to be shown to the public, Marthinus Basson needs to clear the air. He lists his worries. The dance feels stuck on. The scenarios of various scenes seem convoluted. There are so many styles of things that it's impossible to fight through to see the shape of the whole piece. Jokes are laboured. The priorities are to streamline and to find ways of using abstraction to simplify things.

Basil Jones offers his support, sensing that this is a moment for unity. The different styles of material should be there to serve the director, whose vision will shape the piece between now and when it opens to the public properly in two weeks' time, he says. Koffi Kôkô speaks up too, but he has decided there is a different imperative. I want to be equal, he says. Being restricted to set pieces doesn't suit him. His dance work is being weakened by the structure of the rest of the show.

Adrian Kohler looks pained, but he doesn't speak. The extended workload is showing in the faraway look in his eyes – even now there are alterations and repairs that he needs to supervise or take care of after hours. In the last week he's injured himself with his own tools twice, and a knock on the head from a puppet led to him wearing an improvised bandage around a cut on his forehead – a bit of bright pink, patterned Malian fabric that was spare from the Queen's *castelet*. After the tension of Saturday 21st, and with this new crisis, he seems too far adrift to contribute sensibly. Everyone's work is now converging into this pressured clash of personalities.

The discussion continues quite openly with the company the next day as Kôkô and Basson try to give sensible notes on the run. It was an exception in being so poor. Each is determined to do everything he can to improve the show, and neither wants to contradict the other, but they both have a lot to say, and they haven't compared notes. The actors and puppeteers surely appreciate the openness of discussing the possible problems and the show of unity, but sometimes seem to be drowning under the weight of information. The short time left before the work-in-progress shows will be spent polishing details and looking at under-rehearsed moments. Fingers will be crossed that the next time the piece is run, the flow and coherence can be found again. This is the environment that Khephra Burns walks into on his first visit to the company since the exploratory workshop in February.

JOURNEY OF THE TALL HORSE

Basson decides that for the first presentation, the company will show only the first half of the show. The second half is less rehearsed, and both Basson and Kôkô are unhappy with the flow of key passages. The exchange of letters between Mehmet Ali, Drovetti and King Charles requires a fluidly shifting focus around the stage, which will only come with familiarity and confidence; and Lyon is still groaning under the strain of its diversity. With everyone concentrating on playing their own moments (and the weight of responsibility on the guillotine not to damage either a performer or the giraffe puppet), there isn't a confidence about the overall flow.

It's a free show, and the audience will be largely composed of students from Stellenbosch University. The presentations haven't been advertised outside the university, except through word of mouth to friends of the company. Theatre productions always start with previews before the opening: it's a chance to continue working on a show but with the help of an audience. But Handspring have found that these earlier windows onto the performance – with up to a week or more of pure rehearsal still available – are invaluable. They offer a chance to find out what resonates with an audience while there's still time to alter and develop things. It's new to Basson, but he is curious about this opportunity to present a sort of first draft for feedback and comment – and of course in his work at the university, he is used to leading students in discussions of work in progress.

There's no surtitle screen here at the H B Thom theatre, so Adrian Kohler prefaces the performance by explaining to the non-French-speakers in the audience (I think we can assume 99 per cent) what's happening in the French-speaking sections. He and Basson make typically modest and charming introductions, apologising also for the colours being too bright. The costumes are being dyed down in stages, and there is more to happen to them, so there may be moments when the puppeteers appear brighter than the puppets they are holding.

The run of the first half – taking the story as far as the giraffe's arrival in Marseilles (and the revelation of the giraffe puppet), the discussions over its transport, and leading up to the departure of the caravan for Paris – goes well.

The Hunt is now quite long. Koffi's continuing work on it has tended to consist of addition rather than replacement. But it takes the action on stage into a different world – much more symbolic and stylised. It's Koffi Kôkô's world peeping through, and it feels like a window into a style of performance that suits the West African puppets especially well – they are designed to express without text. Even if the audience can't always follow the sense, they are impressed by the strangeness and potency of the movement, blending all of the simple but brilliant Malian technology: the lion costumes, the *castelets*, the stilt-walking with head-dresses, all combined with the human form.

But what the story brings us, what the play brings to us, is a metaphor. Behind this situation, this story, we can live, we can see the human being's curiosity, the human being's, sometimes, ignorance. Ignorance, because they've never seen something like this. And also how the human being can be passionate about something he discovers, and then, behind this, definitely also talk about slaves. Because this reminds me also how they caught the slaves, one hundred years before.

Koffi Kôkô

In the feedback session afterwards, this sequence stands out as the one that most of the students want to talk about. The group of students, who have volunteered to discuss what they thought they saw, didn't really follow the narrative of the Hunt – although the image that closes it, of Atir holding the two 'baby' giraffes, is fairly explicit. Many think it's too long and confusing. It's not the first time that someone has noted that the lion costumes don't look especially like lions. Visually, they are an extraordinary whirling burst of movement, strands of grass flying in all directions. But from a story-telling perspective, they're not very helpful. They're made from a cotton jerkin, with a backbone stitched into it, projecting behind the wearer like a tail, and a dome-like mask that covers the wearer's head, also made from the same cotton in bright red or yellow. Hanging off the whole thing is a great quantity of grass-like strands. For this indoor work, the grass-like bark that is normally used has been replaced with strands of plastic from woven sacks, scrupulously dyed in a variety of soft browns by Téhibou and Yacouba (the dust carried by the real thing was too much to bear) but under the lights this looks just as good. These costumes aren't figurative representations of lions. However, with the right quality of movement (Yaya has shown us how), they can inspire. Kôkô has seen other possibilities in them and has had them move in various ways, including settling to lie down. To the untutored, and, crucially, in a context where this level of abstraction is the exception rather than the norm, the human figure inside the grass is the most identifiable part of the image. They

The giraffe puppet's first appearance on stage

appear as extraordinary, animalistic, whirling men, covered in hair, or grass, or sunlight.

The Marseilles chanting is, inevitably, a problem for the audience as well as the performers. Even with the radio mic, no one can hear Basil as the Prefect, and his presence is confusing matters. It's become the scene that all of the performers dread, and despite their running the sequence at least once a day, it never goes

The whirling grass of a Malian lion costume

right first time. Even if it's properly performed, the question remains whether or not it's the right thing to do with that section of story-telling. In other circumstances, Marthinus would have hoped to answer that question early in rehearsals: as soon as the company had got the rhythm, he would have been able to look at it and alter it to best effect. He's still waiting for that opportunity, and still insisting that they try to get it right. I sense that perhaps he's stuck defending a position he's unsure of. 'No, no no, it will work,' he says, brushing off doubt.

Koffi Kôkô's input to this sequence has added new shades to its potential meaning, but it hasn't made it more understandable – perhaps the reverse. The awkward result is something that looks like it's supposed to make clear and witty sense, but is in fact chaotic, uncertain and impenetrable.

The key collaborators have their own questions to ask about various parts of the show. Koffi Kôkô is unhappy with the 'Dem Bones' song that the French scientists perform, and asks that Marthinus and he work on it tomorrow. Khephra Burns, for whom this has been the first real sight of a section of the piece in action, is a little perplexed. He sees that the company are finding different stories and different interpretations of the scenes than he had initially intended. He's resistant to these lines of development taking precedence over what he sees as the true core of the story.

Marthinus is still trying to tend and examine the different interpretations and versions. 'It comes from many different angles,' he says, 'so it's like a mosaic that you're putting together, and then when you step back, it really doesn't read in the way that you expected. So that happens on many levels; it happens on the level of script, and it happens on the level of music, and it happens on the level of colour, and it happens on the matter of lighting, and so forth. So [even when] you finish a subsection, it doesn't necessarily mean that that sits very well in the larger picture.' Speaking specifically about the script, he says of the different scenes in the play: 'They're not the same. I don't find that the stuff is written in the same way. It works like a film, where you're working with impressions and each one has a very different need. I think it...again, it makes for a kind of a mosaic; and what hopefully you get is that some will be coloured red, and others will be coloured grey, and that when you step back it makes for a very nice picture – but some of them will be grey and others will be red.'

When a writer has been as isolated from developing a piece as Burns has been (and it's many miles from Cape Town to New York, even in the information age), these missed connections shouldn't be unexpected. In the rehearsal room, decisions get made about the meaning and playing of a scene that take the playwright's original intentions and run with them. Theatre is always a collaborative process, and even more so in a piece like this, where so much meaning will be carried in the timing and gestures of the puppets, rather than in words.

Burns is the first to admit that he is a novice playwright. 'This has been a learning process for me,' he cheerfully asserts a few days later. 'This is really only my third theatre piece. 'Cause I did a play for Harry [Belafonte], and then I did a jazz cantata for two voices, which was performed on stage. But this is as much as I've been involved from a writing point of view in the theatre.' Burns is modest (I think modesty might be a condition of employment with Handspring) about his output in a variety of forms, including scripts for speeches and for television and feature films, as well as prose editorial, journalism and stories. But financial constraints have prevented Burns from being present throughout this process, and so he's missed the ongoing conversation inside Marthinus Basson's head over what the scenes might and could mean. The developing meaning of a given moment makes demands on the next one, and Burns has not been able to offer his perspective on this evolving transformation.

The story of Atir will contain various elements. These might include his growing relationship with the giraffe (which is sometimes a job, a nuisance, subsequently a companion and finally a friend), his friction with authority figures like Drovetti and St-Hilaire, his journey away from home and his sense of self. It should contain many other strands that make him identifiable as a complex human being facing an extraordinary situation. To a lesser extent, each of the other characters, however minor, will have many stories too. One of the skills of the playwright is to interweave these strands in such a way that they support each other. And another is to allow space for the piece to be finished in the rehearsal room and in the moment the characters meet an audience.

In this instance, Burns's script must take into account that Kohler's and Coulibaly's puppet-carving allows these characters to speak without words. The same can be said of Basson's and Kôkô's staging. Khephra has left space for visual story-telling mainly in self-contained sections: perhaps he thought that by doing so, the text-led moments would remain more or less as he'd conceived them.

Khephra's initial confusion at how his play has been transformed passes fairly quickly. He's a practical man, and as Basson takes him through the thinking behind the alterations, he grasps the reasons for the compromises. Crucially, they seem to agree on what the core story of Atir is: Atir is a man of principle who has had everything taken from him by the slave traders – his family, his property and his freedom. Although technically not a slave, his life is out of his control. The journey with the giraffe presents him with the opportunity of fame and influence. His celebrity and exoticism in France is a world away from his modest African life, and even though he is only the man who feeds the animal, he's tempted and in some important way, corrupted by the materialistic values of the French. It's his silent companion the giraffe who provides the key to his salvation: in her hour of crisis, as she escapes from the mob at Lyon, he starts to realise what values he has been losing.

Burns describes it thus: 'The core of the story is a journey from self, away from self, and then back to self. Y'know, he's left his village, and he gets further and further away. He wants to get back, by the time he gets to Paris he gets back to himself. He also realises that his village is most likely no longer even there, and the only connection he's going to have to home is this giraffe…you know, and that's what prompts the decision to stay there.'

It's a clean, romanticised engine with the ability to drive this show. I'm not sure that the script's structure, still showing the strain of so many reconceptions, supports it. There might be more truth in Burns's later comment: 'The script was constructed like a puzzle, with interlocking pieces that reinforced these [same] elements and ideas throughout.' It's an image that connects with Marthinus Basson's idea of the mosaic, and one that accepts the disjointed nature of the writing.

The build up to the second work-in-progress is rocked by something much more concerning than script conferences when Philani Mbana, who's been back with us this week, suffers a fit. It's the first time he's ever experienced anything like it. Of course everyone stops. His sudden fall at the foot of the stage sends a shock through the whole rehearsal. Yaya takes the initiative in calming him down – he says he's seen this before. Philani has been drumming in the show and there are many stories about how djembe drummers can be affected like this. Whether you're one of the people who believe in the power of the djembe or not, it's clear that Philani's been under some extraordinary stress outside the rehearsal room, and the gloomy darkness of the theatre, with its tense atmosphere and drive for work, can't be helping. The performers, already tense, are terrified by this event – some are weeping. But Leigh Colombick, the stage manager, has a cool and sympathetic head, and she takes over from Yaya in tending to Philani. He needs to see a *sangoma*, a traditional healer – this affliction is considered to be something that can't be healed by Western medicine alone. Of course, plans for the day are affected, and any hope of trying to take on the second half of the play that evening is abandoned.

The atmosphere of concern over Philani inevitably seeps into the performance. Despite work on the Scientists' dance, the audience still spot that it has nothing in common with the rest of the piece. Eclectic as Basson's and Burns's visions are, this is a hundred years from their 1826 setting, and also decades from the museum location in 2004. Some comments on it are simply practical – it wasn't done in tune or in rhythm, for example – and although the audience liked the injection of energy the music brought, there's no point in including something like this unless it's well-executed. If this is to remain in the show, the choreography will need to be drilled – another time-consuming job.

Comments on the Hunt and Savannah continue to revolve around its length. The young spectators also think the Soirée's too long. Although it's one of the funniest scenes, largely because of the energy and brightness of the characterisations, the scene doesn't have enough story or structure on which to hang the long series of jokes and references. Sometimes an audience can pinpoint the problems when the directors are too close to get perspective, and here they may be right. Even the actors, after five weeks' rehearsal, aren't following the text completely. The idiocy of the guests is clear enough from the puppetry and characterisation – but St-Hilaire's superiority is expressed through a demonstration of vocabulary.

Unfortunately this implies a hierarchy based on education, not intelligence. St-Hilaire is having fun at the guests' expense, but Burns's invitation to the audience to join him relies on a common understanding of his complex language. It's a surprising choice as a way to build a comic scene in a production that has aspirations to tour internationally. The production's only current engagements are here in South Africa: in Cape Town, Pretoria and Johannesburg. In Stellenbosch, many of the audience have Afrikaans as their first language. The first languages of the South African cast include Xhosa, Zulu and Sotho – and this will be reflected in the audiences in the other cities. To second-language French-speakers in Mali, this could be simply impenetrable. And making a language-heavy scene reliant on an extensive Latinate vocabulary is not only politically problematic, it also makes Bheki Vilakazi's job more difficult. In his first appearance, these jokes could make the character come across as pompous, rather than witty. This poses a threat to a scene which needs to introduce St-Hilaire as a sympathetic character.

Everyone is determined to finish the week with a public run of the whole show and so the afternoon of Saturday 28th is taken up with a rehearsal of the second half concentrating on technical business – backstage movement, scenery moving and blocking on stage.

The second act builds to the guillotining in Lyon, the big special effect that uses the height and impact of the shelves. The system has been tested with all the actors two or three times, and everyone knows their job by now, so this is a fairly straightforward reminder. Once Yaya is standing clear of the drop zone and is holding the giraffe's head in a safe place, a cue is given for Enrico Wey to release the cable. It's crucial that everyone pays attention during this moment, even while conveying the chaos of a mob baying for blood. Yaya needs to lead the giraffe's head through the doorway that forms the bottom of the guillotine's frame, and with his help, Téhibou needs to control the giraffe's neck as it lowers and gets into position.

The cue comes, the cable is released, and down falls the block. As before, it bounces impressively as the cable hits its limit. But Adrian rushes forward. He's seen the blade hit the giraffe neck. The performers are frozen while he lunges towards the puppet. He's panicked and furious at Yaya, who has positioned the head too high in the frame, but manages to channel his adrenaline into checking the integrity of the neck.

There is no replacement for the giraffe neck, a one-off mechanism that's the fruit of many months of speculative engineering work. It's a system that Adrian Kohler has devised himself from first principles and it is almost certainly the most impressive thing in the show. To remake it would be crushing for him, as well as

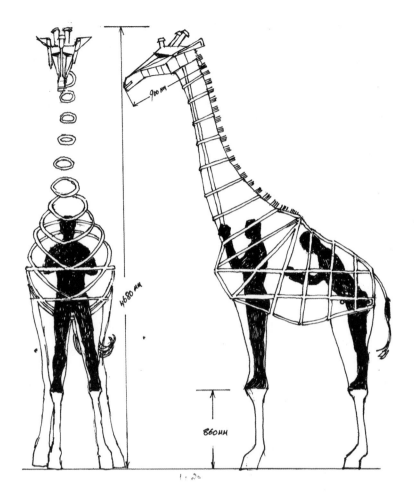

Adrian Kohler's design for the giraffe puppet in 2002.
The neck mechanism would be changed completely from this design

taking several days. We've made one or two adjustments to strengthen it, but it is built for lightness, and so is delicate. Yaya is contrite. The cane and carbon fibre rods that make up most of the structure of the neck prove to have been flexible enough – it was only a glancing blow, and the impact would have done little more than push the neck out of its way. Hands are shaken and Yaya makes sure he knows exactly where the mark is. Even looking through the restricted eyeholes of the mask, he won't make that mistake again.

The blade is hauled back up and this time everyone stands still while Yaya guides the head to the correct position, poking forwards in front of the frame, and gives the cue. Up flies the cable, down flies the block.

Basil Jones, Craig Leo and Adrian Kohler demonstrate the giraffe's neck at a post-show workshop

But this time it doesn't stop. It crashes down on the neck, right to the bottom of the channel.

Téhibou is off his stilts as quick as he can to inspect the neck. There are tears in Adrian's eyes as he prepares to assess the damage. This time there isn't even anyone to be furious at. The metal cable that held the block – and stopped the blade – is capable of holding its weight many times over. But it has been rubbing against a piece of ironmongery on its passage through a pulley and has worn away. Neither Adrian nor Wesley France can believe that they didn't see – or check – this crucial piece of safety equipment, despite all their assessments of the risk involved in this effect.

Miraculously, the neck has survived. Kohler's skeletal design to make the neck light and flexible has proved its salvation. The guillotine block must have landed in between two of the horizontal vertebrae that hold the light stretched fabric of the giraffe's skin. Connecting these and running the length of the neck are pieces of flexible rod and strings running through slender tubes. These must have taken the impact and, except for cosmetic damage to the 'skin', the workings of the neck are intact. The tall horse has got off lightly, but clearly there's no prospect of showing the guillotining tonight.

The audience for the last work-in-progress showing is much larger than the handful who attended the first two. There must be more than 200 people in the auditorium, giving a boost to the actors, who are pulling together in the more familiar first half. Characterisations have more detail and subtlety, and there's a greater resolve and confidence in their ability to put the material in the right order. The second half is much scrappier, slow and tentative, but it will still be good for them to know that they've put that material in front of an audience. This time feedback is invited from the whole audience, and many stay to offer comments.

Without surtitles, the audience can't tell who or where the King and Queen are. Of course, with the simultaneous translation this won't be as much of a problem, but some of the difficulty is inherent in the big design choices that were made right at the start of the process. Adrian and Yaya decided that it shouldn't matter which of the two styles the puppets were carved in – but here, the audience absolutely have to understand that the thin, orange, young-looking man dressed like an African hunter is the King of France. It would be crass to have him dressed in a golden crown (he is, in fact, often wearing his crown, a traditional hunting hat decorated with cowries). Will maintaining an open attitude to the collaboration prove incompatible with creating something clear and satisfying for an audience? It's easier to identify the towering height of Marie-Thérèse as a figure of importance, but it's still an imaginative leap to associate her signal-red hatchet face and torpedo breasts with the Queen of France, 1826. But language is the largest obstacle to the audience. The oddness of the different types of puppet can be absorbed by a visually literate audience, but it's far more disorientating when a single character in a scene is speaking in a different language to the others.

The problem is multiplied because Burns has used language itself as a theme in his scenes. Atir and St-Hilaire have a language barrier to conquer, and these two characters' relationship via the mute Sogo Jan is the heartbeat of the story. Burns has scripted scenes in which Atir, Clothilde, and St-Hilaire's lines are all spoken in English, but are to be understood by the audience as being different languages. It happens quite suddenly: one minute, everyone who is speaking in English understands one another, and then in the next scene, one of them, who also appears to be speaking English, can't understand the others. It's not the first time it's happened in a play, of course; as a convention it's uncontroversial, and like everyone who uses this convention, Burns hopes to get some laughs from it.

Yaya Coulibaly with the King of France

But in few other plays where this device is used do characters also come on stage speaking French, but whom the audience should understand as communicating freely with those speaking English. 'How do you tell the story,' asks Basson, 'of a man who speaks Bamana, and then Arabic, who goes to Paris, and then doesn't understand French, all done in English? If this was done visually, somebody could speak in rings, and somebody could speak in lines or dashes. And then visually it's made clear. And then it becomes poetry. Visual poetry... But you can't do that on an ear. That does call for something else.' We're being asked to ignore the real, actual language barrier, but then to impose an imaginary one on what we see. There's enough material for a whole avant-garde play about misunderstandings. And here it's only a detail in the bigger picture.

The audience are dazzled by the look of the piece, with all the variety and scale of the puppets, but they find the story difficult to follow. Of course they can see that the giraffe is taken from Africa and brought to France, and then

What the international collaboration brings is a completely new way of looking at what you do. The danger of mixing what is essentially a folklore tradition, and a sort of hybrid, Western, inverted-commas 'sophisticated' theatrical tradition, of what we do, is that the folkloric gets sidelined. Because of the narrative needs of the piece, and the performance needs of the piece. But yesterday, I saw them mixing in a very real way. That Queen of Yaya's is magnificent, as a structure, and what he's doing with the King: the mixture of the two, and the way the hyenas come in, with those masks… I wouldn't have been working with that if it wasn't for this collaboration. I wouldn't be seeing that.

Adrian Kohler

taken to Paris, but almost every other element of the story – Atir's flirtation and liaison with Clothilde, the political backdrop, Drovetti's scheming, King Charles's love for animals – seems to have lost someone or other in the audience. It's an indication of how much more work will have to be done in the last week and a half. But almost at the end of the feedback session, a lady speaks up to offer some unreserved encouragement: 'It's a new fable for me, and a very powerful one. This giraffe is a symbol. It's one with profound social and political resonance.' She asks that the team are careful not to distract from this.

It's only one comment, and one person's subjective view, but it chimes with the intentions of so many people here and what they are straining to achieve. It has a powerful effect on several members of the team, and Adrian Kohler later fixes it as one of the key moments in his understanding of what he's helped make. 'Who's it about?' he asks after the play has opened. 'Now I know it's the giraffe. Hearing from the audience that it was a profound story about a giraffe was very important. It's great to hear it from someone else – that despite all the pyrotechnics, that still comes through.'

THE BEGINNING OF THE FINAL WEEK

in Stellenbosch has a real sense of purpose about it. Monday 30th starts with a rallying speech from Basson that's reminiscent of Koffi's divisive demand for consistency on 21 August. This time, it's met with resolve. While the company warm up and prepare, there is a conference for the creative team.

Adrian is already feeling more positive, after a week in which the collaboration seemed to be stalling. 'Our need to do it was to work with [Sogolon]. And last week I was thinking: that's not a strong enough need, in a way, when I felt that we had a stage full of stuff that was hard to lift off the ground. You know, just to want to work with a group of people because they represent a unique African tradition of puppetry – that's not a strong enough reason to make a play.' The adrenaline of the public performances has given the company confidence, and a Sunday away from the theatre leaves them refreshed and conscious again of how much impact this production can have.

The meeting sets targets. Koffi Kôkô must agree to shorten the Hunt sequence, and introduce shadow puppets of giraffes to allow more overlap of different movement qualities. The request comes again for Craig to be released from working in a *castelet*. Kôkô agrees to these proposals, and adds that he wants to cut back on the use of the lion costumes.

Basson also has some major changes to make to the climactic Presentation scene. The movement of the Queen, riding the large *castelet*, has been awkward and halting – it is the only time that Busi Zokufa, who provides her voice, is asked to manipulate the tall pole. Basson also wants to bring more colour into the picture by keeping the *merens habitables* of Fifi and Jolie, two Parisian ladies in the scene. But Busi is also inside one of these, so she will have to voice the Queen from inside a different puppet, and Basson looks for someone else to assign the pole to. It's Enrico Wey, the intern who has become the ASM and guardian of the backstage area. It's not the first time that Enrico has been asked to involve himself in the puppetry, and somehow, in the course of reallocations of labour over the last two weeks, he has now ended up holding the Queen's pole in all of her scenes, including her appearances in silhouette as a shadow puppet.

Most of the work to be done is straightforward. It's based on familiarity with the moves and lines, and on cleaning up emphasis, focus and the technical

Castelets mounting: one of the audience's favourite moments in Koffi Kôkô's Hunt

aspects of the puppetry. The detail of the puppetry can be forgotten or postponed indefinitely when things are going badly, and it's fair to say that rehearsals haven't proceeded according to plan. Basson goes to meet with Khephra Burns to discuss the textual changes that have been made – and more edits that he'd like to make – leaving Koffi in charge of the theatre.

Once Koffi has worked on the Hunt, Basson will be able to go through the piece step by step, implementing the small edits that he has agreed with Khephra to improve the flow of the play. He and the company are equally keen to avoid major changes at this point. The only scenes with real problems are Marseilles and the Scientists' song, and it's becoming unlikely that Philani Mbana will be able to rejoin the company – Basil Jones begins to call the substitute drummers he's been keeping on standby.

Koffi's work on the Hunt takes the whole afternoon. No one is sure why, perhaps not even Koffi himself. The plan had been to implement changes to this sequence, the Caravan and the Presentation, and at least to visit the troubled Scientists and Marseilles this afternoon. But to Kôkô, any change prompts a complete reconception of the sequence.

The new Savannah sequence has a single lion at first, followed by two others, then shadows of giraffes and the 'real' giraffes, before the dance of the *castelets* that leads up to the actual hunting. There is serious fallout from the need to get Craig out of a *castelet*. Instead of three stilt-walking giraffes, Koffi and the other collaborators have decided that there should be only two. Zandile Msutswana, as the least experienced stilt-walker, is asked to take over Craig's *castelet* instead of remaining on the stilts. Zandile is popular throughout the company, having taken on all sorts of challenges, and learnt her stilt-walking and puppetry with grace, ability and good humour. But it's a surprise to see how disappointed she is to be taken off the stilts. Craig tells me that she'd been saying only a few days previously how the stilt-walking was her favourite part of the piece. From the audience, however, she was still shaky on her feet, and there's very little free time now for her to practise and improve her technique. Seeing Zandile's disappointment takes the energy down a little bit more in an afternoon that started brightly but slumps into slowness.

These are relatively simple changes, but they take hours to implement and the can-do attitude of the group ebbs, to be replaced by a familiar fatigue and loss of drive. The end of the day is further delayed by the need to inspect a costume parade of the puppets. Hazel Maree is the puppets' costume designer and has made costumes by hand for each one. If she's to make any final alterations, she needs to see them under theatre lights today, and discuss them with Adrian and Marthinus. Most of the company help to prepare and present the puppets for this post-rehearsal process – another chance to add to the list of work that still needs to be done in the workshop at this late stage.

There are now only two days' rehearsal before the puppets and set are to be packed up and sent to the theatre on Thursday. Rehearsals are scheduled alongside the production team's 'get-in' – the moving of the set into the theatre before technical rehearsals start on Tuesday. From then on, the schedule will be punishing, leading up to the first preview on the following Thursday.

The two last days in Stellenbosch are a familiar mixture of rhythms. Koffi dominates; the scenes he is in control of are still some way off both the precision Basson wants and the essential energy that Kôkô wants. But when he sees something that isn't right, he spends as long as it takes, explaining, demonstrating, altering, explaining again, until the performers are exhausted just from listening. Meanwhile, Fourie is working hard with the replacement drummer/ASM, Vuyo Mgijima. Each of the Newspaperman's speeches has a different rhythm on the djembe and Vuyo has a lot to pick up. He's a bright young Capetonian, and although he takes to his drumming duties more than to his responsibilities backstage, he's unfazed by coming into this process so late and takes the learning of new skills in his stride.

After one more attempt to reconstruct the Scientists' scene from the ground up, Basson and Burns agree that it is too distant from the rest of the piece to make sense and it's taken out. The two of them are working well together. Khephra is practical, generous and happy to contribute changes that might benefit the play. I don't think anyone really regrets the Scientists' scene going, although there must be a few people who regret the amount of time spent trying to get it right. Composer Warrick Sony and video animator Jaco Bouwer, especially, worked hard on creating the soundtrack and animated backdrop to this sequence.

Zandile Msutswana on stilts and strapped into her mother giraffe frame

The energy levels are low and some of the company are starting to feel ill. It's been a titanic struggle with the material and the difficulties of bonding the languages and cultures together, and now, just as the company has started to develop a way of working together, it might be too late. I think they miss the adrenaline of working towards a public performance after last week; the audience next Thursday night seems far away. The leaders of the group are visibly feeling the fatigue too: Adrian Kohler seems withdrawn; Basil Jones, with last-minute producing work all around him, is anonymous except when he's on stage; Koffi Kôkô is as enigmatic as always. At other times exuberant, Marthinus Basson seems withdrawn and anxious.

An attempt to run the show late on Tuesday starts brightly but stutters to a halt at the interval, with concentration sagging. Emphasis shifts to scheduling breaks rather than work sessions, and most of the performers are released on Thursday afternoon while Leigh, Enrico, Wesley France, Simon Mahoney and, inevitably, Adrian pack the puppets. There's a lot of stuff in this production.

Having cleared out of the theatre, but with nowhere else to go, there's a rehearsal on Friday 3 September in the foyer, with the big, bright African winter-sky streaming in through its tall windows. Although working in the theatre has allowed access to the set and given Wesley France the chance to experiment with lighting, the company have been out of natural sunlight for most of every day of the last seven weeks. The change of environment is invigorating and helps the focus. Only a few puppets have been kept from the packing to be worked with today. Without the physical distractions, the actors can relate to each other and realise how well they actually do know this material. A run of the lines in Lyon shows that the structure Marthinus has been looking for really is there.

Buoyed by this success, it's inevitably time to address Marseilles. Marthinus starts to talk once again, but in a way he hasn't since he first introduced the idea, about the build in the chanting. If the company can't find the colours and shifts in this sequence now, it may be too late. The system is not proving elastic enough to accommodate Basil's lines as the Prefect. But worse, the scene *looks* bad. The puppets aren't relating to each other. So haunted are the performers by the memories of endlessly repeating this chant, that it has lost all connection with the action that it's supposed to represent. Adrian has an idea. He cues up one of the first exercises that this company did with the puppets, back when they were first being introduced to their mechanisms: the Chinese whispers. The situation is the same: each puppet has something to communicate – but this time it's the impending arrival of the giraffe.

The puppeteers begin, and quickly become aware of how much more they can do with these puppets than when 'Chinese-whispering' six weeks ago. Their control is sharper, more detailed, more subtle. And instead of the brakes-off frenzy and cacophony of the scene as they've been rehearsing it, the puppeteers find something else. Characters begin to emerge, peeping nervously around pillars and street corners, spreading the word, gossiping, listening and passing it on. Freed from the drum's rhythm, there's time for the puppets to express their thoughts. Adrian is involved in the exercise as one of the puppeteers. Marthinus lets it run on, longer than any of the puppeteers can have expected. The whispering continues. The crowd begins to move organically, splitting into bunches and shifting onto different levels. The puppeteers are making patterns and images on stage in the service of their story – and this time Basson doesn't intervene with suggestions. Their familiarity with the material really helps; the amount of subtlety they start to pull out of those few lines is beautiful, and they easily evoke the atmosphere of a French fishing town undercut by nerves. The sheer quantity of story in the play, and the pace at which it's told, means that there's very little scope for scenes like this in the production, in which story is told visually, simply by means of well-observed and skilfully executed movement of puppets in space. It's a timely glimpse of what these performers themselves offer. And Basson is brave enough with his time to let it run out of energy naturally. All of the puppeteers keep focus – Busi Zokufa, Craig Leo, Téhibou Bagayoko, Fourie Nyamande – until eventually, it's Kohler himself who opts to drop out and break the spell. There's a spontaneous smile from all around the room. Basil Jones, perhaps thinking that this will be a new basis for the scene on stage, emphasizes the need for the puppets to take looks out front, to share their thoughts with the audience. But however persuasive this energy is, Basson decides that it won't fit into the flow of scenes that he and Kôkô have created at that point in the story. He needs this sequence to keep its rhythm and forward drive, and he asks them to apply the level of detail they have now discovered to the original drummed structure.

The group divides as the day continues. Adrian Kohler takes a group of puppeteers to another room to work on puppetry detail in the fragment of the Lyon scene in which the two children execute the cat. When it's been practicable during rehearsals, the group has been split to allow the puppeteers to work with Kohler on technical aspects of manipulation – exercises and repetition that Basson doesn't need to be present for.

When Adrian and his group return, they find Basson, Kôkô and Coulibaly looking at the final scene. After the giraffe is presented to the King, the scene shifts to its stable at the menagerie. Atir enters to say his farewells to his companion. He has been richly rewarded by the King, and aims to return to Africa to find his home village again. He walks out of the room. But something unspoken changes his mind. While he is off stage, we look at the giraffe, alone for the first time, still and silent. Adrian has always guarded this potent moment closely, a moment for the audience to acknowledge how sensitive they have become to the tiniest movements of this puppet. The giraffe doesn't speak, and it barely moves, but the audience take in a great deal. Atir re-enters and makes up his habitual bed with the giraffe – the historical Atir stayed in Paris until his death. He is subsequently woken by Dr Konate – the Malian archaeologist from the framing device; Atir has become Jean-Michel again, the French student who came to research the story of his ancestor.

The focus is on the leave-taking. Up until now Basson and Kohler have been playing with the idea of a bed at the giraffe's head height – a lovely image. Kohler had installed a ladder on the end of one of the shelving units, allowing Atir to climb all the way to the top, and bed down there. The height of the unit is designed specifically to allow the giraffe to rest its head on top, next to the sleeping Atir. But the climb up is long, and the climb down, when Konate arrives, seems even longer. For all the satisfaction of seeing a human being at the top

Fezile Mpela with Sogo Jan

of the high shelves, the sensitivity is lost in the delay. Instead, they decide to look at Atir bedding down at the giraffe's hooves. But something new is happening in this room. Marthinus Basson and Koffi Kôkô are discussing how the story might best be told, trying things out and showing each other different possibilities for the farewell. Each of them is consulting Yaya Coulibaly on his opinion. It might be a feature of the architecture: without a big auditorium to hide in, it's no longer as easy for the three men to discreetly avoid each other. It might simply be that, having seen each other's commitment, the trust between them has grown. There's open discussion of how the crowd in the Presentation can disperse so that the action moves smoothly into this scene. Kôkô reflects later of Basson: 'It was the first time I worked with him.' On this last day in Stellenbosch, all three men have relaxed and remembered their desire to work together.

This refreshing of the spirit of connection is a breakthrough, and it seems appropriate that it takes place before the unique way in which the day ends. An animist priest in Benin as well as an exponent of ritual dances, Koffi has asked to perform a ceremony in order to bond the group's energy, to heal the unsettled energy that has been present since the alarming incident with Philani Mbana, and to address the occasional divisiveness inside the company. He explains that this ceremony would normally be conducted at the beginning of a rehearsal process, or when a company arrived at a new town. Today will be appropriate, he explains, as the company moves from Stellenbosch to Cape Town. It's a ceremony that celebrates a new beginning. 'It's not a magical African thing,' he says with a smile, conscious of the diversity of belief in the group. 'It's a gift.'

JOURNEY OF THE TALL HORSE

When you see the giraffe reach down, to nudge Atir with his hoof, and he says, 'Tomorrow, tomorrow,' the wonderful thing about Atir then is this: Atir is transformed into a puppet.

Yaya Coulibaly

The ceremony is partly an offering to the spirit Legba Eshu, the guardian spirit of roads and doorways, and partly an offering from the group to each other. Kôkô contextualises with a parable about travellers. Legba, attending the doorway, is the first spirit you meet when approaching a place, and represents communication and humility. When the company have humility, they will listen to each other; and the lines of communication will open up. The traveller who does not treat the small spirit Legba with respect will not succeed when he attempts to make offerings to grander spirits. A modest gift is enough. Normally, says Koffi, each participant would bring a small item – a piece of fruit or a miniature of alcohol or perfume. But because the company haven't had a lot of free time, he's asked Leigh Colombick to buy some things for all of us. Participation in the ceremony is optional, but no one opts out. There is some scepticism, but a blend of curiosity, respect for others' beliefs and a desire to show comradeship with the group keeps the company together.

Each participant holds an offering. Koffi asks that they imbue their object with a hope for the group as a whole and a hope for each of the other people sitting in the circle, around a square of white cloth. The ceremony begins with some incantations by Koffi and Yaya (who seems familiar with it). I think Yaya feels that he is one of the spiritual leaders of the company, and as a performer he will continue to be with the group after Koffi has left. I'm sitting in the circle too, up in the Edwardian-styled bar area of the H B Thom Theatre, where, I suspect, nothing quite like this has happened before. Holding our little satsumas or bottles of scent, we're looking occasionally at Koffi but mainly across the circle at each other. The prayers and incantations take some time as we reflect on each other. Looking at each person one by one is a humbling experience. It's easy to have a hope for the people in the company you know well and talk to frequently. You know how they could be happier. But looking at the people you don't communicate so well with, you need to ask questions: about what you hope for them, about what you

Part of Adrian Kohler's workshop/studio in Kalk Bay. At the far left, a giraffe shadow puppet
Photograph by Enrico Wey

think they hope for themselves. And then Koffi and Yaya are starting to come round the circle, sprinkling each of us with perfume and talcum powder, and touching us with a cowrie shell. And as they are passing, a teacup of water and a little miniature of gin are also being passed. Each of us takes a tiny sip from each, except the good Muslims, who pass on the gin. As the shared drinks pass, we each lay down our gift on the square of white cloth, and kiss it three times. Some shyly, some diligently, some with a fond smile that suggests it might all be nonsense. The priests sprinkle the gifts with waters and with the talcum powder, and the white cloth is folded over the gifts.

Legba is also the spirit of crossroads, and the offerings should be left at a crossroads at the edge of the city – and those who leave it mustn't look back at it. Later that evening, Basil, Adrian, Khephra and I stop at a crossroads on the edge of Cape Town. Cars are flashing past, and we wonder how we'll put the package in the middle of the busy intersection, until Khephra (the New Yorker) just gets out of the car, runs directly into the middle of the crossroads, puts it down, and runs back, dodging the traffic. As we drive off, there's a silence.

JOURNEY OF THE TALL HORSE

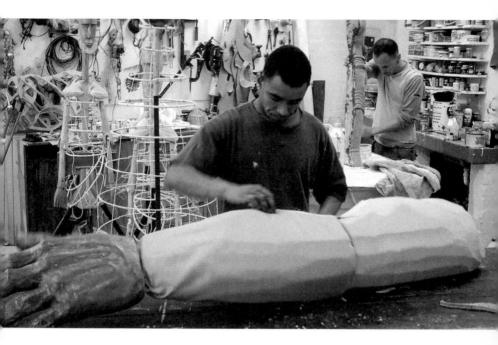

Assistant puppet maker Kevin Willemse working on Mehmet Ali's arm in Adrian's workshop.
In the background, Soirée puppets are drying, and Craig Leo makes pieces of set dressing

Spring has arrived in South Africa at last, after a winter that's had more than its share of rain. The cast have two days off, while the crew get busy installing the show in the Baxter Theatre in Cape Town. But it's a busy weekend at the workshop in Kalk Bay. The shadow puppet of the Queen isn't reading clearly enough against the projections. Adrian had drawn it freehand – a cartoon of the puppet. This time, an accurate silhouette is taken from the puppet itself. It's not always the best way to get a clear image, but the odd proportions of the Queen's long neck, sharp nose and protruding breasts are so distinctive that it's the key information the audience need to read the image. Stylised giraffe shadows are required for the new Savannah sequence – and both Basil and Khephra are conscripted into helping with this. Adrian is remaking the intricate shadow puppet of the Eiffel Tower. The closing image of the show is a silhouette shadow puppet of the giraffe transforming into the Eiffel Tower – dramatising the anecdote that it was from this giraffe that Eiffel took his inspiration. There are so many holes in this puppet that it needs to be stuck onto Perspex, and Adrian isn't happy with the version he made earlier in rehearsals with the helpers at the university: 'There were loads of students around,' he grins shyly, 'and I rushed it.'

Strange as it may seem, the young giraffe puppets that he was apologising for in the first week of rehearsals are still not quite complete. Each week, the new work, adjusting head-dresses or fixing Mehmet Ali, has knocked them back down the schedule, and although they have been functionally complete for some time, no one has seen how they will look. To become part of the same world as the large giraffe, their patterning needs to follow the same logic. The large giraffe's body is covered with black stretch netting – like the fabric that tights are made from. It allows the puppeteers to see out and partially obscures them, but still leaves a reasonably solid 'skin' for the animal. With this over the puppet, the audience can choose to focus either on the shape of the animal or on the operators inside it. Patches of pale silk have been stitched over this dark backing, so that the effect is the inverse of a real giraffe's pattern. The smaller giraffes don't have operators inside, of course, but for continuity, Kohler has also had the wooden giraffe statuettes, that represent the babies in the Hunt, painted like this: pale shapes on a dark background. The young giraffes need to be covered and patched. As with the larger giraffe, the patches are shaped to accentuate the structure of the sculpture rather than being a literal representation of a giraffe's markings.

There are a few hours' rehearsal on Monday 6th in a gym in another part of Cape Town – there is a busy international conference at the Baxter, leaving no spare spaces to rehearse in. The Malians are rested and refreshed, and even Adrian looks better from a couple of days based at home. Basil has been struggling with getting the programme proofs edited and sent to the printers over the weekend, and hasn't had a chance to be with his script. But only he and Fezile are anything other than bright. 'I was at a wedding yesterday,' the slightly bleary actor confides.

Basson suggests that they run the whole show in a simple square, marked out by the lines of half a basketball court. There's no furniture and no shelves to push and, of course, there are no puppets here. Once again, all of the puppeteers are liberated by working without the puppets. They have an opportunity to connect with their characters directly, and, lighter on their feet without anything to carry, they enact all of their blocking with an emphasized crispness. Téhibou and Yacouba probably get the least out of it. They have been rehearsing without the giraffe for

JOURNEY OF THE TALL HORSE

weeks now, walking in the appropriate configuration with Téhibou pointing a stick in place of the giraffe's neck and head. Fourie begins to pull chairs into the space, to represent the shelf units, so that there will be a marker for their position. Later, he starts to bring more in, to represent the wheeled flight cases, and then to represent other pieces of furniture and even cardboard boxes. By the time the show gets to the end of the first half, with the loading of the caravan to leave Marseilles, the court is stacked up with chairs, like the Ionesco play. Fourie smiles guiltily and tries to drag them all off as part of the caravan, in character.

What's most fascinating is how the puppet-less puppeteers engage with their characters and take the stage. Some hold up a hand in front of them, as if gripping an invisible puppet. Others take the space themselves and act the character. It's the most experienced puppeteers – Basil, Adrian and Yaya – who aren't thinking of the puppet when they're giving the performance. Some performers vary their approach according to which character they're playing. Very often it's the minor characters who are invisible puppets.

It tallies with something that Adrian discussed with me halfway through rehearsals, about what develops in a puppeteer as they learn. 'I think a kind of instinct with the figure. You know what its possibilities are, you know what you can demand of it. Things like eye-lines, you know that that's something you eventually have to take care of, even if you're just learning the part now, and your eye-line's a bit off, you will eventually start correcting that… Yaya and us, we can pick up his puppets or our puppets, and, once he's got round the difference in technique of our puppets, he's, you know…he knows what to do with a puppet.' We had been talking about what happens to a performer as they become a better puppeteer.

'Puppeteers, I think, find their character in a different way,' he said. 'They find it through the puppet. An actor does a lot more… I don't know. They find it more in their head I think – the puppeteer finds it more in the puppet. I think they're the same task ultimately, but, with the puppet, you have to work with the limitations of the figure. And so you can't settle anything while learning your lines, because what the puppet has to be able to do underneath that does alter the lines a lot.' What we're seeing in the young puppeteers is this process in action: they're visibly linking the delivery of the lines with movements of their imaginary puppets. But in Adrian, his Handspring partner and Yaya Coulibaly, the puppetry is so familiar or instinctive, the limitations already so much a part of their characterisation, that it's no longer an obstacle to embodying the lines. And the characters are as vivid without the puppets as with. You can see Bheki Vilakazi, as St-Hilaire, a character who acts opposite a lot of puppets, enjoying for the first time the opportunity to benefit from an actor's staple: looking the other characters in the eye.

Adrian Kohler (with a bandaged head) and Basil Jones   Photograph by Enrico Wey

Marthinus Basson is in command of his personnel again, and he finishes off after this encouraging run with a brisk, upbeat session of positive notes. He's keen not to swamp his actors in comment, and is also in a hurry to get back to the theatre where he's needed in order to continue the technical preparations with Wesley France. Just as he reaches the end, Adrian Kohler wants to ask about the playing of the final moment between Atir and the giraffe – he felt it had been rushed. Khephra Burns also has some thoughts on it, and Koffi Kôkô responds too – everyone has a different opinion. This is the scene which was created for the first time on Friday, and which has had almost no rehearsal. Without any lines, the actors are negotiating subtle shifts of emotion without many signals to give each other – and, in this run, with a giraffe missing. Basson doesn't want to get drawn into this discussion, but after Koffi has given his prescription, Burns begins to echo Yaya on 21 August, demanding that Marthinus have the final say. 'It's an acting moment,' says Burns, 'and I feel the director, not the dance master, should be directing it.'

This might be the worst thing that could have happened to Marthinus at this moment – seconds away from leaving a happy company the day before the technical rehearsal. For all his calmness, this is the only moment when he nearly says something he might regret. Even though he won't be drawn on a definite instruction in this context, he lets his exasperation show; not with the performers, but with the collaborative team. 'There are too many people stirring the one pot when we must leave things to develop,' he says quietly as he stands up and gathers his papers, adding, almost to himself, 'and for me it is becoming a big problem.' Possibly he's coming to the end of his patience. But it's only a fraction of a second before he's back in command of his voice and the room:

'We have enough time to let it develop. There are a hundred and eleven good ways of doing it, and we can try some.' He pauses. 'And if they don't work, we can try another, till we get it right.'

Basson wants the company to rest before the technical rehearsal. The 'tech', as it's known, is a legendarily tiring and time-consuming process. While the actors have had weeks to create their moves and get used to the sequence of events, Leigh Colombick, Simon Mahoney and the crew will have only a few hours to learn and practise all of the lighting, video and sound cues. Meanwhile, a crew member will move curtains backstage to obscure or reveal the video projector, or to raise and lower the screen which forms the back wall of the set, each with precise timing. The screen, when pulled up, forms a large opening, used at key moments such as the entrance of the large giraffe puppet. So, for the tech, the actors are put at the service of the stage management and operation team, who get the chance to co-ordinate their cues with the action on stage. It's also an opportunity to adjust the blocking of the performers to work best with the shape of the particular theatre and with the lighting. The performers will be on stand-by for many hours.

The only thing Marthinus wants to spend some time on before the tech is Atir's relationships. Fezile has found it difficult to locate himself in the chaos of the multilingual puppets, and probably feels (quite reasonably) that he hasn't had as much direction as he might expect for a role of this size. There are only two characters in the story, Atir and St-Hilaire, who are portrayed by actors rather than puppets. Why? Basson has no doubt that it makes the characters stand out from their context. 'It's better for them to be people I think. I don't think they should have been puppets. Because I think the story is told via puppets.'

The hope is that, by placing a human actor at the centre of the narrative, Atir's story will pull the audience through, until they find that they are also following the story of the giraffe. He is the barometer of the moods that the team hope the audience will share. However, it's clear that Fezile's interpretation of Atir's story is

Because that relationship... [between Atir, the giraffe, and St-Hilaire] ...for me, if that can be settled, then everything else can hang off it; even a glittering chandelier needs a good kind of fixture to the roof, otherwise it crashes. And that's what I'm looking for, is that very strong point from which everything can dangle.

Marthinus Basson

The young giraffe (operated by Basil Jones, Adrian Kohler and Busi Zokufa) with Fezile Mpela

in flux, and we've seen a number of different approaches to it during recent runs of the play.

Marthinus takes an approach to his relationship that I haven't seen from him before. It's quite different from the style that sees him helming a large group of performers – allocating business, moves and giving line interpretations, as he did in the early stages of rehearsals. It's different again from the emphasis on rhythm, focus and energy that he has tried to teach the performers as rehearsals continued. It's one of the oldest, simplest and most effective tools: asking questions and letting the actor do the thinking. He and Fezile sit down, and he invites Fezile to tell the story of the play.

Mpela understands the exercise, and he chooses to tell the story exclusively from Atir's point of view – more precisely, he tells Atir's story. He talks about Atir's family in his West African village, and how his parents were killed when Atir was taken by the slave traders. He talks about how Drovetti bought the young slave in Alexandria and how he slowly gained his master's trust in the service of the French embassy there. He talks, with the emphasis on the social and economic world, about the power of Mehmet Ali, and how the mission to transport the giraffe to Marseilles fell to Atir; and then how it became necessary for Atir to remain with the giraffe on the way to Paris. The story goes that the giraffe never learnt to trust another human enough to accept milk from them – and the giraffe never grew out of drinking milk.

Fezile does one extraordinary thing in his telling of the story, which reminds me of his histrionic performance in the first full run of the play. Again, it's difficult to work out his motive. He always speaks of the giraffe as a piece of property, never mentioning the developing bond between the animal and Atir. Adrian Kohler and Koffi Kôkô are not there in the room, although giraffe-operators Téhibou and Yacouba are (possibly not following the swift English). Mpela has heard Kohler and Kôkô talk about the love between the giraffe and her handler many, many times – to them especially, it has been perhaps the most important aspect of the play. He knows that most of the creative team see a crucial part of the play's dynamic as being the 'love triangle' between Atir, St-Hilaire and the giraffe. Both Atir and St-Hilaire initially see the giraffe as an object – Atir as a commodity, St-Hilaire as a scientific curiosity – and both of them grow to love her. Eventually, in Lyon, their relationship is defined by their jealousy over Atir's bond with Sogo Jan. Avoiding this strand of the story is perverse, not least because the ending relies on his loyalty to the animal: why does Atir not simply return to Africa having been richly rewarded by the French King? This relationship is clearly in the script and has been at the centre of many conversations about the character's motivations.

By avoiding it, Mpela seems to be deliberately rejecting the guidance that Kôkô and Kohler (and Basson on many occasions) have offered him. Or maybe he's just having fun with his long-awaited moment of rehearsal – exercising and testing Marthinus by taking a perverse position on the text.

Basson knows the rules of this game well enough. He doesn't call Mpela's bluff, nor show surprise, but continues gently asking questions. Fezile lays out his unhelpful interpretation of events, and Basson leads an inquiry into those motives in order to test it to destruction. I think Fezile knows what the end result of this process will be: by starting with the 'wrong' answer, he ensures that the discussion goes into plenty of detail. He's always been a very intelligent and often mischievous spirit; he's easily bored and likes to challenge himself – although this seems an unhelpful time to be tiring out the director. Basson begins to probe Atir's motives: why does he fall for Clothilde? Why does he stay with the giraffe at various points in the story? Fezile has found an almost watertight set of motivations that work in parallel with those discussed up until this point. Atir is a resourceful and reliable servant to Drovetti, far from home in a foreign country: Sogo Jan is a reminder of Africa, and a valuable piece of property. With Mpela calmly unbudging on this point, Basson has to move on. What does Atir feel towards the giraffe? Fezile keeps it non-committal: in his version, Atir is an unsentimental businessman. 'A sense of love?' asks Marthinus, finally. 'No.' replies Fezile, as if it's the first time he's really considered it. 'A sense of loyalty.'

It's an amazing stunt. There's a possibility that I'm mistaken; that in all the time that Mpela has watched Basson exhausting himself trying to bring the puppet sequences up to speed, he's been mulling over his character's motivations and has genuinely found himself shifting to this view of the character. Fezile is a thorough and skilled analyst of character and situation. I've discussed the character with him a number of times, often lending emphasis to this part of the relationship, but I've never felt this level of cynicism before. He continues to refer to the giraffe as a 'responsibility'.

I'm surprised that Basson doesn't do what he usually does when he lacks the time to persuade, which is simply to explain his interpretation. But Marthinus's relationship with Mpela needs to continue with mutual respect. I know he also regrets how little time he's been able to spend with Fezile and Bheki, and maybe allowing this session to take this form is some sort of penance. As we've seen, he's also not a man to invite conflict. The stalemate continues, but the relationship has altered. Each time Basson gently offers a softer relationship, he makes a choice not to challenge Fezile, and each time Fezile rejects the offer, he feels a little more in control of his director. It's a power struggle, and Fezile needs a bit more power and confidence if he's to face an audience in two days' time. If this is the way he's going to get it, Basson is humble and practical enough to take it on the chin. He continues to give the last say to Mpela, each time implying (but never actually asking) that he should take the more orthodox and obvious interpretation of character. Fezile won't accept Basson's interpretation over his own in this session, but eventually the two are reconciled enough to move on to examine a couple of the 'hundred and eleven possibilities' for the wordless farewell to the giraffe.

The relationship between Adrian Kohler and Yaya Coulibaly has been at the heart of this process from the beginning and it's under strain throughout this week. No one knows what has prompted it, but Yaya is solitary and uncommunicative. Basil and Adrian, anxious at the best of times, are worried that it's to do with the poster, which arrived at the weekend. The poster had gone to press during the week of the work-in-progress shows. Basil had been caught between Philani's sudden attack, various other producing pressures and his own need to prepare for performance – and made a bad call on the credits. As is traditional in South African theatre, the writer, director, choreographer and set designer are credited. Of course, Sogolon and Handspring are both credited as co-producers, but because Adrian Kohler is also the set designer, this means that Khephra, Marthinus, Koffi and Adrian are all named, but Yaya isn't. Yaya has a lot of dignity, and it's credible that a slight like this would mean a lot to him. On the other hand, it could just be nerves as he builds up to this performance. On stage in a foreign country, he will be performing in French to non-French-speakers. None of us knows his routine. Whatever the source of the frostiness, Basil thinks that he's taking it out on Adrian. As far as I can see, Yaya seems not to be speaking to either of them. There's a lot to do around the theatre, and Adrian especially, with his design and puppet-finishing responsibilities, is absurdly over-committed. He takes it personally, as if he is responsible, when there is dissent or unhappiness in the group, possibly because he thinks they wouldn't be here doing it if he hadn't wanted to do a show about a giraffe. And so at this time, as well as fulfilling his responsibilities liaising with Wesley France over the lighting and production management, he's fretting over all the members of the company. Wesley knows how to handle Adrian at times like this. But Adrian doesn't know how to handle Yaya. It's a long way from the time I heard him say, 'Every time that I have a conversation with Yaya, I realise how lucky I feel to be working next to him… I mean, he is a person of such grace and, you know, so gentle in the negotiation of the collaboration.' There are few conversations between them over these couple of days, and when there are, it's more negotiation than collaboration.

Adrian, convinced that Yaya's mood is a response to the poster, is exasperated – this had nothing to do with him. He'd rather be off the poster himself, he says. Basil makes a speech to Yaya, which I haltingly help to translate. Yaya is working on making adjustments to a *castelet*. He listens patiently and says that there is nothing wrong. So I go back and ask him again when Basil isn't there. No, says the Malian, he has no quarrel with Adrian. 'He's the one person here who is like a brother to me.' But there is a tension about him and, whatever the germ of it is, the two men have reached a breakdown, with neither willing to accept it. To Yaya, Adrian is avoiding him, and his own pride doesn't allow him to approach Kohler and ask him what's up. Instead, he makes a gesture by implementing an adjustment to the large Queen's *castelet* that Adrian manipulates. The *castelet* is made up of a network of bars, one of which bashes Adrian's foot when he's walking, and some weeks ago Adrian asked Yaya if it could be removed. It's an article of basic respect between craftsmen that neither Kohler nor Coulibaly make changes to each other's puppets without permission from the original maker. Adrian sees Yaya making the adjustment to the Queen *castelet* – but it only reminds him that it's nearly three weeks since he asked for it to be done.

It's a low day for Adrian and he's seeing the worst in everything. Tomorrow, the exhibition of puppets from Yaya's collection opens in Cape Town. The South African Minister of Culture, Dr Pallo Jordan, will be present. Basil, Adrian and Yaya will need to take time out of the technical rehearsal to attend – and the prospect of Handspring and Sogolon arriving in this sullen, uncommunicative mood on the eve of their opening is hardly inspiring. Elsewhere, the performers are feeling optimistic and excited, but here, where so often there's been the best relationship in the collaboration, there's suddenly an alarming rift.

Wesley France, production manager and lighting designer, is working almost nocturnally this week. It's entirely in keeping with the good fortune experienced up to this point that a double-booking by the Baxter is keeping the company out of the theatre during the day, when a conference is taking place. So technical rehearsals are taking place in the late afternoon and evening, with the technical team often working literally all night to prepare. This affects Leigh Colombick, Enrico Wey, helping Wesley with setting up, and Simon Mahoney, supervising his own work as the sound designer, technician and operator. Yacouba Magassouba can also sometimes be found here. He's a budding lighting designer, in somewhat more straitened circumstances, in Bamako – and seeing how France designs with a large rig like the one at the Baxter is fascinating for him. Finally, Marthinus Basson is often on site during the night. The limitations on time mean that by Wednesday evening, detailed technical work has only been done on a little over half the play.

Basil Jones, Yaya Coulibaly and Adrian Kohler with the *castelets*

We had many workshops. In Bamako, Mali, we had a workshop of fifteen days. I told Adrian everything I knew then. After that, the show was possible. *Tall Horse* is not the project of one individual. It belongs to all of us. No-one can say: 'It's mine.' This is an encounter between people with the same desire: to make a piece of work.

Yaya Coulibaly

The lighting states for the last third of the play have yet to be plotted (the process by which France and Basson look over the lighting designer's states and agree or adjust them). But the schedule and good sense demand that the performers and technicians have a dress rehearsal regardless. They need to get through the piece at full speed before the audience arrive tomorrow. At 9pm it starts, and it's as uncertain as anyone might imagine.

Sitting in the stalls, Marthinus grits his teeth, willing the company to remember the flow of the play as they negotiate the new space. It's a different shape and size from the H B Thom – much larger. There's more space in front of the foremost shelf units. In Stellenbosch, coming downstage of the shelves put the actors quite close to the audience. Here, the performers need to come much further forward. Some of these adjustments are coming on the hoof as the dress rehearsal proceeds. It seems inevitable, with all the actors on stage so distracted, that something will go awry. And so it proves, when someone forgets to move shelves, and Basson, against all protocol, leaps up on stage to position them correctly – it'll cause even more confusion if he lets them stand in the wrong place. The company are all relieved to have got through it, but it's no triumph. The director's notes session goes on until 1:45am. A weary cast go back to their lodgings, but the director has to settle down to finish plotting the lights.

The first preview is a charity event in aid of the International Womens' Club. AngloGold Ashanti have draped the impressive 1970s foyers of the Baxter with logos and posters. The house is full, and the audience seems wealthy. It's also predominantly middle-aged and white. The company know what they have to do – and there's a tradition that a bad dress rehearsal leads to a good first performance – but even they must be staggered by the response to the show. There's a spontaneous round of applause for the tall Queen on her amusing first entrance, jogging in on the comic *castelet*, and another for the arrival of the hulking Mehmet Ali. And again and again, almost for each new puppet and successful scene. Perhaps it is a circus after all. The response couldn't be better news for the company, who are understandably buoyed by receiving a standing ovation. The second preview receives similar acclaim.

The truth is that the previews aren't the best these performers have managed, but the impact of the audience's enthusiasm is great for the tired puppeteers and actors. After a lengthy rehearsal period performing to the director and

Adrian Kohler backstage, making adjustments to Mehmet Ali's legs   Photograph by Enrico Wey

choreographer, the actors can finally connect with the people for whom the show
has been made.

Basson, Kôkô and Burns, and Kohler, Jones and Coulibaly can compare their
expectations with the actual response of an audience. Basson's playfulness and
Kôkô's poetry are beginning to find a balance, and the company can identify
new difficulties to overcome. Those of us who've been so close to the puppets
for so many weeks have sometimes forgotten how striking they are – and how
impressive the act of animating wood into apparent life can be.

Adrian Kohler knows what he likes in his sets and general aesthetic, and
Handspring productions in the past have tended to be understated, brooding and
stylised. For years his puppets have not been painted; just carved from jelutong
and coated in a clear sealant to guard against staining. The deep-gouged style he
now carves in has emerged in response to this. The light-coloured, matt surface of
his puppets has allowed them to stand out strongly against a muted costume and
set, and the lines of the gouging emphasize the planes and curvature of the face.
You might expect a lined face to make the puppets look old, but I've always found
these grooves reminiscent of the folds of bark. This is what it would look like if the
wood had grown into the shape of the face.

Kohler also isn't afraid of his puppets getting a knock or a scrape. Many of
them, especially ones which have toured a lot, have scratches across them, and
there's a certain beaten, natural quality. This, too, serves to connect them to the

material they're made from. In a purely practical context, the gouge lines catch the light. As the puppet's head turns, the shadows leap and roll into different hollows, lines and pits of the face, giving a shifting texture that reinforces the illusion of life.

But for *Tall Horse* things have been different. The *maaniw* and *meren* of Yaya Coulibaly's tradition are brightly coloured. Dynamic painting in vivid hues combines with the strong lines of the carving to give these puppets life and vitality – the figures vibrate with tension. The painting isn't naturalistic in colour or shading: puppets have faces that are flat yellow, blue or pink. Detail on the head is often rendered in a brightly contrasting colour: strong red, white or black lips; bright white teeth; the rims of eyes or eyebrows given strong definition. All of this is in contrast to the fabrics used to costume them. Mali is world-famous for its extraordinary printed fabrics, and the puppet showmen use some of the most beautiful to honour their figures.

The animal heads for the *castelets* are even more abstracted. Bamana puppet sculpture includes figures of great simplicity – carvings abstracted for recognition – as well as abstracted, stylised and patterned designs of enormous complexity, like the much-prized and celebrated antelope head-dresses called *Ci-Wara*. A Bamana sculptor (like a Bamana audience) is familiar with many different styles of rendition. The *castelet* heads have bright, multicoloured patterns that play with the lines and shapes of the sculpture in ways that are abstract as well as figurative. Horns might be candy-striped or painted with lozenges. Eyes are sometimes surrounded by a series of concentric circles. Patches of a single colour are often covered in dots of another. And finally, especially if they are to be used at night, the *castelets* are frequently dressed with metalwork – sheets and strips of embossed and beaten gold. (The metal is actually gold-coloured tomato tins, but it recalls Mali's glorious history as the centre of the gold trade. When Mansa Musa's expedition to Mecca, in 1324, stopped in Egypt, his porters were carrying so much gold that the Egyptian currency collapsed overnight.) The bodies of the *castelets* are dressed in combinations of fabrics, in ways that are not at all about imitating the hides of antelope – Bamana design is not about simple representation. Mary Jo Arnoldi writes about how this decoration balances with the sculptural form: 'While *Sogo bò* sculptures may be flamboyantly painted in order to energise the masquerades, these decorations must never totally obscure the basic form. Shape-defining and shape-enhancing features must be kept in a dynamic balance.'[1] These puppets are as fabulously decorated as Adrian Kohler's are modestly plain.

To strip the Malian puppets of their colour would be to completely alter their design. And just as Adrian has used his drawings of puppets from Yaya's collection

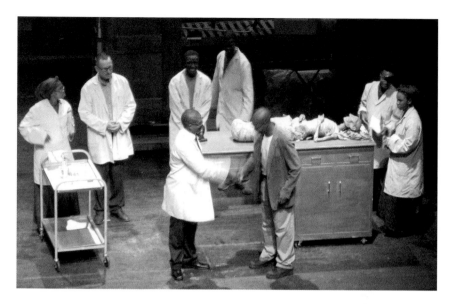

The first scene (with the 2005 cast): Dr Konate (Bheki Vilakazi) welcomes Atir (Sandile Matsheni); behind them, the museum attendants

to inspire his carving of puppets for this show, acknowledging the origin of these complex rod puppets in the Malian tradition, he's willing to stretch his practice into colouring his puppets too. Adrian's style of puppet-making has been altered for this production more than his techniques of manipulation. But if Yaya's puppets are being used in novel ways, they are made just as they would be in Bamako. 'The only change we've made is to hollow them out,' he notes. 'At home we don't do that. That's interesting. I've hollowed out lots of these puppets, but it's interesting to see this little problem that this poses in use: when the puppet takes lots of knocks, we have to make time for a lot of repairs. Normally at home, when a puppet is used in a show, it must not break. When a puppet breaks in a show, it's because the spirits are without… [*Laughs*.] …the ancestors are angry with us. That's important. But it's not rigid. The puppets for this, we've been given the freedom, we don't have this constraint… It's a collaboration.'

Curiously, neither Kohler nor Coulibaly have been keen to pick up brushes and apply some colour. Enquiries to Yaya about the colours used in the Bamana tradition have always been brushed off – 'It's not important,' he says, though even cursory research suggests that, in traditional performance, it is very important. And so, as Kohler sacrifices the plainness of his puppets, Coulibaly sacrifices the strictures on the decoration. Kohler has decided that not only does he want colour on his figures, he also wants to use the glossy enamel paint that works so well on the Malian figures in daylight.

The framing device of the museum has added another layer to the discussion about the look of the puppets. In the fictional museum, all of these objects are old, recovered puppets. And so, while bright colours might still be appropriate, so would marks of use and signs of age. By the time I came to Cape Town for rehearsals in July 2004, most of the puppets had been given a dark, chalky undercoat, in a range of tones that went from light grey to nearly black. It gave the puppets from both styles a connection, as well as providing a good undercoat for the enamels. Gradually, in late-night painting sessions after rehearsals, puppets began to acquire colour. Ladies at the Soirée became a rich ochre. The King took on a bold orange, and the Queen her forceful red. Yaya always laughed at the painters' nervous enquiries about the choices of colour, smiling indulgently and offering supportive words. The painters came from the company: Leigh Colombick, Enrico Wey, myself, sometimes Basil Jones, and sometimes Marthinus Basson. Yaya managed to avoid the sessions and, although Adrian always stood nearby, he invariably found something else that needed his attention. He'd supervise colour mixing, but never put brush to wood.

Quickly the colours of the figures became intimately linked to their characters. Once combined with gold leaf on her crown and her magnificent neck, the redness of the Queen became symbolic of her temper. The electric blue of the Fashion Designer gave him an other-worldly air that reinforced his arrogance. The same blue was applied to all of the puppets in the Lyon scene, giving it a visual unity – sinister and moonlit, with the cultish townspeople determined to destroy the giraffe. The enamel has been thinned a little to allow the undercoat to show through, and applied with streaks, giving the painting a weathered quality. The story of the play is about looking into the past, and the puppets that are used to enact it feel as if they have an untold history of their own. But the enamel paint offers difficulties. Glinting in sunlight, the rich enamel colours give the figures great definition. But on stage, they are foregrounded in all sorts of other ways, including lighting from more than one direction.

Wesley has found that the colours he usually uses to bring out Adrian's puppets don't work for this production. Instead of textured, matt-finished figures which are all broadly the same colour, he now has a combination of different carving styles to deal with, all painted in reflective paints. Yaya's puppets are smoothly-finished, and many of them have strong, jutting brows that invite deep shadows across where their eyes would be (sometimes there are no actual carved eyes). These shadows can be very dramatic. But the paint gives reflection in the focused theatre lighting. And when the colour used is a deep one, France is put in the difficult position of wanting to throw more light on it – but being unable to, first because he is starting to over-light the puppeteer, and second because the amount of glare from the shiny enamel is making the sculpture difficult to read. A number of the puppets are repainted in lighter tones: a rich purple initially used on the bloodthirsty children of Lyon is over-painted with the same pale blue as their parents, for example.

And in a brightly lit scene, the flat colours can dominate too much. The blue of the Fashion Designer is so bright that the subtlety of the carving, normally such an advantage when Kohler and France collaborate, was lost. In the closing days of rehearsal, with all of the puppets painted by others, Adrian lost some of his reticence and began to implement changes himself, laying a thin, white chalky top-coat over the enamel on the Fashion Designer. It has the required effect – to dull the glare and regain some of the useful matt quality he's used to – and it reads as a patina acquired with age. Shoe polish has now been applied to most of the puppets to age them further and introduce more shading to them. It's a compromise on the authenticity of the simple, flat colour used in Mali but, as in so many respects, the direction of the collaboration has been decided by the venue in which the production will be performed. Yaya's grammar and traditions are developed for a specific locale and environment, and here they need a little adaptation.

Balancing the stage image in a production where the puppeteers are visible is a delicate job. Kohler and Jones consider the image of the character to include the figure of the puppeteer – consequently they don't wear black hoods or attempt to conceal themselves. But the primary focus is the puppet figure, and so the costumes worn by the puppeteers tend to be in muted shades. Phyllis Midlane, the costume designer for the performers, has been finding contemporary clothes that can be dyed down for the puppeteers (although it's been a rather more involved process creating costumes for Atir and St-Hilaire). In contrast, the puppets need to stand out from their manipulators. The cue here has been taken once again from Yaya's collection. The fabulous patterns of Malian printed fabrics work so well on his puppets, even cut in simple designs, that for the collaboration the company are interested in taking them further. Hazel Maree has made costumes for Adrian Kohler's puppets before, and she creates beautifully cut patterns that flatter and bring out the exaggerated proportions and movements in his engineering. In a nod to the work of British/Nigerian artist Yinka Shonibare (in which figures from British history and classical art are reimagined, their costumes tailored with decorative West African textiles), the costumes for *Tall Horse* are designed in period style, using printed fabrics. Many of the fabrics are imported; others are hand-printed by Handspring in their workshop.

The final part of the stage image is Jaco Bouwer's video work. Projection is important in Handspring's visual vocabulary. For their frequent collaborator William Kentridge, it's an essential part of his expression, and the rich animated sequences of charcoal drawing that he created for their collaborations provided a narrative that balanced with what happened on stage. In *The Confessions of Zeno*, Handspring played with live projection of shadow puppetry. Using the video camera to capture shadow puppets operated at different distances in front of a white background gave the shadow image depth as well as clarity. In *The Chimp Project*, drawn animation and recorded shadow puppetry combined in sequences that made the most of their own stylistic restrictions – in the same way as the company does with its three-dimensional puppets.

Jaco Bouwer isn't trying to replicate Kentridge's style. He's collaborated with Marthinus Basson in a number of capacities in the past and has an understanding of theatre from the perspectives of director and actor as well as a visual artist. His contributions on screen are always well-judged, and it's notable how much time he spends in the rehearsal room, watching the stage action take shape and discussing in detail with Basson how the projection work can complement it.

Bouwer's concept picks up on and develops a number of visual themes already present in *Tall Horse*'s aesthetic. He sees a link between the pattern of the giraffe's skin and the patterns of the Malian fabrics. He sees it again in the straight lines of the shelving units of Kohler's set and in the lashed-together gridwork of roots or canes which forms the bodies of both the *castelets* and the giraffe. As we've seen, the pattern of patches on Kohler's giraffe follows the lines of this grid, because he too is interested in the relationship between formal and natural patterns. Alert to this theme, Bouwer finds it everywhere, and it resonates particularly strongly with Khephra Burns's interest in Enlightenment science's classifications. Although the beginnings of the Enlightenment predate the play's action by some time, Burns relates the Linnaean system of taxonomy, via the Europeans' desire to control and formalise, to their colonial administrative structures – Europeans ordering and controlling Africa and the world. St-Hilaire was France's pre-eminent naturalist at the time. His work in identifying homologous structures in vertebrates (the pattern of bones in a hand, a paw, a hoof, a wing, a paddle are essentially the same, although altered by adaptation to their environment) paved the way for

Some of Jaco Bouwer's video images

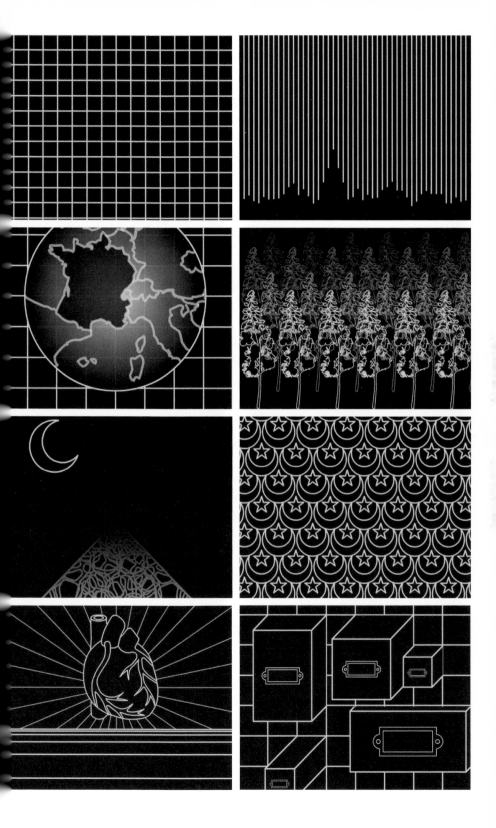

Darwin – and it's true to say that his life's work was about identifying patterns and classifying differences and similarities.

The grid isn't restricted to the Europeans. Of course Islamic and African cultures have been amongst the pioneers of mathematics and geometry and, as Sogo Jan travels through Egypt and as the plot refers to Ali and the Sultan of the Islamic Ottoman Empire, Bouwer's use of lines and patterns draws heavily on the repetitive patterns of ancient Islamic art. The interplay of symbol in his visuals implies a complex relationship between the Christians and the Islamists.

Bouwer's work is based on line and on ways in which a simple line can form into patterns, shapes and optical illusions suggesting depth. The line he uses is a uniform green. The shade is taken from a photograph of Mali that Adrian Kohler came across in his research.[2] The photo shows an interior, lit by a strange, otherworldly, green glow, thrown from a modern neon light but also evoking sunlight through a shade. The same shade of green you see on old-fashioned radar screens and computer monitors, it seems at once dated and ultra-modern. The green lines keep a sense of modern perspective on the period action. Kohler has allowed it to be the only bright colour on stage, repeating it in illuminated emergency exit signs and torchlight.

He also sees it from a different perspective: rather than a line explored until it creates pictures, he sees images reduced to the simplicity of line. 'Jaco's done an amazing sort of process of reduction on images,' he offers. '[They're] lovely, simple images.'

The video is projected onto the large screen, centrally located on the back wall. Tall shelves on rollers slide to either side of it to expose the screen. Bouwer develops a narrative of the line. The first thing we see is a rigid perpendicular grid, accentuating the right angles of the shelves. Later, the lines that draw themselves on the screen use angles and intersections, forming into repetitive straight-line patterns. Then the intersection of tangents brings curve into the vocabulary of symbol. In a sense this is a process of simplification and definition: countries, hills, rivers, mountains and homes reduced, like a three-dimensional map, to a shape made with lines. The line drawings are always restrained and minimal. Even when a beautifully detailed skyline of Alexandria unfurls, with spires, minarets and harbour, it consists of outlines alone, with no shading or texturing; at other times, plain lines carefully angled offer an illusion of depth and perspective in the stable.

The wall of green light draws decorative patterns which relate symbolically or metaphorically to what's happening on stage. When St-Hilaire dictates a letter to the King expressing anxiety about the journey through Lyon, a map of France on the wall behind carries a dotted line which proceeds to Lyon, at which point a stylised guillotine blade falls from nowhere and cuts the whole image in half.

Opinions have been mixed on how the projections work with the overall stage image. For many people, one of puppetry's attractions is its age. It's a sort of heritage activity, like traditional national dances or bead-work. This is perhaps even more the case when the puppets are carved in wood – a real craftsman has made these puppets in the same way his ancestors might have, with sharpened tools, held by hand. Kentridge's charcoal drawings also have a traditional quality (although the thought behind them and the material in them is utterly current) in their texture, reminiscent of woodcuts and sketched Renaissance cartoons. You can see the weave of the paper in them. The shadow puppetry in *Zeno* and *Chimp Project* uses an aesthetic that predates the camera technology that's making it visible on a big screen. I think that some of the initial surprise that greeted the style of Bouwer's animations came from preconceptions of what puppet-theatre shows should include. These are unashamedly computer graphics. Bouwer's simple line is versatile but restrictive; it relates to the restrictions that Kohler and Coulibaly offer themselves by using wooden puppets. If the stiffness of the puppet and its limited mobility force the puppeteer to define the most effective movement for maximum expressiveness, Bouwer's decision not to include texture or colour in his palette forces him to stretch the concept of line while preventing it from becoming clumsy.

The myth of traditionalism in puppetry is truer for Yaya than for Adrian. Handspring puppets use polystyrene for their lightweight bodies. Their construction involves the use of power tools for precision cutting and drilling. The mechanisms often use metal rings and fishing wire. The giraffe head and neck is made using fibreglass rods and lycra netting. Adrian's puppets would never survive a run without two-part epoxy glue to patch together the breaks of fingers or ribs. He certainly feels a connection with tradition in his work, but he's not enslaved to it – he's happy to use modern materials like latex and foam in his construction where they give the best effect. Yaya is consciously guarding a tradition, but Sogolon also makes puppets with contemporary materials for some of their shows. The puppeteers have a respect for the skills of their predecessors – and the old materials are sometimes the best ones for the job – but it's naïve to suggest that they are or should be restricted in what they use.

However, in the work-in-progress presentations at the H B Thom in Stellenbosch, some of the audience suggested that the brightness of the screen was distracting them from the stage action, and that's a concern that has to be taken seriously by the director and designer. Wesley France had a solution: a lightweight black gauze

Stage Manager Leigh Colombick preparing boxes   Photograph by Enrico Wey

hung in front of the plastic screen would diffuse and soften the brightness of the image. But it alerts Adrian Kohler to the way video has become part of the creation of the piece without an explicit decision having been made to include it.

'Because we've been working with video, we always feel we've got to have video, and one's always got to have these elements, and I was thinking yesterday that we don't have to have such a multi-dimensional [show]... I love what Jaco's doing in this piece, but it's just that we have got used to the fact that video engages the audience in a way that we feel is sort of...contemporary. And so therefore it's...you know...better. [Laughs.]' In the end, the video has added an extra layer of signs and symbols for those in the audience who enjoy them to decipher. But Bouwer would be the first to define it as a supporting layer, and if the green is a distraction, he is willing to try another approach. For one night only at the H B Thom, the company performed in front of drab khaki lines before the energetic green returned.

Jaco's other main difficulty has been to co-ordinate the sequences with the action. In the Nile section, for example, it's the screen that charts the passage of days, with some beautifully simple and resonant images, like a flash of lightning that becomes the Nile on a map of Africa, or stars in the sky that join up to form a vast, rigid firmament, which then seems to tilt in relation to the ground. But because this sequence runs continuously during the scene, any variation in the scene's length means a re-edit is necessary for Jaco. He tries to keep these to a minimum – his sequences tend to come at the beginning of a scene and unscroll a background that can then fade or rest – or, notably, in the case of a forest, he begins with a chaos of identical, overlaid line-drawn plants, which slowly un-draw themselves, disappearing one by one until only one remains. His job in the run-up to the first night has been to keep track of all the changes and re-edit his material to match up. He then needs to co-ordinate this with Leigh Colombick, who will be the one pressing play on the laptop.

The third night's performance is the premiere. A show of this size would expect more than two previews, but it's the gamble a small producer has to make. And despite their combined international standing and the support of AngloGold Ashanti, Handspring and Sogolon are in a big theatre which they need to fill to balance the books. The reviews are essential for ticket sales in a small city like this – and tickets need to be sold early for word of mouth to get going.

NOTES

1 Arnoldi (1995), p.102.

2 In *Mon Afrique: Photographs of Sub-Saharan Africa*, photographs by Pascal Maitre (Aperture Press, 2000), p.37: 'A room in a Hausa-style palace. Low-relief geometric patterns on the walls lit by a wall-mounted fluorescent tube.'

8

THE FIRST NIGHT IS ALWAYS A TENSE affair, but the company are able to channel their nerves. Partly this is down to the warm-up. During rehearsals, at least the first half-hour of the day was dedicated to a physical and sometimes vocal warm-up. Limbering up the body and getting rid of excess tension can bring the company together in common activity and focus them on the day's work. Now, as the company start to give performances, the warm-up works to do all these things and to energise them for the show. The connection between these performers on stage will be essential to the success of each performance, and most of the company are committed to doing the warm-up properly.

At various times, different people have been involved in leading the warm-up. Koffi Kôkô's were thorough and strenuous. They gave a tiny glimpse into the sort of rigorous physical discipline, control and stamina that would be involved in working with him full-time on one of his dance pieces (and underlined why most of this cast would be incapable of being part of such a company). Téhibou's were also memorable: vigorous aerobic workouts that got the blood pumping around the body and left those much less fit than him heaving on the sidelines. But mostly, the task of leading the warm-up has fallen to Craig Leo, who has a patient, gentle, knowledgeable style of instruction that lends itself well to teaching and supporting the group. He also has the sort of mind that remembers and understands the exercises. As time has gone on, he has found a selection of stretches and exercises that appeal to and suit this group.

Both before and after the warm-up, different actors have their own preparation rituals. Some are pragmatic: checking their props and puppets are in the right place. Fourie, Basil and Busi all have to queue for Simon Mahoney to fit them with radio microphones, to give some of their roles extra power: Fourie needs one for the Newspaperman, and the other two to give the large puppets voices to match: Basil for Mehmet Ali and Busi for the Queen. Yaya Coulibaly doesn't go near the dressing-room. His whole ritual takes place in the wings: he changes there, by one of the props tables, and occupies that little corner, by the downstage-right entrance, as his personal area. It's also the place where the King puppet is stored when he's offstage and where Yaya changes into his costume and mask for Polito.

The group coheres graciously now. Remembering how the company split down cultural and linguistic lines in July, it's encouraging to see how everyone defers to Craig for the warm-up, with Yacouba's good-natured smile of enthusiasm raising a response from anyone it's aimed at.

On this first night *Tall Horse* is the best it's been so far and the company are rightly proud

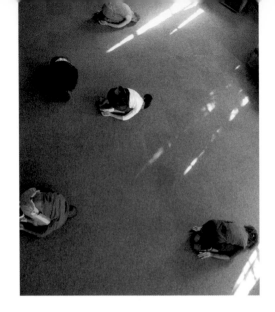

A company warm-up

of themselves. The previews and opening performance of any piece of theatre are moments of discovery for the directors as well as the end of their journey. The curiosity and collaboration of rehearsals alter the piece from its makers' first intentions, but it's the audience who reveal what has actually been made. Those of us who have seen all of the rehearsals and the struggles and discoveries that have happened in them, Marthinus Basson and Koffi Kôkô included, are the least qualified people to know whether the piece is successful or not. While they can look and continue to give direction, support and advice to their performers, the audience are the judges – and they are enthusiastic.

As the press reviews slowly leak out over the next few days, and once the production goes on to Pretoria and Johannesburg, they are unanimously positive. The *Star* calls it 'one of the theatre events of the year…a glorious Pan-African artistic experience'. Other critics describe the piece as 'groundbreaking' and 'a startling revelation'. That's what you hope for, and it is a reminder of how extraordinary it is to see either of these companies: Bamana puppetry is seldom seen outside Mali; Handspring's productions, although regularly on tour, usually play relatively short engagements, and puppetry of this standard is very rare.

Puppetry is the focus of most of the reviewing, and is always given the sort of glowing reports that are the benchmark of both Handspring's and Sogolon's work. As is often the case with a piece of theatre using puppetry, some reviewers are surprised to see what they had perceived as a children's medium tackling a

Drovetti bows to Mehmet Ali: Adrian Kohler, Fourie Nyamande,
Yacouba Magassouba, Nana Kouma, Zandile Msutswana, Téhibou Bagayoko

complex, epic story. None of the reviewers or audience that I hear from have any difficulty with the mixing of puppet styles – what seemed the biggest challenge at the outset has been successfully overcome. Moreover, the large number of puppets, and their ingenuity and beauty, make this a real event: a spectacle that audiences feel they'll never see the like of again. Word of mouth, and consequently ticket sales, are good.

Of course, there are still difficulties.

The political strand of the narrative is hard to follow, even now the audience can read the French parts of the script on the surtitles. This material depends on letters from the Sultan of the Ottoman Empire being lost *en route* to Mehmet Ali, and letters from Drovetti being lost *en route* to King Charles. The first set are 'lost' because Ali doesn't want to receive them (they command him to intervene in Greece). Burns has the second set sent by carrier-pigeons, which the hunting-mad King shoots down for the Queen's pigeon pie. In the end, a message finally arrives in Paris from Mehmet Ali, inviting the French to make an alliance with Egypt

JOURNEY OF THE TALL HORSE

against Ali's superiors in Turkey. But, regardless of the gift of the giraffe, the French have already ordered an attack on the Turkish fleet at Navarino, and the march to Greek independence is on its way. The gift of the giraffe hasn't altered Marie-Thérèse's realpolitik.

Which is quite hard to follow even when it's the main focus of attention. Burns, sensitive to the potential danger of these scenes being dry, has livened up the King and Queen through their comic relationship, with the domineering Marie-Thérèse forever criticising Charles for forgetting to behave more like a king. There are good laughs in these lines, including some pointed comments on contemporary US foreign policy, but this relationship is in stasis, and the gags take our focus away from the action of the scene. When Burns wrote the script, he also didn't know that these lines were going to be delivered in French – which limits the audience's perception of lightness.

Politics is also the domain of Newspaperman. Newspaperman, a vibrant outlet for Fourie Nyamande's exuberant streak, delivers updates on the giraffe's journey and geopolitics direct to the audience. Here, too, Khephra Burns loves to toy with the language and rhyme:

NEWSPAPERMAN Invasion!
International Political Equation:
The Turks take Greece,
Anti-Islamic sentiment peaks.
Mehmet Ali's
The most hated man in Europe
Except in Lyon
(Where King hate is sure up)
And prognostications
In anticipation
Of the Turk's devil leopard
Say the long-necked beast
From the East
Might soon be deceased.

Nyamande, assisted by Basson's suggestions and accompanied by Vuyo's drumming, loves to make these quirky speeches as entertaining as he can. He's a winning performer and a natural show-off, and he forms an easy bond with the audience. But even though the audience do love him, they don't necessarily follow what it is he's just said. At the crucial political moment – Charles considering Mehmet Ali's offer of an alliance – Newspaperman bursts in with this:

Fourie Nyamande   Photograph by Enrico Wey

NEWSPAPERMAN News flash:
 Egyptian fleet trashed.
 European forces storm
 The port of Navarino.
 But does His Majesty know
 Who let the dogs out – woof woof woof.
 Many boats lost
 The Pasha pays the cost
 For Greeks who seek to be
 Their own Boss
 But who let the dogs out – woof woof woof.

The irreverent reference to the 2000 Baha Men record is prompted by an elliptical (mis)quotation of Shakespeare by the Queen earlier in the scene – 'Hounds and foxes, Charles. In Egypt's case, lions and natives. It's time to let loose the dogs of war.' Newspaperman's moments of unexpected modernity are a regular hit with most of the audience. But the plot development – that the Queen has commanded the fleet's attack – is lost. Khephra is unrepentant, and his defence of his work is simple: 'The audience are having a great time,' he says.

The awkward scene at Marseilles is still more sound and fury than an effective piece of theatre. Some of the chaos is conveyed but little of the subtlety that Khephra had at one time anticipated. Even now there are some nights when the actors fall out of rhythm.

But if the political and historical background in the play isn't coming through completely, the fable of the giraffe, its real backbone, grows stronger with each performance.

Fezile Mpela's game with Marthinus Basson continues. Now that the play is up and running, it's for Fezile (as it is for all the performers) to calibrate his performance in response to the audience, while still playing within the range he's agreed with the director. Fezile has an instinct to play Atir as a little more like himself – charming and knowing – than the rough-edged slave that might have more historical accuracy, but he knows how to make a sentimental connection with the audience, and his performance is well-received. As the run continues, he finds the connection with the giraffe more and more – and Téhibou and Yacouba, in return, are able to develop the strand of performance that establishes Sogo Jan's reliance and affection for him. Making the bond between them the emotional centre of the piece is a real achievement and it makes the moment when he seems ready to leave her a far more affecting and effective climax than the drama at Lyon or the ceremony of the presentation to the King.

Other delights continue to develop in the execution of the production. The Soirée becomes one of the benchmark set-pieces. Marthinus's entry to the scene via the guests proves more and more revelatory. With so much text spoken by the guests (even with cuts), it can be difficult to pick out the principal focus – that St-Hilaire's passion for his work and his desire to see the giraffe lead him to offend the polite society of Marseilles with his curtness. But the vitality and hysteria of the guests makes a wonderful (and carefully-judged) circus. The swoops and sweeps of the crinoline skirts as Craig Leo and Busi Zokufa manipulate the ladies, and the affected bobbing of Fourie Nyamande's and Nana Kouma's male guests, have found real crispness, and this neatly offsets Bheki Vilakazi's portrayal of St-Hilaire. When they began rehearsing this scene, he had to overact to get noticed amongst the excitable puppets. Now that they're tuned to a level, he's able to bring his performance down, and his normality amongst the madness lends him authority.

The Fashion Designer is another satisfying set-piece: an outrageously camp and demanding diva who offsets St-Hilaire's dryness as the giraffe is prepared for its

The Fashion Designer in his moment of glory –
Craig Leo, Adrian Kohler and Basil Jones manipulating

journey across France. In a flourish that has the audience whooping, the designer is so hard to please that he even shrugs off the ministrations of his secondary manipulators, sending Basil Jones (on his left arm) and Adrian Kohler (on his legs) flying across the stage – which of course leaves him almost helpless until they return. His speech is a torrent of petulance that has haunted the principal manipulator Craig throughout the rehearsals, as he has tried to memorise it and time its forceful emphases with the slick movements executed by the three puppeteers. But communicating with an audience is different – the crowd enjoy both the virtuosity of manipulation and the dynamic character.

JOURNEY OF THE TALL HORSE

The company's hard technical work is paying off. One of the quiet time-consumers of this rehearsal period has been the cat-killing in Lyon, and it is a model for co-operation across the language barrier. Basil Jones works the cat, and the children are operated by two puppeteers each: Nana Kouma and Craig Leo manipulate the sweet little girl, and Zandile Msutswana and Adrian Kohler are on the bloodthirsty boy. With no text, the difficulties are different from the co-ordination of movement and speech that is the challenge with the Mehmet Ali and Fashion Designer systems.

This is pure visual storytelling, so precision is demanded if it's to be convincing. Although all the cues are visual rather than reliant on hearing English, there are awkward and fiddly props to deal with. The first moments are relatively straightforward as Leo and Kouma combine to stroke Basil's cat. When the boy appears, things have to run very smoothly. On each puppet, each manipulator has one arm. The girl (using Nana's hand) grabs the cat's head, and Basil lets go of it, concentrating on flailing its tail to convey the struggle. Meanwhile, the boy, using Adrian's hand, pulls the guillotine up from its hiding place. Nana, using the girl's hand, now needs to steer the cat's head and control rod through the narrow opening of the guillotine so that Basil Jones can retake it on the other side. Meanwhile, the girl's other hand, held by Craig, is steadying the guillotine, as is the boy's hand, held by Adrian, on the other side. Zandile, operating the boy's head and right hand, is keeping the audience focus, chuckling. Once the head is through, Nana has the trickiest job. Letting go of the girl's hand, she needs to find a slender metal pin in amongst the fur of the cat's neck, and remove it. Basil now has one hand around the front of the guillotine, holding the cat's head control, and one behind, making a frenzy with the tail. When the pin is safely out, Nana reaches up for the string that holds the guillotine blade, and gives a cry to cue the others. Zandile, as the voice of the boy, lets out a blood-curdling yell of her own as Nana pulls the string. The small blade falls, and, with the pin already safely released, Basil is able to pull the head and body sections of the cat apart. The head 'bounces' on the ground, the macabre children laugh, and the audience, fairly reliably, laugh along with them.

A lengthy version of the scene had the children playing catch and keepy-uppy with the head, but the flow of the scene demands that only a moment later, the children have to get offstage – which, with five bodies cramped into a small area, is as difficult to organise as the rest of this tightly choreographed sequence. It's one of the unsung triumphs of the performance that the audience aren't aware of the complex mechanics that go into this modest little moment.

Nana Kouma and Busi Zokufa with the children of Lyon

Any concern over whether the Bamana puppets were being used 'authentically' also proves to have been misguided. Seen in the context of the whole play, it's clear that they are using their specific and dynamic strengths to serve the story – and there's not much more a carver could ask. Basson's strategy of looking at them to see what they *can* do, and then using that, works to their benefit, and I think that with few exceptions, Yaya would agree. Puppets are practical tools of performance, and while these Bamana figures have developed in response to a specific performance environment and style their strengths are carried in the design of the figure. Adrian said that Yaya 'knows what to do with a puppet', and the same comment can be applied to these puppeteers working as an ensemble: Coulibaly and Kohler have, at different times and in different ways, helped and encouraged the puppeteers to find the expressiveness of the Malian puppets; Basson, as he has always offered to, has responded to what works on stage. His eye for an entertaining visual sequence has been applied, without favour, to both the Sogolon and Handspring puppets, and where they have combined, he and his team have found new ways of using both of them.

If Fezile and Bheki could be forgiven for feeling hard done by in rehearsal time, Téhibou Bagayoko and Yacouba Magassouba in the giraffe have had even less. Wherever there is text, there will have been several conversations between Marthinus and his actors. The giraffe has no lines, and for the most part Marthinus's direction was simply to indicate to the boys where they were to stand. If there were specific cues – to bring the head down to nudge Clothilde here, or to turn away from St-Hilaire there – these have been indicated, but the thought that links them has not. The two boys also have the curious job of following on from other puppeteers performing the same character: in the Nile sequence, Busi Zokufa, Adrian Kohler and Basil Jones combine to work on the intricate mechanisms of the young Sogo Jan. Téhibou and Yacouba have become among the most respected in the company, partly because of how modest and thorough they have been in carrying out their work in the giraffe, and partly because, now that the company are performing the whole show, it's easy to see what a terrific achievement it is for them to perform in the giraffe for such a long time. Perhaps because the giraffe is an oasis of passivity amongst the chaotic relations of the humans there's been much less discussion in rehearsals of its thoughts and attitudes. The giraffe has a unique and powerful character journey. Koffi Kôkô expresses it well: '[She] observes all. All of this story. She is totally innocent, but can do nothing. And finishes, having her only relationship with the person who killed her mother.'

With another puppet, the puppeteers would be looking for secure sequences of movement to build their performance around; finding the timing and expression of their thoughts with adjustments of the wrist, arm or head. But getting into the giraffe takes time, and standing in it is far from comfortable. The neck is extremely heavy, and Yacouba, at the back end, is bent forward. The boys found out what can happen if they rush into the giraffe or stand around on it for too long on only the second day of rehearsals. While Marthinus gave notes to other actors, Téhibou casually crossed his stilts, enjoying the extra stability that being strapped to a second stilt-walker offered. But Yacouba made his own foot-shuffle, and, with Téhibou's stilts snagged against one another, the pair overbalanced. The whole giraffe, cage and all, crashed to the ground. The boys were embarrassed and apologetic, each admitting guilt, and the frame survived the impact – but it was a timely warning not to expect them to stand around in the giraffe for too long. Since then, the two puppeteers' experiments have kept time with their skill. And so, many rehearsals have seen them off stilts, outside the puppet.

Téhibou's job inside the front end of the giraffe is the more straightforward, and strenuous, of the two. It requires strength and sensitivity, but he seems to have plenty of the first, and he can develop the second by rehearsing the scene without the heavy neck. He's often to be seen coming on stage holding any long object in its place to keep the discipline of expressing himself at a distance of several feet. Yacouba's work is more technical. Adrian Kohler puzzled for a long time over how to distribute the controls in the giraffe puppet. Ordinarily, one person would be the primary manipulator on a multi-person puppet. It means that the character's thoughts can be clear, and the secondary manipulators can follow. This leading puppeteer would control the head, the breathing and, in a human figure, whichever arm was most comfortable. So, on this principle, Téhibou, as the front of the giraffe, would control the head mechanisms along with the neck. But it takes both arms to hold the neck up and move it around. There is a lever inside it, between the main grips, that allows Téhibou to swivel the head from side to side, but it quickly became apparent that to loosen his grip on the main neck controls meant losing the close control that would be needed to benefit from the swivel. The lever, which is very nicely made and works with brake cables, was used once or twice in the February 2004 workshop, but as far as I know, it hasn't been touched since.

Working in conjunction with the main neck movement, the nodding control determines the level of the giraffe's eye-line. Kohler experimented at some stages with this as a loose string for the front operator to work, and later with it attached to the front operator's own head – so that when he pulled his head back, the giraffe would look up, and vice versa. But it was found that, apart from being difficult to attach, this was too much affected by the movement of the main neck joint: every time the neck stretched forward, the string from the operator's head would get pulled tight – and the giraffe's head would lift.

The giraffe's other key ways of expressing itself are its ears and tail. Adrian has made moving tail-joints before and has found that a great deal can be said with a well-judged tail-flick or wag. This, it's clear, will be the job of the rear manipulator. There are in fact two controls for the tail, set into the giraffe's frame with convenient levers. In addition to these, Yacouba operates the two controls leading up to the giraffe's head – for its up and down movement and for its ears. This is an incredibly difficult connection for two performers to make. For a puppeteer to play another's secondary arm is difficult enough. With text, or some other cues to work around, it's possible to hold back and gently discover when to make a movement in order to ornament or support the primary manipulator's work. But here, the two must co-operate in the subtlest movements of the character, all the while strapped to each other and wearing stilts.

It's impossible to say who is the primary manipulator on this puppet. Certainly, Téhibou takes control of the main movements and, as the front legs, also leads

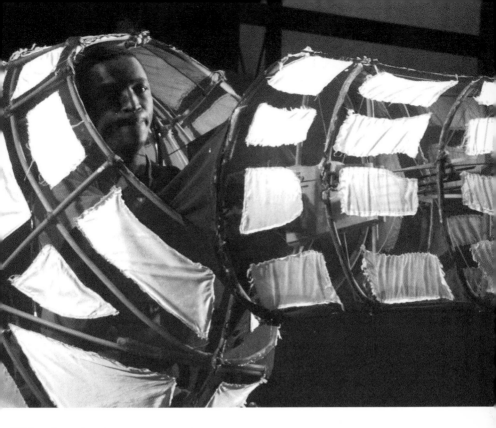

Téhibou Bagayoko Photograph by Damien Schumann

the figure when it travels. He's the more visible of the two. But it's Yacouba who is doing the 'speaking' – the delicate, crisp, expressive flicks of the ears or swishes of the long tail. Marthinus Basson almost never talks to them about these movements except where they directly inform the scene.

I sometimes wonder if Téhibou and Yacouba have benefited from not speaking English. The ferocious detail of Basson's ebullience has buoyed, confused, enthused and challenged all of the English-speaking performers, and bewildered Nana Kouma. But Téhibou and Yacouba seem to have understood early on that Marthinus's gushing stream of directions can be complementary alternatives; speaking to a group, he is often trying to offer multiple ways into a single idea. They have settled into a patient, receptive rhythm, keen to move on and try the next thing, letting the wave of language pass them by. I'm sure they have discussed Sogo Jan's character with Yaya, and recently I have been talking to them a little about how she responds in certain situations. But, overall, their linguistic isolation may have allowed them to at least partly stand above the chaos, just as the silent, ruminative giraffe stands above the chattering human beings in the fable. 'The giraffe represented… There was something else I was playing with and that is that

Sketches for an early idea for the giraffe by Adrian Kohler, with operators standing between the legs, able to lift the entire animal off the ground

Bamana and Dogon sayings about silence,' reflects Khephra Burns. 'That in silence, there's wisdom: you know, silence opened up many paths, and speech, language, confused them. They have lots of sayings like that, that in silence there's wisdom, and too many words is foolish, you know. So we've got all these languages and y'know, miscommunication, it even happens with people speaking the same language. Because there's no guarantee that the words we choose to express the feelings and emotions we have will trigger the same feelings and emotions on the other side, you know?' The mute wisdom of the giraffe communicates itself to the audience better than almost anything else.

Apart from the hard physical exertion and the telepathic bond they are developing, Adrian Kohler has a new mechanical challenge for Téhibou and Yacouba to take on. The giraffe puppet has always been thought of as having legs. As rehearsed, the puppeteers' human legs and stilts have projected from the bottom of the body cavity, breaking the image of the animal a little: the puppeteer's

JOURNEY OF THE TALL HORSE

leg goes down about as far as the giraffe's knee, and below that it's all stilt. The giraffe legs will partially obscure this picture, making it much easier to visualise the complete animal. These legs have been with the company in rehearsals all along, but Adrian hasn't yet designed a successful attachment system. For a photo-shoot, which the boys undertook slightly precariously in high winds standing on the beach, the thighs were attached to the frame with swivels, and the bottom part of the leg was simply stretched with fabric to the base of the stilt. It completes the picture when the giraffe is at rest, but it doesn't do what Kohler would ultimately like, which would be to reproduce the natural movement of a giraffe's leg. He's spent a great deal of time over the last twenty years developing complex and beautiful mechanisms to imitate the joints of animal legs, which can be seen in the slender legs of the young giraffes. But these hinged structures are controlled from the top, and require the full attention of a puppeteer's hands and fingers. Even then they are difficult to manipulate, as anyone who has tried to operate the young giraffes as they're walking will admit. Hinged legs for the big giraffe would need to move automatically, responding directly to the movement of the puppeteer's leg. It shouldn't be impossible to design. But the proven system in use on the young giraffes depends on the leg being absolutely straight at all times, and fixed so that they're perpendicular to an axle which can be set into the body. The axle for their front legs is attached in a central ball-and-socket joint that allows it some swivel. But the legs are always parallel to each other, and the strings and elastic retaining cords that control their movement can run directly down the leg – a system of levers working on a single vertical plane. On the large puppet, the legs of the puppeteer move in a much less predictable way: the bottom of the system is constantly twisting and altering its angle in relation to the top. If anyone can devise a way to make this work it's Adrian, but with all of the various crises piling up over the weeks, there's never been time for this creative task.

Khephra Burns, a guest in Handspring's house at the time, recalls how he encouraged Adrian to finish the legs, discussing the design of swivelling universal joints with him. They wouldn't be able to solve the big design challenge, but they could fix the existing legs on in a way that wouldn't impede the stilts. 'One half hour before curtain time on opening night, Adrian and I were backstage desperately cutting and grinding away on the giraffe,' he remembers, 'but we got the legs on, and they worked! There was no time for the puppeteers – Téhibou and Yacouba – to do a test run. That night when they came on stage with the giraffe was the first time they had had the new legs on.' The swivel-mount on the leg is bolted to the giraffe's body. Because the leg is dressed with the same stretch lycra as the rest of the body, it can be pulled to the bottom of the stilt and tied off. It's the same basic system as the version for the photo shoot – not the perfect movement, but the image of the giraffe is completed. Kohler was anxious about how the extra pull on the cage might affect Téhibou and Yacouba – but they took it all in their stride.

It's clearer now that the legs are on how stylised the giraffe is. Its pattern, cut according to the intersecting lines of the canes that shape its body, and rendered in negative, beige on black; the angular lines that sculpt its head; and now the straightness of the simple legs, hanging on the side of the torso. In most ways, except for its rough proportions, it doesn't resemble a giraffe. But its motion has a poetry, and the puppeteers offer a characterisation, that is unmistakably a giraffe. Appropriately, it is perhaps the crowning achievement of this collaboration. Inspired by the Malian tradition and referencing the *castelet* in its basic design, it uses all of Handspring's technical ingenuity in its extraordinary neck. But to work it has needed the strength, stamina and patience of Sogolon puppeteers and the gentle direction of both Yaya and Adrian, alongside the narrative expertise of Marthinus Basson and the movement of Koffi Kôkô. When it's come to working with the giraffe, it's often seemed that all four of these men have held themselves back and left it to the others – but they have all made a contribution, and it silently carries all of their input. The giraffe is a success, and it's inevitably the emblem of *Tall Horse*, which also finds itself a success.

Characteristically, Yaya Coulibaly is conscious of the symbolic importance of the opening of the production. 'The South African Minister of Culture came,' he reminds me proudly. 'The representative of the Malian Embassy in Pretoria came. When you see them together here, you can see that Handspring and Sogolon are quite small in comparison. It becomes a big international co-operation between Mali and South Africa. But also for the African continent.'

And just as the story of *Tall Horse* didn't start in Cape Town in February 2004 but five years earlier, it doesn't end with the opening in Cape Town; nor with the changes that Marthinus Basson, Handspring and Yaya Coulibaly agree to make to the show while its run continues in the State Theatre in Pretoria and the Dance Factory in Johannesburg during the weeks that follow.

For all its African upbringing, *Tall Horse* was conceived in the United States as an international piece of theatre. The generous sponsors, AngloGold Ashanti, always envisaged this as a South African-Malian collaboration which would play in both those nations. The production's life will depend on how it's received by the rest of the world's promoters and programmers (and the difficulty of synchronising the schedules of both companies). Over the course of his time as producer of Handspring, Basil Jones has made connections with programmers in most parts

Adrian Kohler

of the world. Their celebrated productions – *Woyzeck on the Highveld*, *Faustus in Africa!*, *Ubu and the Truth Commission*, *The Confessions of Zeno* and the opera *Il Ritorno d'Ulisse* have, between them, played at most of the major international festivals. The name of the Sogolon Troupe of Mali also opens doors to those interested in bringing authentic African theatre to their audiences. A number of those programmers and representatives come to see *Tall Horse* in its initial form during this three-venue run.

The whole team are anxious about these visits. The seven-week rehearsal period has been just enough to get the show on stage, but not really long enough to make it the best it can be for taking to the world. Jones, Kohler and Basson are often engaged, in the aftermath of the opening in Cape Town, in discussions on what the show could and should become. Its development could go in a number of directions. It could become more of a spectacular. It could become a smaller, more focused piece, with a greater proportion of time devoted to the relationship between the political and the private. There could be more dance. There could be more text from Khephra Burns. In the short term, of course, there's not a choice as to what will happen. Koffi Kôkô is due to return to Europe soon, and Burns has work to do in New York. What changes are to be made will be done in stolen moments in the theatre. They will be modest changes to improve the flow and sense of the show as it stands. You get the impression, when you hear Basson talk, that he feels the job is not quite finished. He can't have anticipated how difficult it would be for this large, diverse company to meld together and make progress on the piece, or what an obstacle the language barrier would be. He's struggled also with trying to integrate Kôkô's different rhythms into his normally high-tempo rehearsal, and with finding the flow through Khephra Burns's eclectic script.

Basil Jones knows that for the production to be marketable abroad it needs to be played without an interval – not a possibility at its current length. The programmers do come, and like what they see, and as a US tour looks more and more likely, it becomes apparent that this is not the final form of *Tall Horse*. The new year will bring a new rehearsal period – and a few more surprises.

HANDSPRING HAS BOOKED THE BAXTER

Theatre for another run. So in April 2005 the company gathers in Cape Town again.

The piece has been programmed into the prestigious Theater der Welt Festival in Stuttgart, Germany in July, and Basil Jones has negotiated a tour of the US in September, October and November, including the Brooklyn Academy of Music in New York and the Kennedy Center in Washington. If it plays well in Germany and the US, there will be possibilities for further touring in Europe and elsewhere. But the production needs to be performed without an interval, at a length of about an hour and a half. Most of the team are enthusiastic about making changes. In 2004, even with seven weeks, the struggle against circumstance and linguistics meant that all the team could do was get the play to the stage. They weren't able to examine fully the balance of the story-telling – how the script, written so far away from the puppets, would fit with them. This period sees an opportunity to rebuild the play around the core of the story so that the structure can support the puppets better. Budgets are tight. AngloGold Ashanti contributed considerably to the original rehearsal period, but for these changes Handspring must balance the books alone. There are just two weeks to re-rehearse before presenting the new version at the Baxter. It won't be possible to fly in Koffi Kôkô or Khephra Burns – Handspring, Sogolon and Marthinus Basson will need to solve the problems themselves. Basson and Adrian Kohler have already worked hard to edit the script to approximately the right length, and it's impressive how much the integrity of the piece remains.

There are changes of personnel, too. It's not a complete surprise that Fezile Mpela has fallen out of love with the project. He'd given a lot of time, and strong performances throughout the run, but a return to it, and another substantial time commitment across 2005, didn't make sense in his busy career. A new Atir has been cast: a young, bright, ambitious actor from township theatre, Sandile Matsheni. Less predictable, perhaps, is the absence of Zandile Msutswana, the young actress who played Clothilde. Her place will be taken by a recent graduate of the University of Cape Town's drama programme, Mbali Kgosidintsi. Nana Kouma, from Mali, will be replaced by a very different young Malian woman, also called Nana: Nana Traoré. There is also a replacement drummer for young Vuyo.

Astonishingly, Basil Jones has managed to find a suitably qualified South African who also speaks Bambara. Glenn Solomon Morton, known as 'Solo', is a white South African percussionist and djembe player who has spent much time in Mali and embraced Bamana culture. The rest of the company remains the same: Yaya Coulibaly, Téhibou Bagayoko and Yacouba Magassouba from Sogolon; Basil Jones, Adrian Kohler, Busi Zokufa and Fourie Nyamande from Handspring; Bheki Vilakazi and Craig Leo.

It won't be easy to bring these four new performers up to speed in the time available. Mbali will have to pick up puppetry skills that Zandile had seven weeks to master. Sogolon does not usually use female performers, but Basil has insisted that Nana Kouma be replaced with a female. Consequently, Nana Traoré will need to learn puppetry and stilt-walking to fulfil Kouma's roles in the play.

The new performers come prepared: they've been studying the text, and Sandile arrives, thankfully, with most of it already memorised. Adrian in Cape Town and Yaya in Bamako have been teaching Mbali and Nana, respectively, the principles of what they will need to do. Both women are thorough and determined not to show up their colleagues. From the first day, Nana Traoré seems intelligent and engaged. Because Téhibou and Yacouba have retained most of the English they learnt on their previous visit, and Yaya's ability to understand English has always been fairly good, Nana is usually the only one with difficulties in following Marthinus – and consequently, is offered plenty of attention. The other Malians are often on hand to give clarifications in Bambara.

Basson finally sacrificed the troublesome Marseilles scene in Pretoria in 2004. It had struggled while it lived, but it died peacefully, leaving a much more fluid transition. Now, as Atir leaves Africa on the boat to France, and we leave behind the heat and the pragmatism of Alexandria, the scene shifts abruptly to the surreal social competitiveness of the Soirée and the introduction of our new major characters, Clothilde and St-Hilaire. It's a dynamic contrast that stresses the gulf between the continents. Although a considerable amount has now been cut – the establishing of the scientists, the popular hysteria preceding the giraffe's arrival, a brief speech by Atir on discovering Europe – it's clear that in a tighter retelling of the story, this works. But by and large the script edits aren't wholesale removals like this one. Some lengthy sequences, in being made shorter, have lost staging ideas: there had been a reprise appearance of Mehmet Ali's giant arms, apparently growing out of the shelving units, during the letter-writing scene in the second half; now, the shorter, simpler version doesn't need to be supported with so much visual ingenuity.

There's no danger of comparison between Sandile and his predecessor, Fezile. Where Fezile built his characterisation around a watchful, grudgingly deferent Atir who cannily climbs the greasy pole to achieve success in Europe, Sandile's approach to his character focuses more on his naivety. Sandile's Atir is an open, guileless man, who finds himself placed in extraordinary situations. This different quality he's found in Atir demands that the other actors reassess the material they have become familiar with. The rehearsals have a new purpose and a fresh energy for the whole company. There will be new sequences, but Basson's unlikely to be led into the same sort of tangential visual riffs that marked his engagement with the material the first time round. In fact, Marthinus's relationship with Sandile is built around frequent discreet conferences. Now that the puppeteers know their routines, they can reacquaint themselves with the detail while Marthinus concentrates on being a coach to the actors.

The first morning is taken up with a read-through of the edited script, and in the afternoon Basson starts work in a brisk, productive, cheerful manner. He begins at the beginning, with the framing scene in the Museum – a sequence that includes everyone in the company. The aim is to show the cues to Sandile, Mbali and Nana, but something else happens too: as each performer remembers his exact movements, this process tests the validity of each 'beat' in the sequence blocked out nearly nine months ago, so that each actor is re-engaging with the 'why' behind their move and the connection between that move and their own or someone else's line.

But this being *Tall Horse*, even in two short weeks there are surprises waiting in the wings. The first is a muscle strain that affects Busi Zokufa. Busi has been at the heart of Handspring's work for twelve years or more, and, given the strong feeling within the company, she is almost like family to the other long-serving members such as Basil, Adrian, Leigh and Wesley. Busi's a large woman and it's not the first time that she's had a strain. This production has been especially taxing, with her inside two *merens habitables*, playing Clothilde's Parisian friend Jolie and the beautiful lady of Lyon. But this pain, which strikes on the very first day, prevents her even from walking. Yaya offers a vigorous massage, and she sits down to watch work continue. The injury immediately affects what we can rehearse. Marthinus, on a tight schedule to get the whole piece rehearsed, drives on to the Nile. Although Busi normally manipulates the head of the young Sogo Jan in this scene, Basson can use the time helping Sandile with the monologue.

One of the textual contractions has been to reduce this from four separate 'days' to a single speech, and Basson and Kohler have edited it to give a sense of a long journey, without the literal punctuation of sleeping, waking or time-

Sandile Matsheni with the giraffe Photograph by Damien Schumann

[Atir] was a specimen, something totally exotic,
for the [French] people. And then we see how the
men around him wonder how to understand him
scientifically, politically. But between this, we see
women from Paris, who see this man, a strong man,
a beautiful man, and they are passionate about him
– like the men are passionate about the giraffe.

Koffi Kôkô

consuming lighting fades. Some of the supplementary action is rendered excessive. So instead of the detailed interplay of boats and birds in the longer *Tall Horse*, Basson restricts himself to one or two boats passing at the beginning and end of the scene. These acquire a symbolic quality, and the scene seems more taut. The loss of the slaves singing behind the boat is a possible source of regret, and when he reads the edits, Khephra Burns is quick to express concern about this ellipsis. In the rehearsal room, however, there's no sense that the issue of slavery has been lost, only the demonstration of it. The power of 'Jonnya Mani' was considerable, and part of its effect came from how unorthodox it was to pause the scene for so long to hear it: the passage of the slaves across the back of the stage felt like an uncomfortable hiatus in the action for the audience. In the swifter version there have to be sacrifices, and this stylistic quirk is one.

The puppeteers don't always greet their puppets like old friends. Craig Leo, for example, puts off contact with his star turn, the Fashion Designer, for as long as possible. The long hours he spent holding its weight while trying to perfect the rhythm of its over-the-top speech flood back to him more easily than the moments when all three operators found themselves working in harmony. Fourie, on the other hand, is pleased to get his hands back on several of his puppets. He begins to bob around the space with the blind man as if we'd never been away.

The company haven't returned to Stellenbosch. This time the rehearsal venue is Hiddingh Hall on the University of Cape Town campus. Marthinus Basson will be separated from his faculty until the show moves into the theatre, with two weeks' leave booked. Having Handspring on their doorstep is an asset for UCT, and the Head of Drama, Mark Fleishman, is an old friend of Basil and Adrian; both he and his wife Jennie Reznek have worked with the company. Fleishman is also one of South Africa's best directors, and Magnet, the company he runs with Reznek, has created many rich and potent pieces. Kohler had said of rehearsing in a theatre in Stellenbosch: 'We've rehearsed everything else we've done in other places. Sort of, warehouses and workshops and the rehearsal room at Handspring in Johannesburg was very nice, but it got very small towards the end of it. To be working in that theatre and, when we needed to have people coming in and watching and stuff [was] a fantastic privilege. And because we're working with those big trundling shelves, we couldn't really have done it in any other way.' The same isn't true now. The focus must come away from the big trundling shelves, and this space has better natural light, is more flexible, and closer to the city.

With Busi Zokufa out of action and Basson working on the Nile sequence, the puppeteers are one short. Adrian moves up one, to the head of the young giraffe, so that Sandile can find out what it will do as he talks to it. Kohler's engagement in the act of puppetry is unlike anyone else's, especially when manipulating an animal. His concentration is so fully in the puppet that his control over his own facial muscles relaxes. His mouth drops slightly open, and he looks amazed, as if he's seeing a wooden head animated for the first time and doesn't trust the object in his own hand. When actors work with puppets for the first time, their ability to manipulate the figure convincingly often relates directly to how much they're able to believe that the puppet is alive. With Kohler, there's no doubt. It's written all over his face that what he's holding is vital and unpredictable. You can sometimes see a similar look on the face of Fourie Nyamande or Téhibou Bagayoko when their puppetry is at its best.

The first production meeting of the re-rehearsals considers the knock-on effects of the textual changes. There's lots for Jaco Bouwer to do. With so many scenes changing length, he needs to make sure that what he supplied last time won't be too long. He suggests that he come in to watch the Nile tomorrow morning, to take a rough timing of the new shorter version, from which he'll be able to condense his four-day odyssey into one smooth sequence.

But when Jaco arrives in the morning, there's no sign of Busi. Working through the scene in bits is one thing, but an accurate timing can't be taken without her. Last year, perhaps the company would have waited. This time they can't. Marthinus gathers Sandile, Bheki and Mbali to do some detailed work on other parts of the text, while Yaya organises Téhibou, Yacouba and Nana to help him reattach the heads to the *castelets*. While the Queen *castelet* is so bulky that it gets taken apart between locations, the others are transported intact, with only the projecting (and decorated) necks and heads packed inside flight cases. The tails are demounted and strapped to the back of the body.

Busi makes her way in, but she's not well. The strong pain-killers she's been prescribed have caused her to oversleep. She decides that she'd prefer to stay and watch what's happening, but there's nothing that she can do to help with the rehearsal, and the main effect is that Leigh, Basil and Adrian are distracted by their concern for her.

It looks possible that Busi won't be able to perform in two weeks' time. If this is a serious strain, it could also be recurrent – and at the moment she is completely immobile. The physical demands of the roles she plays mean that it's totally impractical for her to go on if she's in pain. Marthinus looks at the Nile and Alexandria scenes to work out who could conceivably cover for Busi. Adrian works the head of the giraffe superbly, with a precision and crispness that bring out all the nuances of its thoughts. Enrico Wey, whose on-stage action has previously been restricted to holding the Queen, hidden by her huge robe, and operating a *castelet* in the hunt, is brought in to take over from Adrian on the legs.

It doesn't feel like a crisis. The weather is lovely, and Hiddingh Hall is a beautiful room to work in. On each side of the room, floor-to-ceiling leaded windows let the light stream in. It's in marked contrast to the sealed environment of the H B Thom Theatre. The relaxed energy of the performers not directly involved in the scene is spreading to those who are working.

But when attention turns to the Hunt, some of Basson's anxieties start to show through. The Hunt was always Koffi Kôkô's territory in the 2004 *Tall Horse*. It revelled in a luxury of stage time, slowly building its textures, varying the tone as mini-stories between the *castelets* unfolded, bringing in danger, calmness, tension and humour until its broader purpose – to establish the savannah and introduce the elegant giraffe mothers – had been achieved almost by stealth. But it ran at fifteen minutes, and with the show being contracted to ninety, something will have to go.

Marthinus has decided to rebuild it from scratch, to see what the minimum length would be. He can use some of Kôkô's elements – but what he's not going to be able to do is create something in Koffi's style. Clarity is the key, and Adrian Kohler is making a contribution too. He's decided that the giraffe babies he carved for the original production are too small to have enough impact on stage. He has made new, larger giraffe babies, each of which has a long neck with a moving head, which can be operated by Craig or Sandile as they take them under their arms.

Basson seems to want to get this session over with quickly and falls into his traffic-orchestration mode, delivering instructions as he thinks them, building up the passage of bodies on stage. First a single *castelet*. Then one mother giraffe crosses the stage. Then two *castelets*, crossing in opposition. The *castelets* come together and bow their heads to drink – one of Kôkô's motifs – and there is time to breathe. Another joins them. The staggered entry builds the atmosphere and allows each of them plenty of individuality – but it's also based on uncompromising backstage practicalities. Basson has cut the lion costumes, so Yaya is free to take the first *castelet*.

His first entrance is a beautiful demonstration: slow, stylised, a genuine dance. The stiff, heavy body of the animal moves with a slow, stately pace, but the movement of his legs underneath it is still light and nimble. Coulibaly is able to combine a brightness and vitality with the slow passage across the space that Basson asks for, and it makes the stage seem enormous – the single *castelet* becomes expressive of a herd in the distance.

Adrian Kohler carving a replica of one of the new baby giraffes   Photograph by Enrico Wey

Basson working at this pace is a baptism of fire for Nana Traoré, who apprehensively gets on to her stilts. Her nervousness shows as she starts to try them out. Most of the performers can remember seeing Nana Kouma and Zandile Msutswana learning the stilt-walking and aren't concerned about her halting first steps, but Yaya's face is grim. Enrico Wey helps to guide her through the moves as Basson begins to change his mind about the sequence of the entrances. Before long the instructions become confused – will the mothers pass behind the stage once or twice? The slow progress of Nana when she walks across the room on stilts means that she hasn't made it offstage in time to come back on. Basson, with an eye on the bigger picture, is moving on to the next phase, but Traoré is still bewildered about his previous decision. For a second, things are reminiscent of last time and Nana Kouma's sense of isolation from the fast-moving, English-speaking room.

Sandile Matsheni holds the two new baby giraffe puppets Photograph by Damien Schumann

But this Nana will not find herself receding in the way that her predecessor did. She's more confident, more verbal, and hungrier to learn about the new environment she's in. While Nana Kouma seemed happiest when surrendering her personality to a dance, Nana Traoré likes to take centre stage. She looks a little lost on Tuesday when raised up on her stilts, but on Thursday, with her feet firmly on the ground, she's given an opportunity to offer a real service. With Busi attending a physiotherapist, Marthinus is about to ask Leigh Colombick to read in her lines for a rehearsal of the first King and Queen scene – in which the world of the Jardin des Plantes invades the framing world of the West African museum. But Yaya stops him. '*Non, non,*' he says. '*C'est pas nécessaire.*' And he gestures to Nana, who reads in the Queen's lines in French. For that day, it's a revelation.

When playing the Queen in French, Busi had been doing something quite extraordinary. She'd found a way to deliver the lines phonetically, and understand the sense of them enough to inflect the language persuasively, without ever really knowing the rules of accent and intonation. She'd worked assiduously with translators and Yaya, learning the phrasing. What Marthinus has never really heard, though, is the lines spoken by a French-speaker and with real force, which is what Nana offers him this Thursday morning.

Busi and Nana deal with the Queen very differently. Busi is a wonderful character and comic actress with years of experience. She took the battle-axe character and turned it into a multi-layered creation: ferocious, vain, coquettish, seeking flattery and obedience. She used skilful timing to give the character a delight in her power that made her rather charming despite the bitterness and haughtiness in her dialogue. Nana, with very little preparation, gives in full what she sees from the lines in that scene: a gale force of ferocity in a powerful, low voice that nearly knocks the King off the stage. For the first time, the stage has an unrestrained West African power struggle between the King and Queen.

Nana's dynamism while standing in as the Queen brings the question of Busi's fitness back to the top of the agenda in another meeting between Handspring and Marthinus. At this stage, it could be anything from a simple strain to a slipped disc. The situation has been distracting Basil, Adrian and particularly Leigh Colombick, who has been ferrying Busi to and from the physio and looking after her outside of rehearsal times.

It looks as if she will remain unavailable until at least the beginning of the next week. Today opened up the possibility of a cast member who could cover for her as the Queen, in the same way that contingency plans have emerged for reallocating her puppetry responsibilities. Marthinus is practical in his assessment. 'It seems to me,' he offers, 'that the problem is a severe one – and it doesn't look like it's going to clear up any time soon.' At times like these, people turn to anecdotes, and stories are told about friends whose problems cleared up immediately, or whom the problem continued to plague for years. Unfortunately, no one here is a doctor, and a firm decision is impossible. But Nana showed enough promise today to suggest that she may be able to handle the role as an understudy. Basson decides to introduce her to some of the other scenes over the next two days.

Even though the aim is to work through specific sections of the edited script, covering for Busi absorbs a large proportion of Friday's work. It's become clear that in the Nile scene it makes more sense for Adrian to continue working the difficult front legs of the young giraffe, leaving Enrico as a direct substitute for Busi on the head. This puppet is also operated by Jones and Kohler, and it may seem odd to put the least experienced puppeteer on the head. But while the legs are operated by trigger and pulley systems, the head is held directly in the hand. The connection between the movement of the manipulator's hand and the thought that's being expressed isn't mediated via control mechanisms – the operation of this part of the puppet is more to do with precision of acting than technical dexterity.

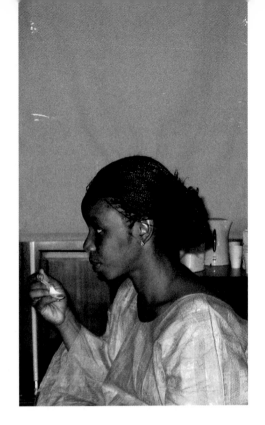

Nana Traoré

Enrico Wey is finding, time and time again, that when a replacement is sought for Busi, he is the one available. When he joined the company as an intern and observer, he probably didn't anticipate understudying for a principal puppeteer on a production bound for some of the most prestigious venues in the US. He takes to it with the mixture of good humour and modesty that seems to be a feature of Handspring's best-loved collaborators. He takes Busi's lady guest in the Soirée scene and both of her weighty *meren habitable* roles: the beautiful lady of Lyon and the Parisian mademoiselle, Jolie. It would be marginally preferable for a female puppeteer to take these roles, but the only one available, Nana Traoré, is otherwise engaged in each case. Mastering the moves and lines is a substantial task but, crucially, Wey is enjoying himself, and he tries to take up as little rehearsal time as possible – he knows the play well already. Compromising him is his habitual regard for the backstage mechanics. It's here that he would be missed if he did step in to Busi's roles: keeping things organised backstage, and helping to cue and prepare the puppeteers for their entrances.

Busi's injury puts the company off-schedule early on in the fortnight. But despite this, Marthinus is at his witty, charming best, and Adrian confides: 'I'm

The Fashion Designer with Enrico Wey
and Adrian Kohler

enjoying this so much more than the first rehearsal period.' There's less tension, and with dozens of performances behind them, more trust between the performers. The key collaborators are showing different sides to their characters. Yaya is bringing more of his relaxed affability into the rehearsal room. In 2004 he was always watchful and protective of his puppeteers and, alongside his witty and mischievous moments, presented a serious side. He's still all of those things and takes his responsibility as a representative of his nation and company seriously, but he's more mercurial now, satisfied perhaps that everyone here has made a significant commitment to the project. Marthinus, with a short period to work in and a clear target, doesn't seem nearly as affected by the ups and downs of the rehearsal day. Perhaps it's simply that, revisiting the project, he knows there are parts of it that work, and so he's rebuilding from a position of strength. Adrian Kohler, as he's said, is looking forward to every day. There's no pressure on him to make new puppets or to worry whether the set design will work, and there's less to supervise in terms of costumes – just fittings for the three new performers. And so he can concentrate on his first love, the puppetry itself. Freed from his anxieties, and having been closely involved in the editing process, he often sits down with Marthinus when he's not in a scene. Basil Jones's producing work-load has hardly eased – he still faces a full desktop each morning and evening – but he's refreshed by the positivity of his partner, and, despite concerns over Busi and the future plans for the show, he is enjoying being engaged with the work again.

Sandile Matsheni is making good progress as Atir, although he has yet to find the performance style that the others have settled into. His experience and instinct come from a more declamatory tradition, and Sandile will often find a strong position and offer the speech boldly to the front. With *Tall Horse*, Marthinus is more interested in subtly observed detail. Even though the Baxter is a big theatre, Sandile will look better in this show by finding the delicate moments of decision and doubt in his speeches, rather than grandstanding. Keen to take these notes, the attentive Sandile starts to experiment with a softer style of delivery.

Meanwhile, Nana Traoré is engaging with the Queen's other scenes. As she's not previously worked with Sogolon, Yaya is particularly anxious about how she performs (and how it reflects on him). He's furious about how badly her stilt-walking is developing – it seems he had spent some time training her in Mali before they came to Cape Town. Perhaps her confidence on the stilts is low because of the foreign environment, or because the wooden floor in Hiddingh Hall looks slippery (it isn't). Enrico Wey, who has not previously been up on stilts, takes up a spare pair one day and begins to learn; and I think the sight of a beginner reminds her what she has learnt and gives her confidence. It's daunting to be the novice in a room where Craig Leo, Téhibou Bagayoko and Yacouba Magassouba stroll around as if their stilts were natural extensions of their legs. So Marthinus's enthusiastic acceptance of Nana as Busi's understudy makes good political sense, helping to rehabilitate her as a representative of Sogolon and of Mali – although Marthinus has been careful to emphasize that Nana is an understudy and not a replacement for Busi.

Because of the Queen's size, Busi didn't originally carry her but instead walked alongside the bearer, presenting a similar picture to the one the audience see with a smaller puppet and a manipulator just behind or beside it. Upright and armless, the Queen has a statuesque simplicity of form: the fabric hangs evenly from the shoulders and, without a body as such, she occupies the role of a totem as much as a character. But her head, although substantial (and quite heavy), is small in relation to her height and, bolted to the support pole in the traditional style, has no articulation. The whole Queen can turn from side to side, but she can't turn or angle her head relative to her neck or shoulders, which makes it difficult to give her detailed animation to go with her lines. She's as solid as rock – and in danger of being as interesting.

With Busi on stage, the audience would often watch the actress more than the looming puppet. The addition of an arm on one side of the puppet, for Busi to

The giraffe [is] at the centre of this storm, there's a war going on, all these schemes, and the giraffe is just at peace always, you know?

Khephra Burns

Yaya Coulibaly and Busi Zokufa with the King's and the Queen's heads Photograph by Damien Schumann

hold and manipulate, has been discussed as a solution. This would offer a stronger visual connection for the audience and would allow Busi to synchronise the lines with gestures more directly. The arm would be connected to the horizontal cylinder that reads as a set of stylised shoulders. Variations were tried in Stellenbosch in 2004: a rigid wooden arm made with an elbow joint, and a soft rope arm from shoulder to elbow or wrist. Yaya Coulibaly carved two hands for the Queen, which are still available. But this plan has always fallen down: as soon as an arm is attached, it breaks and distorts the natural fall of the fabric. The shape suddenly looks clumsy – the thin line of the stick arm weakens the composed, abstracted figure. Working with Nana on the Queen reawakens these experiments.

Nana is trained as an actress, and so her instinct is to play the characterisation in her own body. Busi Zokufa is also trained as an actress, but her many years of puppetry enable her to channel her characterisation either into her own body, into a puppet, or just through her voice. It's a particular skill, and it's rare even for puppeteers to be providing the voice, live, for a character that someone else is manipulating. In *Tall Horse*, it's a relationship that Adrian Kohler has had to develop, first with Zandile Msutswana and subsequently with Mbali Kgosidintsi, the actresses playing Clothilde: for many of her scenes he is the main puppeteer, while they provide the voice and manipulate one arm and her hips. But even there, the two puppeteers are close together and can use physical contact and the body of the puppet to communicate with one another. With the Queen, Enrico Wey is standing under the fabric holding a three-metre pole with a head and shoulders on it, while Busi (or Nana) is several steps away. It's not a ventriloquial trick that Nana needs to master. Instead of inviting the audience to study her expressions and physicality, she has to learn how to direct their eyes across to the head of the Queen puppet while she is speaking. It's the opposite difficulty from that of the actors in the show, such as Bheki Vilakazi. While they must talk to the piece of wood and not the person holding it, Nana must learn, when playing the Queen, to speak, not to the King, but through the Queen, who, in turn, directs focus towards the person being addressed. But of more concern is Nana's delivery of the lines. Yaya has been introducing her to the text, and Nana is keen to take her chance. But what was a quibble in the first scene is becoming a concern as she approaches the others. Nana tends to speak each word in a line with equal force. She enunciates crisply and projects well, but the meaning of the line gets lost because there's no inflection.

The production is being revisited by some experienced hands. Last year, extra puppetry sessions focused on the different puppet control systems; by exploring their possibilities, the manipulators would be more versatile on stage. But now there is the potential to take the scenes forward, and Adrian wants to target Mehmet Ali. Having looked at a video of the production in 2004, he's excited by the prospects of this huge puppet, but isn't satisfied with the level of connection between the head, breath and arms. It's partly because of the bulk of the object. As we saw, Basil Jones has a mighty job trying to manage the frame, supporting it by a variety of means: balancing it on the flight case, holding it in his belt and transferring some of its weight to his shoulders with a harness. As well as this wrestling, he has to speak the lines, manipulate the head's direction and angle, and tilt the body forwards or backwards when appropriate. Meanwhile, Téhibou and Yacouba, on the arms, are pulling him in different directions as they try to use gesture to support the words.

On returning to the sequence, it seems that the three of them have developed different rhythms. Separated by the puppet's body, they can't see each other, and it's easy for their work to diverge. Yacouba is decorating more words in Mehmet's speeches than before. Mehmet's right hand (on his side) used to make a gesture to stress certain words; now it's more like a conductor's baton, beating out the rhythm of his lines. Meanwhile, Téhibou and the left arm are fully engaged with Mehmet's mood, rather than the detail of his speech. Adrian begins to lead sessions on reconnecting the three manipulators.

The multiple support systems are actually making Basil's job more difficult, and the harness and belt are removed. As discussed in 2004, what's really needed is some sort of swivel-joint at the base of the main rod, so that the puppet's 'spine' can lean in each direction without slipping across the flight-case on which it rests. Adrian has a new idea. A steel pin in the base of the spine could slot into a (slightly larger) hole in a reinforced metal plate on top of the flight-case, allowing the spine to lean in all directions, without a physical obstruction on top of the case. It works, and gives Jones a more secure base from which to connect his words to the work of the Malians. It's also decided that Basil will have a new control: a string to work the moving mouth of Mehmet. Adrian had originally made the puppet with a moving mouth, but it had not been used in this scene, only in the second half of the play, when Mehmet's head alone is seen dictating a letter to the Sultan. Now that moving the body has become easier, a puppeteer of Basil's experience should be able to integrate lip-synch movement into his performance.

Adrian's style of direction makes a change from Marthinus's. Where Marthinus's interest lay in the spectacular and visual poetry of the puppets and in the narrative flow of the story-telling, Kohler wants to work with the puppeteers on perfecting each small moment. He wants to put the right move in the right place to direct focus or to emphasize a line and connect the action of the three manipulators. This means that there will never be enough time – there is always an adjustment that could be made.

It's similar to the intense work that he, Basil and Craig Leo needed to do to find the detail in the Fashion Designer sequence. 'Craig did a lot of work on the text at home, but involving a lot of changes, sometimes within a line, and the figure just can't go there,' Kohler says about the relationship between puppetry and text. 'It's much cleaner if you make fewer. And I think the puppet does pull the lines into perspective. And in a good way, because even for an actor too many changes in a line is not a good thing.' Yacouba's instinct, like Leo's was initially, is to illustrate too many words or concepts. Craig Leo found himself liberated with the text when he ornamented less of it.

Because these puppets are strong as sculpture, they are able to hold their positions longer than other figures. Puppetry can look at its best when it involves the movement from one fixed position to another; the audience responds well to a series of strong visual images, accompanied by a sequence of words that relate to it. It may initially seem that close imitation is the way to make the puppet most alive, but, just as actors shape their performances around decision points in a text, a slight formalisation allows the flow of feelings to be understood as a digestible sequence of intentions.

But puppetry demands a greater discipline and crispness in executing those changes, especially when the puppets are operated by more than one person. Most of the puppets that Kohler earmarks for extra work involve several people.

Despite the diversion of Busi's injury, Marthinus Basson keeps the rehearsal process on track, and by the end of the first week Sandile, Mbali and Solo have seen the whole play from the inside. In a good mood, Basson works briskly without letting the performers feel rushed. He's helped in this by Yaya's, Yacouba's and Téhibou's rapidly improving English. He's also very well organised. He's already been through the changes to the script with Jaco Bouwer and Wesley France, who have a good idea of how it will affect their work in adapting the video and lighting. A previously longish scene involving the French royal family is now a brief snapshot – and so, rather than clearing the whole stage, Basson moves it to the front of the stage and cuts smoothly into something else upstage; this affects the lighting sequence substantially. There's a new nimbleness to the story-telling. An awkward series of scenes involving the Prefect of Marseilles and St-Hilaire, revealing the large giraffe, discussing the practicalities of transporting the animal to Paris and preparing it for the journey, has seen relatively little editing but shifts fluidly from scene to scene. Whereas before a real location was established for each of these scenes, now the theatricality of the ongoing conversation is foregrounded and the location becomes unimportant.

The process of this rehearsal is not purely removing and editing. As the play is made shorter, it needs to be rebalanced with different points of focus – and as Marthinus, Adrian and Basil reflect on the first version, they decide that one moment that never quite asserted itself properly was the presentation of the giraffe to the King and Queen of France. Khephra Burns uses the scene to illuminate the comic relationship he's been developing between Charles and Marie-Thérèse. Throughout, Charles has preferred to hunt or to spend time with his animals than to pursue his royal duties, and his wife has hauled him up for lack of attendance to protocol. Burns shows St-Hilaire inviting the King to thank Atir, a black man, at the public presentation. Marie-Thérèse is horrified, but Charles overrules her, and so Atir has his moment of glory and is rewarded. The scene ends with the revelry sweeping past and Atir left behind – the world continues and, despite his brief moment of 'equality', the African is forgotten. At the end, the music that was adding the grandeur to Versailles, as Koffi called it, gave a sense of great pomp, although not revelry. Basson and Simon Mahoney had brought up the volume of the music to smother Atir's attempts to speak to the King, the royals processed away, and Atir had been left alone with Sogo Jan. But there was something missing: the climax of the story of the giraffe as she too meets the King. Burns's script ended the scene with Atir's exclusion, skipping over an enjoyment of the real conclusion to Sogo Jan's story. Marthinus wants to reinforce this moment, reinstating some of the dancing of *castelets* that he has removed from the Savannah and using them to end the presentation with an upbeat, festive demonstration of what the Malian *castelets* can do.

'Solo', Glenn Solomon Morton, will be more than just the drummer. He's contracted to work as an ASM, with Enrico Wey backstage, as well as using his djembe to accompany Fourie Nyamande on his Newspaperman speeches. But with Enrico stepping in to cover Busi's puppetry there are new absences, and Solo is proving an enthusiastic candidate to step forward and take them on. Particularly welcome is his willingness to step into a *castelet*. Solo's time in Mali among the Bamana means that he's particularly keen to connect with Yaya. Just as we reach the last afternoon of the first week, Solo approaches him and asks for some instruction in using the *castelet*. Yaya shows him a couple of steps, puts him under the heavy frame and begins to give instruction in Bambara, which Solo also speaks. Yaya is enjoying teaching and enjoying his pupil's determination to perform well – later Solo tells me how in his conception of Bamana society it is the role of the younger man to be obedient to the elder.

Yaya calls for Solo to trot, to rear up, to run in circles, to alter the spring in his step, to bend down, to run again. It's an impressive display, more so because of the amount of energy the athletic Solo is expending on a hot day. Yaya continues; Solo doesn't ask to stop. The *castelet* comes alive as Yaya's brisk commands control its rhythm and Solo bobs keenly, waiting for the next call. It becomes like a circus trainer working with a real animal, as the antelope *castelet* capers and leaps at Yaya's calls. Soon, everyone in the room is watching only this demonstration, and Solo works for at least twenty minutes – the others usually complain after five in these cramped cages. Yaya is delighted, enjoying himself unselfconsciously as he challenges and teaches. It's Marthinus Basson who realises that what we are watching is the scene between the King and his animals that can become the climax to the story.

Over the following days, the scene is refined into a sequence between the King and three of his animals. Yaya's way of holding the King in a belt is a new adaptation of his own tradition that has come from this collaboration: he's seen Handspring use a belt-harness to support tall objects and has applied the idea to his own manipulation. It means that he can use both of the King's hands at once: the King can gesture and even clap his hands. So Yaya is working with minimal restrictions as he starts to recreate and adapt the genuine energy that he found when playing with Solo.

The sequence emerges smoothly from the presentation of Sogo Jan to the King in Paris. Having addressed Atir, the King is satisfied to see his wife leave – it allows him to engage fully with his new animal – and he shows the giraffe how he commands his existing menagerie. Once again there is a fluid movement between contexts without an explicit marker. Atir and St-Hilaire step back to the periphery as the King speaks to his most important confidants and begins to make them play. The three *castelets* are inhabited by Solo, Fourie Nyamande and Craig Leo, and the sequence allows them to demonstrate their favourite and most individual moves. The King barks commands in Bamana: 'San Fe!' as they rear up; 'Dugu Ma!' as they bend down[1]; and an extraordinary trilling cry of 'Kiri kiri kiri kiri kiri kiri kiri kiri kiri kiri!' as they spin spectacularly. The giraffe looks down at it all indulgently. After so much plotting and anxiety, this exuberance transforms the ending of the play. The stately stiffness of the formal presentation and the quiet emotion of Atir's farewell to the giraffe are now balanced and given energy by an intervening moment that simply celebrates these wonderful puppets. It's also a rare moment of unmediated Malian work (although Basson does need to keep

The giraffe looks on as the King (Yaya Coulibaly) commands his *castelets* (Craig Leo, Solo Morton, Fourie Nyamande)

a lid on its length) between one of the classical Malian *marionnettes à tige* and their *castelets*. And finally it gives the story of the King a satisfying ending. At this moment, all of the quirkiness that Khephra, Yaya and Marthinus have contributed to the King's characterisation falls into place. It's easy to see in this moment of pure play why he treats his politics, his marriage and his people so flippantly – how could they compare with the joy he sees in his animals?

Many of the current discoveries develop from a principle Marthinus was conscious of in 2004. Khephra Burns's script told a whole story by itself. But once the puppets were on a stage, the story changed. The design, the look, the movement of the figures offered new challenges that the frenetic crisis-resolution of the first rehearsal period couldn't always resolve. So part of the rewriting process has been to find places for the puppets to exist alongside the text, and to complete their stories. Unfortunately, economics determine that Khephra is isolated from the rehearsals again. He has received the proposed rewrites that Basson and Kohler have made since the original opening, and of course from his distance, many of them don't make sense. His original vision has been reshaped, and he has regrets about seeing sections go. 'Being away from the company at times when changes were being made to the script and performance,' he reflects, 'was probably the most difficult part of the process. The collaborative process worked best when all of us were there with the company and had input into the script, direction, performances and changes.' The need to shorten the running time means that some political intricacies are treated in less detail – for example, a lengthy sequence illustrating the difficulties of communication between the Turkish Sultan and the Pasha Mehmet Ali has been compressed. There are inevitable cuts to the Soirée and to the opening scene in the museum. In each of these cases, verbal humour is being replaced by visual theatricality – a more direct humour, expressed in gestures and looks. It's very rare to find a playwright who really uses the minimum number of words, and the stylised gesture of these puppets means a great deal can be said without being spoken.

Khephra also regrets (and resists) the loss of the guillotine climax to the scene in Lyon. It should be a dramatic high-point of the show, but the events of the rehearsal and the play's structure have been conspiring against it. First, the main strand of the play is a picaresque narrative – Adrian's 'road movie'. The heroes move between successive events which are rarely linked. Clothilde returns to haunt Atir and the giraffe, giving the illusion of continuity, but all that has happened is that she has been dragged into the slip-stream of their progress. The second strand of narrative – the plot involving Mehmet Ali, Drovetti and the Queen of France – does have structure and development, but as the secondary focus and because of its intricacies it doesn't always feel like it. So Lyon arrives out of nowhere: there's no build-up, and this terrific moment, where the symbolism of necks reaches its conclusion, can feel random and indiscriminate. As Burns has said, this is his first stage-piece of this complexity. In rehearsal, hearts stopped when the blade fell twice on the neck of the giraffe – but in the theatre, they often didn't. The construction of the play isn't preparing for the moment fully; the construction of the special effect is making it vulnerable. In a climate of unsentimental discipline, it's removed.

Narratively, there's still the threat as the blade is revealed, and the removal of contrived stage mechanics frees up Basson's placement of performers, allowing him to engineer the chaos and hostility of the Lyon mob more effectively. Restricted and partially masked by the guillotine, the giraffe wasn't able to fight back against the probing, poking crowd. Now, it can move from nervous skittishness to panicked kicks and swings of its head as the Lyonnais mill around it. The fictionalised falling blade was always a fudge. Symbolically, the blade fell thrillingly. But no real reason was offered as to why the blade didn't sever the giraffe's neck.

And concerning Burns most are changes to Newspaperman's character. The South African audiences related well to Fourie Nyamande's affable, mischievous journalist, and Basson's idea to set his speeches to drumming gave him immediacy as well as a cheeky authority. But the audiences had trouble following the politics: so some of Newspaperman's speeches have been rewritten or adapted by Basson and Kohler to help the audience keep up with the action. Basson has also tried to strengthen the role as a stage presence by bringing rhyming to Nyamande's character in the framing device. All of this is a surprise to Burns, who's understandably concerned about the new lines in his script. 'Since my name is on the script, I feel any lines that audiences judge as stinkers and credit to me should at least be mine,' he observes. And with a smile: 'On the other hand, I'm quite willing to let them credit me for those lines suggested by Marthinus and Adrian that I did like and kept in.'

So while the company rehearses, with Solo learning the rhythms to accompany Fourie's lines, Khephra is composing his own revisions. They are often better written, and are inevitably more in keeping with the tone of the original text – but, like the original text, they can be elliptical and hard to follow – not an advantage for a character who is the most direct line of communication to the audience.

To take a company from Africa to Europe means extra work for Wesley France, composing the surtitles in the appropriate languages. All that's to come. But this production has to play in the United States and, more urgently, in Cape Town, where the audiences will be expecting to understand the English that's spoken. Plenty of attention has been paid to the accent of Busi Zokufa when she speaks French, but the mixture of accents among the English-speakers is also a concern, judging by feedback from last year's shows. Most of the black South Africans speak English as a second or third language, without the crystal-clear Anglicised vowels that Fezile, Zandile or Mbali learnt at drama school. The accents aren't difficult to follow in conversation, but deciphering them all at once can be problematic for the audience. And if it's easier to understand an accent when looking at the person's face, here we are usually watching the puppet. Vocal skills are crucial to a puppeteer. Fourie, Sandile and Bheki attended sessions in Johannesburg, before rehearsals started, with Fiona Ramsay, a celebrated South African actor and broadcaster, to help them clarify their diction. Marthinus Basson has been keeping pressure on these three – the actors with the bulk of the text between them – to bring their vowels a little closer towards an English accent. As the token British member of the company, I've been involved in this work. I find it bizarre to ask these professionals to alter their accents to make them closer to mine. It's almost like asking them to re-learn the language, substituting different vowel sounds for the ones they have been using happily for years. We're also working on diction and simple vocal clarity in projection.

Vocal clarity is a particular concern of Basil Jones, who raises the stakes in this second week by introducing a specifically verbal warm-up to the morning routine.

There's a touch of the schoolmaster about Jones as he presents a large board with difficult words on it and invites the company to say them together. But it's a completely positive response, led partly, I think, by the enthusiasm with which the Malians join in with the exercise. Immediately the purpose shifts from correcting the pronunciation of individuals to training the whole company to speak English in a similar way. Not much is going to be achieved in a single week but, hopefully, through the performances and over the tour habits will be formed.

In 2004, in the H B Thom theatre, it was difficult to know what the weather was like. In a break or at lunch-time you might see the sky, but the working environment was entirely artificial. Most of the time the outside wasn't much worth seeing; in a South African winter, clouds hung gloomily over Stellenbosch. Enrico Wey had been with the company for nearly a week before the cover lifted enough for him to see that the plain the town sits on is surrounded by mountains. But in the theatre, the tungsten-lit atmosphere was perpetual and changeless, and a little bit gloomy too. Not being able to perceive the passage of the day made long sessions on the same scene drag and contributed to the tensions and listlessness.

Hiddingh Hall couldn't be more different. The late Victorian colonial-style architecture provides tall windows along either side of the room. And this time, with summer heading into autumn, the weather is largely hot and beautiful. It provides the opposite difficulty. With the bright sun shining into performers' eyes, the blinds are shut to block it out, and there is relatively little artificial lighting. The light canvas of the blinds filters the sunlight, and it's like the inside of a beautifully timbered marquee on a hot day: dreamy and soporific. This atmosphere, though more pleasant, is no more help to collective concentration than the theatre's flattening of time.

But this year the deadline is looming more urgently, and along with the other shifts of temperament as we approach the second week, Basil Jones has arranged for a translator to be present. Perhaps this will help communication with Nana over the Queen. Janni Donald is ideal for the job. Janni travelled to Mali to meet Yaya and help him select puppets from his collection for the exhibition which accompanied *Tall Horse* in 2004 (and is now on show in AngloGold Ashanti's Gold of Africa Museum in Cape Town). She curated the exhibition in each of its venues. She is also a puppeteer and a French-speaker, having studied in France, and so has an understanding of the process the company are undertaking. Since she wrote the article about Bamana puppets I referred to in Chapter 3, she has married, and is now Janni Younge. She's available for most of the week, and when she isn't she makes sure that her husband Luke or her friend Bérénice is present to cover for her.

It's a different situation from the translators in Stellenbosch. Yaya, Téhibou and Yacouba are much more comfortable with English than they were then, and they know the rhythms of Marthinus Basson better. He, in turn, has developed a pidgin vocabulary to direct them in. Director and giraffe can reach an understanding quickly using simple terms – and the performers are sensitive enough, and familiar enough with the material to interpret his simplicity in the spirit it's intended. It's only occasionally that Yaya has wanted to discuss a concept in more depth and I have had to reach for the French-English dictionary. But it's time and habit that has allowed these three to develop a practical working relationship with Marthinus. Nana doesn't have this benefit and, to her, his outpourings (accompanied by minimal translation) must be as perplexing as they were to Nana Kouma who preceded her. Janni will hope to keep Nana from feeling isolated, and it's with some optimism that work begins with her on Monday.

The catch (and the point, really) of more fluent translation is that it allows Nana to answer back. Previously, her responses to direction were limited – now she's able to ask more questions. And as Janni translates more of Basson's thoughts, there is a far greater flow of information. This may or may not be a good thing. 'It doesn't make the process any quicker,' he observes after a session in which he's had to wait while his words and hers have been repeated in another language. But it levels the playing-field between the performers, and the Malians enjoy having someone else whom they can talk to in French.

A surprising amount of time is spent working with Nana on a single scene. Khephra Burns was interested in using the museum as a trophy room for the hunter King, and had scripted a scene in which the Queen, taking some beauty treatment in rollers and a face-pack, is mistaken by the King's minister for an *objet d'art* (a more plausible scenario given that the puppet Queen is a piece of sculpture). In execution, this turned out to be more difficult than expected. Although the Queen is simply a pole with a head and shoulders on it, draped in a large piece of fabric, it is a long pole and a large piece of fabric. Stood up, she was too high; laid down, the form of the fabric was broken and the figure was weak. A late inspiration was to think further about her status as an object.

For a big wooden Queen, undergoing a beauty treatment shouldn't involve rollers and powder puffs; rather, the puppet would be taken to pieces and cleaned with brushes. Kohler quickly made a set of stands to support the Queen's separated head, breasts and hands on a table. Fondness for the idea of a face-pack meant the introduction of a latex mask to pull the dirt out of the cracks, and Craig Leo, originally detailed as a beautician, became a restorer instead.

The stage picture is strong: the Queen's head is physically separate from her breasts and arms, and each are treated as objects by their manipulators (Craig Leo and Busi Zokufa). Her head can be swivelled on its stand, and her arms are able to gesticulate from their stand or be brought to her face by the puppeteer. To be able to see her spread out on a table emphasizes that her rigidity and remorselessness are features of her personality, and not just of her physical architecture. She is at once the Queen of France and the object that represents her.

Nana isn't used to puppets, and this deconstruction of puppetry relies on familiarity. I'm not sure it makes sense to her why the puppet is dismantled and laid out. Busi's long experience as a performer and puppeteer meant that she was able to enjoy calibrating this scene: how little needs to be done to ensure that the parts of the puppet remain objects; when to use voice alone and when to give it emphasis by lifting a hand or moving the head; how to keep a character 'alive' when it moves so little. At a time when Basson is straining for a sense of progress and achievement, the breaks of rhythm forced on them by translation are even more frustrating. For Nana, juggling increasingly specific direction on her manipulation with the ongoing debate over how to inflect and stress the text seems to be too much.

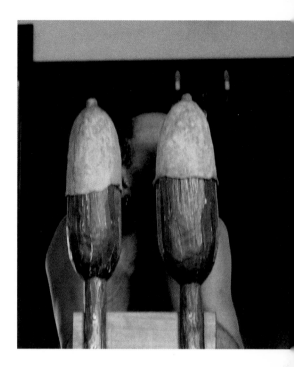

Craig Leo, behind the demounted breasts of the Queen dressed in their latex covers

It's the second Tuesday before the company finally runs the whole play. Basson might have hoped to do it to end the week last Saturday, but Busi's injury meant that wasn't possible. The first triumph is the length: almost exactly an hour and a half. Basson and Kohler's educated guesses when making their edits have proved accurate. This is great news: it means that their energy can go towards developing and working on what is there, rather than looking for further cuts. Another reason for the urgency of doing a run is Sandile Matsheni. This is the first time he's experienced the arc of Atir's journey. He's been working patiently around the drama of Busi's substitutions and is building up his version of Atir. His journey is a single story – each decision affects all of the others – and he will want to experience the whole piece as often as possible before it reaches an audience. Téhibou and Yacouba's connection with him comes quickly; the work they did with Fezile when he was finding the character means that they can help Sandile find his own strongest moments. The other newcomer, Mbali Kgosidintsi, has a trickier job, switching between different characters. For her and for Nana Traoré, taking on a run also means understanding how quickly they needs to swap puppets in a transition. Clothilde dominates Mbali's work in the performance, but she also performs one of Mehmet Ali's concubines, a boat on the Nile, a carrier-pigeon, a porter in Alexandria, a child in Lyon, and more. Mbali has prepared carefully, though, and copes well. Nana, with just as many changes of character to manage, is less certain of the sequence of events, and for her this chance to see how the different scenes connect is doubly valuable.

Solo Morton also enjoys the run. His main priority is to stay in time when accompanying Fourie, but he has been willingly involving himself with many other parts of the show, not least his intelligent and energetic engagement in the *castelet* sequences. But he has difficulties outside the rehearsal room. He's moving from place to place and doesn't seem to be eating properly. On Wednesday evening, after the rehearsal, he is found collapsed in the corner, muttering weakly. He hasn't eaten or slept properly for days and may have been sleeping rough – he's waiting for a friend who has offered to let him stay at her place. Solo seems to enjoy the attention his eccentric behaviour can arouse. He likes to dress in Malian clothes and looks very striking, a tall, well-built man with a shaven head, peaceful demeanour and a ready smile. He enjoys debating the relative benefits of different life-styles. Fully nourished, he's articulate and discerning, quick to understand, happy to work hard without complaint and always ready to help. But in this state, he's a concern. His speech is slurred, his vision unfocused as his eyelids droop. And he's also fiercely proud. It's all anyone can do to get the information out of him that he's not been sleeping properly. After some food, he is stronger, but even then he refuses almost all help. Basil tries to book him a hotel room, but he refuses to sleep in it.

As Solo has his first flutter of weakness, the rest of the company are working late with Jaco Bouwer. Bouwer, Basson and Adrian Kohler have found an opportunity to transfer some narrative into visual form, using shadow puppetry recorded into the video image. This sort of two-dimensional language inside the projection

Stills from Jaco Bouwer's animated shadow puppetry sequence of the caravan

(rather than live, as in 2004 when some of the Queen scenes were played with a shadow on the screen's backdrops) adds another layer to the visuals.

Kohler and Bouwer are directing and filming a shadow sequence of the caravan leaving Marseilles. In the long version of the show this was the pre-interval scene. The large giraffe had been revealed, and the decision had been made that she would transport herself, by walking, to Paris. The whole company came on stage to give a sense of the grand convoy, carrying and stacking piles of boxes plucked from the museum shelves. The convoy is a large part of the giraffe's story: from the cows that were brought along specifically to provide milk for her, to the hangers-on who followed from town to town. The original version of the play tried to convey the arduousness of the walk through a series of speeches delivered by St-Hilaire.

Adrian has made a set of simple shadow puppets: torn, black silhouettes with rough edges to match the rough but evocative lines of his carving. Only the figure representing St-Hilaire has a movable part: the arm holding his walking stick is hinged. The puppets are moved slowly along a thin horizontal cord against a white screen. Bouwer films the puppets themselves rather than their (less distinct) shadows. It needs several takes to get the shots he needs, and there are so many figures that the whole company, including stage manager Leigh Colombick, are needed to animate the figures. Even Bheki Vilakazi is included. Ever since the first week of rehearsals in Stellenbosch, he has been asking to use a puppet.

Despite Solo's discomfort, it's enjoyable to see the whole company engaging in the animation of the shadows. There was a time when asking the Malians to join in might have seemed counter-productive; where being inclusive would mean the job taking twice as long. But trust has genuinely built up between these companies, and especially through their puppet manipulation. Adrian allocates the puppets carefully – he's keen to make sure that Yaya is given one of importance – but he knows that all of his company are capable of performing them.

The difference from 21 August is marked. The division between the performers has been redefined now, and it's the new company members – Mbali, Nana, Sandile, Solo – who need the support of old hands from either company. Yaya has also found a way to feed in to the piece's direction, giving his perspective in notes sessions after a run. With this re-establishment of trust comes a coherence in the ensemble story-telling that has sometimes been lost in the complexities of the story.

In a run on Thursday, the shape of the first half delights Marthinus Basson. There's still work to do, but the performers are gaining control over their material and the story they are telling. Basil's classes in diction are also bearing fruit, with a marked improvement in the clarity of the vocal delivery.

It feels good to spend the last week working on small improvements: tightening up the pace of one scene, developing the detail of puppetry or nuance in another. Marthinus Basson may not have expected to be in this place by now – especially at the weekend, worrying about Busi – and perhaps it's the company's good progress that allows him to be calm as Nana continues to struggle with the Queen's material. Tellingly, the politics have changed. It was Yaya who suggested that Nana step up to cover for Busi. Faced with Nana's delivery difficulties, Marthinus has been patient, and it's Yaya who's been shortest with her when a note isn't taken. She herself seems determined to offer what her directors are asking for, but it's as if she is being asked to learn and perform in a completely foreign style – and communicating through a translator. Faced with a recurrent problem, everyone with the ability to communicate with Nana has their diagnosis, and the babble of advice can't be helping her. Eventually, Yaya discreetly asks Marthinus if perhaps we're spending too much time on rehearsing Nana's understudy performance, when there is work to be done for the whole company.

The Queen will no longer appear as a shadow puppet. Yaya is happy to break with the convention that she is always riding, and he, Adrian and Marthinus prefer the image and impact of her entrance on stage, rather than the looming silhouette that hung behind the King in 2004. Now Adrian himself carries the pole, with Solo walking in train, billowing the Queen's robes gently behind her.

On Friday 22nd, Busi Zokufa is well enough to return to the rehearsal room and is clearly not giving up hope of performing. It still looks a bridge too far to ask her to engage in physical work, but it's encouraging to have her there observing, and her voice could yet be available for the Queen. But even this would require her to come on and off stage with the puppet, and if she strains her back or leg again she could be completely immobile. So work with Nana slowly continues – her instincts continue to lead her to speak without inflection, especially where the text takes her outside her own French vocabulary. Busi keeps track of how the scenes are developing. It's almost inevitable that Enrico Wey will cover for her puppetry, especially in the tough physical roles like the heavy *merens habitables* of the Lady of Lyon and Jolie. He makes sure that he finds time to discuss the sequences with her.

The Friday afternoon ends with a masterclass for UCT students, keen to see how Mbali, who graduated from their department the previous year, is getting on. It's an enjoyable release for the company too. The old hands have taken on the cuts and changes fairly easily, and in the pleasant, warm weather a run before lunch has been a little under-powered. An audience is just what they need, and the bubbly and excitable students are eager to see what the show is all about. February 2006 will be the 25th anniversary of Handspring, and Basil and Adrian talk about the history of the company and the collaboration with fluency. Téhibou, Fourie and Yacouba are shamelessly charming in playing to the crowd, and Yaya is both statesmanlike and flirtatious. It's lovely to see how he engages with an informal crowd, even working through translator: it's Marthinus who invites volunteers up to try their hand at manipulating the Malian Soirée puppets, but it's Yaya who steps up to tell one of them that she's a natural and invites her to join his troupe. She blushes to her roots. Marthinus leads a session of demonstrations and commentary; he feels connected enough to the puppets now to introduce and comment on the difference between them, something he would have hesitated to do in 2004.

The puppeteers show the tricks of the puppets and are gratified to be reminded how much impact they can have: the three-man teamwork behind the Fashion Designer's droll camp; the spectacular whirling of the *castelets*; the grace of the *merens habitables*; and of course the majesty of the giraffe.

Saturday is the last day in the rehearsal space, and there is an edge of fatigue after a long week. Sandile is working hard to keep a grip on the journey of Atir and add more detail to his performance. The sessions generate small but telling improvements: clarifying the flight patterns of the pigeons; adding detail and crispness to the movement of the Marseilles citizens, who, robbed of their chanting, now listen fearfully to the unreliable reports of Newspaperman; and ploughing energy into the scene between Fifi and Jolie. This scene is an exception in that both performers are new to it: Nana Traoré is new to the whole show, and Enrico Wey, covering for Busi, needs to learn it too. The long-necked *merens* require practice to animate convincingly, and, with the puppeteer's view restricted to a small window in the front of the costume, and the puppet's head a metre above them, it's difficult to aim the puppet's eye-line, walk backwards, or position the puppet correctly on the stage. The lack of confidence translates into a tentative energy between the characters, which could be fatal to a scene about their thrilled anticipation.

The familiar organisation of Leigh Colombick and Wesley France finishes the day. It's traditional on a Handspring tour for the puppeteers to be partly responsible for the safe packing of their puppets, and Leigh allocates each of the many flight cases (complete with a packing list) to two performers. Today will be their opportunity to establish that they can pack their cases – this will save time on the road when it needs to be done late at night after a performance. Enrico, still the ASM despite his new responsibilities on stage, assists with this organisation and the loading up of the van.

Getting the show into the Baxter again seems like *déjà vu*. The technical team and backstage crew are pleased to see Adrian and Wesley again so soon, and from their perspective not much has changed. The set is the same; the lighting-rig has changed a little; but they are expecting this to be an easy process for the company – reviving a show should be a quick job.

Seeing the set is a revelation for the newer cast members. Sandile looks up at the four-metre shelves. 'Oh. They are big,' he concedes. 'When you said shelves, I thought…' He, Nana and Mbali make sure that they get as much time in the space as possible, working discreetly around Wesley, Leigh, Simon and Enrico. Previously, their entrances have been from one corner of a room into the middle of it. Now, with the furniture of the theatre around them and an auditorium to gaze up into, they can get a feel for how much ground they need to cover, and what sort of impact they will have when they do so. Mbali is always keen to practise her manipulation of Clothilde; and Nana can't wait to get up on stilts and acclimatise herself to the stage floor.

Wesley France has found himself plotting lights in unsociable hours again, and the schedule this time is even tighter. The whole technical rehearsal needs to take place in an afternoon. In 2004 the technical took a day and a half, and was still not finished. Even though the show is now two-thirds of its original length, to complete it in the four hours set aside is a challenge. The first preview is the next

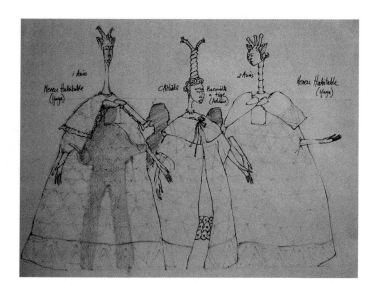

Adrian Kohler's design sketch for the scene between Fifi and Jolie and a pregnant Clothilde

day, and Marthinus Basson isn't here. His leave has come to an end – during the daytimes, he needs to attend to his teaching commitments. So if he's to see the dress rehearsal it will need to be this evening.

Somehow the tech starts late, with costumes and props still being placed, and it seems that there's going to be little opportunity for the company or the technical team to get used to the changes. But with the pressure on, the company respond with great focus. The organisation backstage, with Enrico there much less regularly now, is the key area, and the experienced hands look after each other. Busi is coming on to voice the Queen, and, with more time backstage, makes sure the puppet is prepared for its entrances. The only serious timing difficulties revolve around a fast costume change of Sandile's and the various rearrangements of the Queen – whether she is being set in a *castelet*, or demounted for the scene on the table.

By their nature, technical rehearsals are draining. The company concentrate hard to get this done and, although several of the changes are hurried through, it's an achievement to be finished in four hours. Téhibou hasn't read the schedule and is devastated to find that there's a dress run to do in the evening. He has given his all, and several other performers also look exhausted as they get hold of a meal.

Solo in particular looks depressed and uncommunicative. His accommodation difficulties seem to have been continuing, but he stubbornly avoids discussion, despite offers from many sides. It seems intrusive to push him on the subject, but now its effect on his work begins to be a problem for his colleagues. Fourie Nyamande, who needs to speak in rhythm with Solo's drumming, has been holding his tongue about his partner's wandering concentration – sometimes falling off the beat and, once or twice, coming in with an unexpected rhythm. In the dress rehearsal, after a long day and apparently very little to eat, Solo isn't at all reliable, missing some backstage cues as well as exhibiting some erratic drumming. Fourie is worried, and all Marthinus Basson can do is ask Solo what's up. But Solo shrugs, brushing away questions.

He's not the only one who hasn't much left for the weary dress rehearsal. Basson watches a series of scenes unfold in which the characters articulate impeccably, but without spirit or flow of thought. One or two still have something left in their tanks. Sandile Matsheni has the most adrenaline. This is his highest-profile role to date, and he will not miss an opportunity to improve it. There are still rough edges on his portrayal of Atir, but his appetite for an audience reaches out to the back of the auditorium. Craig Leo, with relatively few changes in the re-rehearsal period, had been losing energy while working in Hiddingh Hall. But back on stage here, he rediscovers his enjoyment of the roles and is one of the few to come out of the dress feeling more energetic than when he went in. Perhaps surprisingly, Nana Traoré is the third person to relish the dress rehearsal. She's not playing the Queen, and maybe it's the weight of that expectation removed from her shoulders that gives her a lift. Throughout rehearsals she's been having trouble hitting her entrance cues on time (understandable when they are in a foreign language) even with her colleagues helping, and sometimes she's seemed listless on stage as a

It's a story, not a fairytale, it's a true story. So you've got to be careful. When you tell a true story, you have responsibilities.

Yaya Coulibaly

Sandile Matsheni and Yaya Coulibaly

scene continued. But the theatre building and the anticipation inspire her, and her manipulation in Lyon and the Soirée has extra focus.

These three are responding to the imminence of the performance of course, but also they're benefiting from the technical atmospherics of Wesley France's lighting, Simon Mahoney's sound (with Warrick Sony's music) and Jaco Bouwer's video projection. The shadow puppet sequence that Jaco shot the previous Wednesday (it's Tuesday now) works very well amongst his two-dimensional line patterning, and Basson and Kohler decide to develop the integration. Jaco arranges to film more shadows: giraffe necks and heads for the Savannah/Hunt (replacing live ones in the previous version) and a slave boat, which he will edit into the background of the Nile sequence. There are other small changes. Because of the cuts, Adrian has handed over the puppeteering of the King's Minister to Basil. The Minister is one of the most distinctive puppets in the cast: instead of legs, he has a pogo-stick, which Adrian constructed out of carefully planed wood and elastic. It makes for a very enjoyable movement, allowing the puppet to bob up and down with its breath when stationary, and to bound across the room excitedly for entrances and exits. But in the streamlining of scenes, the opportunities for bobbing have been curtailed, and some of his exits now take place across other characters' lines (notably the Queen's, whose appearance often frightens him into leaving). In the long version of the show, the solution had been to allow pauses in the Queen's lines to allow him to bound in his noisy way off stage (and let the audience enjoy watching him). Now, watching how it holds up the scenes, Adrian makes a slightly shocking suggestion: to remove the pogo-stick.

Like losing one of our favourite toys, it's difficult to agree to the suggestion. But this will solve the awkward pacing of those scenes. The pogo-stick was a charming character trait, but removing it won't change what the Minister does or why. In fact, without the long, heavy stick, the Minister's movements are liberated. Basil still animates him using the bouncing movement, conveying the zealous, panting sycophancy that Khephra had written into the character's lines. But now he can slip and slide unctuously into the scene, bounce as required, and grovel his way out silently while the Queen roars at her husband. Adrian and Basil have always said that the Handspring puppets are descended from the Bamana rod puppets, and here, returning to the characteristic simplicity of the leg-free Malian design allows for a flexibility where designed sophistication had only restricted. It reminds me of the lessons that Handspring hoped to learn by working alongside this ancient puppet tradition, and also of the sacrifices that Khephra Burns has been making as his sophisticated script has been boiled down to this more minimal version. It's two-way traffic, as we see whenever Yaya admiringly handles one of Adrian's finely-crafted figures. But Handspring have definitely been invigorated by what Sogolon have brought to *Tall Horse*.

Craig, Basil and Fourie are first to the warm-up for the first performance, and Nana and Sandile are close behind, well energised. With the technical rehearsal so short, Wesley France is still taking a few performers aside to show them adjustments to their positioning which they can make to best exploit the lighting.

On the opening night, Sandile makes a great connection with a young audience – a big contrast to the middle-class, middle-aged first preview of the opening in 2004. The first *Tall Horse* seemed a grand theatrical event; this time, the production reaches a wider audience. Word-of-mouth has been spreading from the first run, and several of the first matinée performances here at the Baxter are for school groups brought in on buses from the townships. It's an initiative funded by the Ministry of Culture, who are perhaps pleased to demonstrate how Handspring, one of South Africa's best cultural exports, are reaching out to bring the influence of the rest of Africa to their own nation. These audiences aren't used to theatre in grand buildings like the Baxter, and they're vocal and enthusiastic when they see the show – most loudly at the sex scenes between human Atir and the puppet Clothilde.

Tall Horse is a different show now. Where the original seemed big and slightly clumsy, this has drive and coherence. There's less of the exploratory eclecticism that came from the alliance of Khephra Burns's sophisticated script, Koffi Kôkô's poetic movement and Marthinus Basson's visual flair. But the unity of this leaner *Tall Horse* was always at the heart of the project: the ancient puppet story-telling style of Sogolon combining with the ingenious puppet-theatre of Handspring to tell an extraordinary tale.

2004, the start of the collaboration, was the tenth year of democracy in South Africa, and the time that saw the project develop was also one of reflection in that country. Cape Town's tourism has never been busier, and quiet Kalk Bay is dominated now with builders developing luxury flats. There's even talk of the old fishermen's cottages, which Basil and Adrian pass when they walk their dogs on the harbour front, being bought up and sold on. The beginning of the 21st century has seen a rising interest in the fate of Africa. *Tall Horse* offers a real artistic meeting between two countries both separated and connected by that continent, and on tour it's a unique example of a united voice reaching out from Africa to the wider world. Alicia Adams had hoped that *Tall Horse* would help to tell the story of Africa's impact on the world. And now *Tall Horse* itself is part of that impact.

It's still a work that will develop as it shows itself to new audiences. Adrian Kohler and Basil Jones are always looking for improvements and always hungry for audience feedback. Yaya Coulibaly and Marthinus Basson love to make a connection with their audiences and are alive to how the piece plays on any night. There will be changes made in the previews and whenever the production arrives in a different place to delight new audiences. The progress of *Tall Horse* has been challenged constantly, by miscommunication, by difficulties to do with place, distance and language, by contrasting styles struggling to find a common rhythm. Like the two puppeteers in the giraffe, strapped together in a cage, the collaborators in *Tall Horse* have sometimes pulled against one another and come close to falling. They've needed to find an instinctive connection to walk on stilts successfully. But in 2005 it began to feel as if the companies were walking in step. And each time a run of *Tall Horse* is set up, the collaboration is renewed, these artists trust each other a little more, and the connection between the groups, on and off stage, becomes stronger.

NOTES

1. Mary Jo Arnoldi's book *Playing with Time* indicates that *Duguma sa* is the Ground Snake character in Bamana mask rituals, and *Sanfè sa* is the Tree Snake.

The giraffe has to remain this fragile, innocent thing. Ultimately the giraffe has to be the strongest throughline. And if she can retain it... and I guess it's an anxiety still, whether we can do it with that puppet... if she can retain some kind of a strength and determination within her complete victimhood. She's removed, and she's taken somewhere. A lot of foolish people circle around her, with their own needs, and their own desires, and their own preoccupations. But if we can see her as the strange and odd thread of the story, then we will have achieved something with it. Because, if she can be poignant, and if she can be dignified, all the way through...

Adrian Kohler

I have a wish; that Africa doesn't stay like the Kalahari. I wish for fraternity, for balance, equality. That is the grandeur I see in the giraffe. The giraffe has the height to look. We can look back on the first world war, on the second world war, on all the wars… If we can agree to shake hands, then we can achieve the grandeur of the giraffe.

Yaya Coulibaly

AFTERWORD

I'VE BEEN PARTICULARLY PRIVILEGED TO ACCOMPANY
this project for so long. Everything in the book is written after the event, from
notes taken throughout rehearsals, and is necessarily subjective and incomplete.
This is only how I remember the personalities, struggles and triumphs of making
Tall Horse. I hope you'll be able to see through my prejudices and fixations and
spot the other sides of the story where I might seem critical or one-sided. Many
parts of the process aren't covered in this book – of course, being close to the
process I would have liked to discuss every scene's development in detail. The ones
which have been focused on caused the most controversy or are most illustrative
of how the relationships between the team changed. There were times when the
production felt like it would be a disaster, and very many more times when it felt
both fulfilling and thrilling.

My first visits to Handspring were part of a Professional Development Bursary,
courtesy of the Arts Council of England, and awarded through the Puppet Centre.
I'd made contact with the company five years before, when they brought *Ubu and
the Truth Commission* to the London International Festival of Theatre 1999 and
conducted a two-week workshop in association with the International Workshop
Festival, in which I was a participant. I subsequently visited them in Munich in
2001, when they were touring *The Chimp Project* in Europe. The relatively low cost
of living in South Africa meant that I was able to stretch the ACE bursary a long
way, but in being able to stay for the full duration of rehearsals I'm indebted to
the generosity and hospitality of Handspring, who helped to cover my costs and
feed me, and generally treated me as a member of the company rather than as
an outsider. Without their support I would certainly not have been able to return
in 2005 to work on and witness the re-rehearsal period that led up to the final
(shorter) version of the production. I look forward to seeing the piece when it
finally plays in Mali, for when I'd like to thank Yaya Coulibaly in advance for the
hospitality he's so often extended the offer of.

I came to this production as an observer, to learn from these major international
artists how they make theatre for adults that combines puppets and actors and
plays to large audiences from widely differing cultures. I've returned having learnt

an enormous amount about their craft, but much more about their humility, generosity, vision and kindness. I very much hope that the reader can see that the company who came together for *Tall Horse* were unified by a desire to create the best possible piece of theatre that could come from their collaboration, without a hint of cynicism. My lasting feelings towards them all are of deep respect and great affection.

I'm very grateful to the following people for helping me establish and maintain contact with Handspring and Sogolon, and for giving me excellent advice during that period: Jessica Bowles (whose suggestion it was to record the experience), Sue Buckmaster, Penny Francis, Tom Morris, Lucy Neal, Beccy Smith, and Lyndie Wright, and to ACE for the opportunity to learn from the best in the world. Thanks also to Janni Younge and Luke Younge who worked with Yaya on curating the Patrimony exhibition and were of great help in conference with him, and to Lusanne Hansen and Pascale Neuschäfer, who helped me as translators in recorded interviews with Yaya.

Of course, my warmest thanks are reserved for Adrian and Basil, Yaya, Marthinus, and the members of the *Tall Horse* company, who made me feel so welcome and gave me so many good memories.

Mervyn Millar

Tall Horse

Performance Script
by Khephra Burns

This is the script of the 2005 version of *Tall Horse* that played in:

Baxter Theatre, Cape Town, South Africa, 27 April – 14 May 2005
Theater der Welt Festival, Stuttgart, Germany, 8 – 10 July 2005

United States tour September – November 2005
Williams College, Williamstown, Massachusetts
BAM Harvey Theater at Brooklyn Academy of Music, Brooklyn,
    New York (Opening event at Next Wave Festival 2005)
Pittsburgh Cultural Trust with African American Cultural Center,
    Pennsylvania
University Musical Society (UMS), University of Michigan, Ann Arbor,
    Michigan
University of North Carolina (UNC), Chapel Hill North Carolina
Eisenhower Theater at Kennedy Center, Washington DC

It is an edited version of the script that was performed in September
and October 2004 at the Baxter Theatre Cape Town, State Theatre
Pretoria and Dance Factory Johannesburg.

Puppeteers	Adrian Kohler, Yaya Coulibaly, Busi Zokufa, Fourie Nyamande, Basil Jones, Nana Traoré, Yacouba Magassouba, Téhibou Bagayoko, Enrico D Wey, Mbali Kgosidintsi, Craig Leo
Actors	Sandile Matsheni (Jean-Michel / Atir) Bheki Vilakazi (Dr Konate / Geoffroy St-Hilaire)
Director	Marthinus Basson
Scriptwriter	Khephra Burns
Choreographer	Koffi Kôkô
Puppet Designers	Adrian Kohler and Yaya Coulibaly
Set Designer	Adrian Kohler
Music Composer	Warrick Sony
Video Animator	Jaco Bouwer
Assistant Director	Mervyn Millar
Costume Designer	Adrian Kohler
Lighting Designer	Wesley France
Puppet Makers	Yaya Coulibaly, Adrian Kohler
Assistant Puppet Makers	Téhibou Bagayoko, Thami Kitti, Nana Kouma, Yacouba Magassouba, Mervyn Millar, Kevin Willemse
Costume Makers	Hazel Maree, Phyllis Midlane
Production Manager	Wesley France
Stage Manager	Leigh Colombick
Assistant Stage Manager	Enrico D Wey
Sound Engineer	Simon Mahoney
Translators	Nellie Orvain-Edwards, Libby Meintjies, Catherine Du Plessis, Janni Younge, Luke Younge
Producer	Basil Jones

ACT ONE

Museum, Bamako, Mali

A storeroom / archive in the basement of a museum in Bamako, Mali. Dr Konate and assistants are attending to the preservation of a dusty old mummy when they inadvertently break a brittle finger from the mummy's hand. An assistant sets it aside near the microscope. Enter Jean-Michel.

JEAN-MICHEL Dr Konate?

DR KONATE Oui.

JEAN-MICHEL Jean-Michel du Tam à la Tour.

The name doesn't seem to ring a bell with Dr Konate.

I wrote you about the collection of artefacts from nineteenth-century Egypt.

DR KONATE Oh! The student from Paris who is searching for enlightenment.

JEAN-MICHEL Actually, I'm doing research on The Enlightenment – the Age of Enlightenment?

DR KONATE Ah! The Enlightenment. Spirit of adventure, age of exploration… (*Snapping the nose off a brittle, dusty mummy*) …progress. Whatever happened with that?

JEAN-MICHEL (*Distracted by what he is witnessing*) Pardon?

DR KONATE (*Grinding the noses to powder with a mortar and pestle*) The Enlightenment. Did they find it? Your scientists were convinced they were finally seeing into the true nature of things. Europeans have ordered much of the world we inhabit and fixed everything in its place: plants, animals, men, predators and prey, 'Enlightened Europe' and 'Darkest Africa'. Those who control the naming of things control our perceptions. And perception is reality, n'est-ce pas? But if you know where to look from you will be able to see.

Dr Konate stirs the powdered nose into a glass of water and offers it to the visiting student.

JEAN-MICHEL No, merci.

DR KONATE Four out of five Enlightenment doctors recommended it.

JEAN-MICHEL No, merci, really.

An Assistant brings tea and little finger-shaped biscuits.

DR KONATE Tea then?

JEAN-MICHEL Tea would be fine.

DR KONATE Well, then how can I help you?

Jean-Michel helps himself to the tea and a biscuit. He sets a half-eaten biscuit down on the counter.

JEAN-MICHEL As I explained in my letter, I'm looking for anything that might relate to a certain slave belonging to the French consul in Egypt in 1826.

DR KONATE Special Collections. You need the key to see them.

A discussion among Dr Konate's Assistants turns into a loud argument.

(*To Jean-Michel*) Archivists. Very passionate about the Special Collections.

JEAN-MICHEL They call this chaos a collection?

Jean-Michel picks up a mummy finger by mistake and takes a bite. Everyone else freezes. Jean-Michel chokes.

TEA LADY He ate the finger.

Jean-Michel reaches quickly for some tea to wash it down, but grabs Konate's mummy-nose concoction and drinks that before realising it.

ASSISTANT He drank the nose.

DR KONATE Monsieur, please, you are devouring our collections.

JEAN-MICHEL You gave me that to drink!

DR KONATE Oui, but I did not give you the finger.

JEAN-MICHEL (*Gesturing with his notes*) I did not come all this way from Paris to Mali to eat and drink mummy parts. Dr Konate, please, my research is important to me. It's...it's personal...

DR KONATE This slave. Was he one of your ancestors?

JEAN-MICHEL Oui.

DR KONATE Then you will soon meet him.

JEAN-MICHEL Am I going to die?

DR KONATE No, you are going on a journey through our Special Collections.

NEWSPAPERMAN (*Whispering to his fellow assistants*)
Comes this curious prodigal seeking
Secrets of the past to play
Among the secrets in our keeping
Where mummy fingers point the way
And a potion made from the mummy's nose
Now peels the veil of time away.

Dr Konate turns and begins pointing out artefacts in the Special Collections. They have been standing in the midst of it the entire time. Dr Konate knows precisely where everything is – in its place. The artefacts seem to come alive as the mummy nose concoction begins to take effect on Jean-Michel.

DR KONATE Voilà! Mehmet Ali, the Pasha of Egypt, is there. Drovetti, the French Consul, here. And here.

JEAN-MICHEL Monsieur Bernardino Drovetti!

DR KONATE Oui. The most powerful Frenchman in Egypt at the time.

JEAN-MICHEL And his slave?

DR KONATE Ah! The slave. We shall come to him. But first, may I present...

Le Jardin des plantes

The King and Queen of France, Charles X and Marie-Thérèse, pass through the storeroom (what is for them their private menagerie). All the puppets and artefacts begin to quiver. Jean-Michel is wide-eyed.

MARIE-THERESE For God's sake, Charles, you're the King of France. Walking doesn't become you. It's not natural. These animals should be paraded before us. Properly groomed and made presentable. Protocol, Charles, protocol. That's the natural order of things.

KING CHARLES X Walking is natural, my dear cousin royal.

MARIE-THERESE Wife. I'm your wife, Charles. For thirty-two years.

KING CHARLES X Just thirty-two? Funny, but I never stopped thinking of you as my cousin. However, Madame la Duchesse, nature has seen fit to give us legs, and I intend to use mine to stroll through the Royal Menagerie and enjoy these lovely beasts.

MARIE-THERESE They smell like the rabble.

The hyenas growl.

Dogs! Don't look at me!

The hyenas growl again.

KING CHARLES X They're hyenas. Dear.

MARIE-THERESE Train them! Oh! Mon Dieu! Animal excrement!

Museum, Bamako

DR KONATE The King's two great passions: his collection of exotic beasts and…

JEAN-MICHEL Mummies?

DR KONATE Exactly. And in Egypt Drovetti was running a thriving trade in mummies, which he sold by the gross and by the pound. After the Rosetta Stone was deciphered, he went from infamous tomb robber to celebrated Egyptologist overnight.

Drovetti has come to life and is now sawing the mummy in half.

DROVETTI I was consultant to scientists and the major museums of the world.

DR KONATE (*Dryly, as Drovetti's legs walk on stage and find him*) Grave robbers and the sons of grave robbers will speak his name with reverence for many generations.

DROVETTI Bernardino Drovetti, Consul of His Highly Christian Majesty Charles X in the Valley of the Nile and proprietor of Mail Order Menageries International, Nile Tomb Excavation and Wholesale Heritage Disposal, at your service.

JEAN-MICHEL / ATIR Drovetti?

DROVETTI Do not take liberties with me, Atir. You will address me as Sidi. Do you understand?

JEAN-MICHEL / ATIR (*To Konate*) Atir?

The back wall slides open; Mehmet Ali emerges from the dark.

DROVETTI (*More insistent*) We're going to the palace on a matter of some urgency – war. It seems Greece has fallen to the Christians. The Turkish Sultan is furious, which puts our pasha in a *posizione precaria* with France.

Jean-Michel is confused, but follows along.

DR KONATE Caught between a French king and Egypt's Pasha, Drovetti was in a rather precarious position himself.

Sultan's Palace, Alexandria

Day. Music / Video-wall (Islamic patterns / Grand mosque / Greece / Cross / Crescent Moon).

MEHMET ALI (*Calling from offstage*) Baris!

DR KONATE Religion, politics, power…

MEHMET ALI (*Calling from offstage*) Baris! Turk Donkey. BARISS!

JEAN-MICHEL / ATIR Disastrous mix.

DR KONATE But profitable.

MEHMET ALI Ah, Drovetti, come. What news do you have from France?

DROVETTI Liberty, democracy…fashion, of course. And the war in Greece. The French newspapers cheer the victories of the Christian insurgents.

MEHMET ALI What does the new king say?

DROVETTI The people support the revolt, and the King does not find them in a mood to be contradicted. They sent his brother to the guillotine during the Reign of Terror, you know, and then ate all the animals in the Royal Menagerie. Some are even calling for a crusade against the Turks.

MEHMET ALI Baris!

DROVETTI Undoubtedly crusadewear will be the hot new look for spring. But real crusades are expensive, with no guarantee that the looting and plundering will bring a good return on the investment. France knows that the Turks can't retake Greece without calling on your army.

MEHMET ALI Baris! All this fuss about a little country with nothing left to plunder.

DROVETTI The question, Your Highness, is what will Egypt do?

MEHMET ALI Baris! Useless envoy.

DROVETTI Quite useless.

MEHMET ALI I need him in Constantinople.

DROVETTI I believe Your Highness had him impaled.

MEHMET ALI Is he dead?

DROVETTI Quite dead.

MEHMET ALI You know that a number of your generals have hinted France would support me if I launched my own war of independence from the Turks.

DROVETTI (*Non-committal*) Hmm.

MEHMET ALI France would find Egypt a worthy ally. I should send something to the new king – a token of my esteem, a gift in exchange for Greece. See what you can dig up.

DROVETTI Might I suggest something living? His Majesty's passion is the restoration of the Royal Menagerie. And I know that he is still distraught over the loss of his prized dromedary, which was eaten by the mobs when they attacked the Tuileries.

MEHMET ALI A camel! Is that all? Just a camel? Send him one hundred with my compliments…and throw in a dozen leopards to give the camel-hungry mobs something to think about.

DROVETTI Atir.

JEAN-MICHEL / ATIR Sidi?

DROVETTI What's our delivery time on a hundred camels?

DR KONATE (*Stage whisper to Jean-Michel / Atir*) Two weeks.

JEAN-MICHEL / ATIR Two weeks to Alexandria, but… (*Aside to Drovetti*) begging Sidi's pardon, that's a lot of camel dung in the King's menagerie. (*Confidentially*) In the Sudan there's a tall horse, with the face of a camel and the spots of the leopard…

DROVETTI Excellent, Atir. (*To Mehmet Ali*) Your Highness, it occurs to me that there is a creature of the most regal stature, which would make a rare gift. I don't believe one has been seen in Europe since Caesar governed Rome. The reason, I suspect, is that they can be extremely dangerous – capable of killing a lion with a single blow from its hoof. The adults cannot be taken alive, as they will fight to the death rather than be captured. I believe they are called develeopars in Turkish…

ATIR Sogo Jan in my mother tongue.

MEHMET ALI Excellent, Drovetti. Excellent.
Do you know why the ancients of this god-forsaken land worshipped the scarab beetle?

DROVETTI I believe, Your Highness, that it symbolised the regeneration of life.

From Mehmet Ali's massive belly beneath his robes emerges the scarab with a ball of dung, which he rolls around the stage.

MEHMET ALI It rolls a ball of dung around, like the sun rolls across the sky. And out of that dung comes new life, the little hatchling beetles. Egypt is a dung heap, Drovetti. But out of that heap of black slaves and the decay of its dead past, we are bringing new life to the present. We're rolling, Drovetti. You and I are the dung beetles of Egypt. And that places us in the company of the gods.

The Hunt

Castelets set up the savannah. Animals grazing, nuzzling etc. They become restless. Hunters enter. Animals stampede.

Two giraffes enter. One of them a mother with her two young calves.

Animal stampede followed by hunters. giraffe kicks at two hunters. They flee, leaving Atir alone on stage. He performs a ritual prayer.

The giraffe re-enters. He attacks her. Felling her. Atir holds up two statues in triumph.

The Nile

Day One. Music / Video-wall (Nile / Birds / Dunes / Boats).

Atir and the two young giraffes are drifting down the Nile on small felucca. One of the giraffes is not faring as well as the other.

ATIR (*To the sickly calf*) Drink. Look at me. I'm strong today because I stole milk right from the cow's udder when I was a boy. See how your sister suckles. She's a good milk thief. Drink like that and give a good report of me to Sidi. We have to help one another. Who knows what the days will bring?

The stronger calf nudges him to get his attention and then looks at the pattern of her markings on her side. Atir sees the pattern too, but doesn't like what he reads there.

Tunga?! You're mistaken. It is you who are going on a journey from which there is no return. You should have paid better attention to your own taamaki. That is your n'dakan, your destiny. My name is Atir. Besides, I have things to do in Alexandria – coffee to serve, mummies to grind into medicine for sick Europeans. There's still a lot of plundering to be done, and Sidi cannot do it all himself. So don't talk to me about a tunga. In two months I will get paid, you will be sailing for France, and I'll be rid of your stupid predictions.

Day Two. Video-wall / Night.

Atir is sleeping. The giraffe nudges him with her foreleg and wakes him up. Atir inspects the markings of the healthy giraffe.

Why am I even listening to you? You're like the women of my village who don't know how to stop talking. (*Nostalgically*) I haven't heard the chattering of woman in my own tongue in many years now.

The healthy giraffe nudges Atir; it wants to be fed.

Look. Already you have made a servant of the one who captured you. That's not the way of things, you know.

Day Three. Videowall (Nile / Pyramids).

The healthy giraffe spits out bottle. Atir picks it up and gives it to her again. She spits it out.

Don't sulk. I was once a slave like you – stolen from my village in Mali by the jonserelao. But look at me today.

The boat rocks. A bird and several feluccas pass behind Atir's felucca. The giraffe is not impressed with Atir.

Today I'm no longer a slave. Slaves are not permitted in France, and the consulate in Alexandria is a French compound. I'm in foreign service…and tomb robbing. At least there are opportunities for advancement. You will see: one day I will return to my village – a rich man. I will return. One day.

Port of Alexandria

Video-wall (Palm trees / Boats).

Sounds of a harbour – loading and unloading. Atir is there with the two giraffes. Drovetti enters, busily going over cargo manifests.

DROVETTI How are the animals? Gifts fit for kings, I trust?

ATIR This one is, Sidi. She drinks five gallons of milk a day. Our milk cows run away from her. But her sister…

DROVETTI Send that one to England.

ATIR But, Sidi, they are sisters!

DROVETTI There's too much riding on them – war and peace, life and death…profit and loss. The last thing we want is a French embargo on Egyptian antiques and African exotica. The weak ones always wither and fade when far from home. It's the expatriate, the adventurer who shapes the world, Atir.

ATIR Na'am, Sidi. Just like the jonserelao.

DROVETTI Jonserelao?

ATIR Venturers, like Sidi. We didn't see them coming, not the Banama, not the Bozo, not the Nubians, not the Sudanese – none of us, not even our gods. Now the villages are empty. But the Sogo Jan can see far...over the horizon. And they tell what they see, here, in their taamaki.

DROVETTI Taamaki?

Atir touches the pattern on the giraffe's neck.

(*Sceptical*) Their markings. And what are they telling you?

ATIR This one tells of a tunga, a journey from which one never returns.

DROVETTI Indeed. (*Indicating her sickly sister*) And this one?

ATIR This one says, 'Big storm coming, many boats lost...even the fish get seasick.'

DROVETTI That one says France, that one England. If it dies, the King can stuff it. It's the thought that counts. You can board Mademoiselle Tunga on the boat to Marseilles, and I'll inform both their majesties how they may amuse themselves at court telling fortunes by giraffe.

Atir is hesitant about setting foot on the boat himself.

ATIR (*To the giraffe*) Go. Get on the boat. Goodbye. I'm not going with you.

DROVETTI (*Looking up from his clipboard*) Problems Atir?

ATIR No problem, Sidi. This one is very happy to be going.

End of Act One.

ACT TWO

Transition / The Journey

Video-wall: Atir and the giraffe on the boat in the tranquil open sea.

ATIR You stick your nose in war that is none of your business, and now because of you I must go to France. When we arrive in Marseilles, I am telling you, that's it, I am done with you. This is out of the way for me, you know. This is not the way to Mali.

NEWSPAPERMAN In Marseilles today,
France got its first glimpse of an animal,
Not seen here since the days of Hannibal,
From Africa's deepest darkest interior,
Making women feel faint and tall men inferior,
A creature whose most wanton feature
Is its twenty-inch tongue.
Even its dung is a curiosity.
Is this gift from the cunning Pasha Mehmet Ali
A Trojan Horse for our King's menagerie?

LITTLE MARSEILLE BOY What are they going to do with it?

NEWSPAPERMAN Ask your mother!
In other news:
Egyptian cloud hangs over Greek insurgents.
Ten per cent discount on household detergents.

The Soirée à la girafe

A dinner party in a most bizarre setting. We are in the salon of the Prefecture. Count Grandeville de Largemont, the Prefect of Marseilles, Lady Clothilde Grandeville de Largemont and select Guests mingle amidst the Count's cabinets de curiosités.

COUNT We live in a world of marvels and monstrosities, and everyone wants to see them.

VALET (*Announcing*) Professor Etienne Geoffroy St-Hilaire of the Department of Quadrupeds, Cetaceans, Birds, Reptiles and Fish, the National Museum of Natural History, Paris.

Applause. St-Hilaire enters escorted by the Prefect's Valet.

COUNT Ah! Professor. We are honored that you have come all the way from Paris to be with us. I am Count Grandeville de Largemont.

ST-HILAIRE Mes hommages.

COUNT (*Introducing*) My wife, Madame Clothilde Grandeville de Largemont.

ST-HILAIRE Enchanté, Madame.

CLOTHILDE You are most welcome.

COUNT Cognac?

ST-HILAIRE No. Merci. I am here to convey…

GUEST 1 We were just discussing the fascination of our age with mammalian marvels and monstrosities.

GUEST 5 An area of special interest to Monsieur St-Hilaire?

ST-HILAIRE (*Transfixed by Clothilde's breasts*) Pardon? Ah, oui. I suppose it is just the spirit of the Enlightenment that fills us with *curiosité*.

CLOTHILDE Vive la curiosité!

ST-HILAIRE For me, the beauty of these monstrosities – any monstrosities – is that the environment shapes them to their function. And even when they have no function, they may still point the way to an archetype.

In the silence that follows, it is clear that no one has understood a word of what St-Hilaire has said.

GUEST 3 That is precisely what I was thinking.

COUNT (*To St-Hilaire*) Cognac?

St-Hilaire accepts, feeling he may need a stiff drink to get him through this. The Count takes a flask of cognac from a cabinet in his chest where his heart would otherwise be, takes a long swig for himself, then returns it to the compartment without pouring any for St-Hilaire.

ST-HILAIRE Merci. So when can I see…

CLOTHILDE (*To St-Hilaire*) I so miss Paris – the fashions, the theatre, the joie de vivre. Have you seen *La Chasse et l'amour* by that young Negro playwright, Dumas?

ST-HILAIRE No, Madame.

CLOTHILDE I hear he's quite dashing and talented.

ST-HILAIRE Madame, may I inquire after the animal which I have been sent to…

GUEST 4 (*Interrupting*) Professor, I hope you don't mind me asking, but do you acquire your mummies through Monsieur Drovetti?

ST-HILAIRE Non, Monsieur, I…

GUEST 3 I purchased one from him last year.

GUEST 1 I hear that he has opened up a new tomb, which has yielded some rather unique specimens.

Collective reactions: Hmm, Really, Ooh, Ahh, etc.

ST-HILAIRE Excusez-moi, but I wonder if…

GUEST 4 I would be interested in a well-preserved pygmy should he ever come across one.

ST-HILAIRE Take care it is not a full-size mummy that has been cut off at the knees.

COUNT I believe that Drovetti has had some difficulty selling the more obviously Negroid mummies.

GUEST 1 True, but he moves the surplus inventory by grinding it into anti-ageing creams.

GUEST 3 Actually…

ST-HILAIRE (*Forcefully*) Dames et Messieurs! Please! (*Regaining his social graces*) I have come all the way from Paris to inspect the King's animal, a gift from the Pasha Mehmet Ali, which it is my duty to conduct safely back to Paris. Can I see it? Now. Please?

CLOTHILDE (*Protesting*) But, Professor, the night is young.

Everyone looks at St-Hilaire as if he has made a terrible faux pas.

COUNT Lady Grandeville de Largemont has her own sense of the natural order of things, which we dare not upset. Cognac?

CLOTHILDE We have in our cabinet a human foot with seven toes, alleged to be of Egyptian origin.

ALL Amazing!

GUEST 1 To what purpose could the good Lord have directed a foot with seven toes?

GUEST 3 But that, I suppose, you might ask of most everything coming out of Africa.

ALL Indeed, to what purpose Africa?

General laughter.

COUNT Everything in life has its purpose. Antelope exist because lions must eat, and Africa exists for the benefit of Europe. Nature has ordered it thus.

GUEST 4 Well spoken Count!

ALL Hmmmm.

ST-HILAIRE (*Sarcastically*) This foot is not unknown to science. It belongs to Homo pedestris oralis majoris whose vestigial pedal phalanges formed a large part of its diet.

St-Hilaire's insult flies over their heads.

GUEST 4 Fascinating!

Chorus of nonplussed reactions: Oui, Umm, Hmm, Ahh, etc.

CLOTHILDE But the curiosité of all curiosités is the very creature which all of Marseilles knows by now is quartered in the stable my husband, our dear Count, had built for just that purpose.

ST-HILAIRE (*Emphatically*) Precisely!

GUEST 1 Oui. Come now, Grandville…

ALL S'il vous plaît. Are we to be the last in France to see this creature?

COUNT Quite the contrary. You shall be the first. Now, If you will follow me, I will show you that which has never been seen before in all of France.

Debut

Music / Back wall opens.

The interior moves away to reveal a stable. Shadows hide the giraffe. Atir brings her out into full view for the company. There is a catching of breath, awe and wonder in hushed oohs and aahs as they look on at this extraordinary creature tended by the exotic, silent, ebony handler. Women with cleavage of milky flesh shining in the lantern light also stare at Atir. He and the giraffe stare back at them, equally mesmerised. The atmosphere in this shadowy barn is erotic and highly charged.

COUNT Dames et Messieurs, I present to you, Le Beau Enfant d'Afrique.

The giraffe enters slowly led by Atir.

GUEST 1 How strange!

GUEST 2 It's so big!

ST-HILAIRE In all my years of scientific endeavour I have never seen a more graceful creature. Camelopardis reticulata artiodactyla giraffidae. Truly a marvel of nature.

GUEST 3 What lovely dark eyes.

GUEST 1 And such long beautiful legs.

GUEST 3 It's so big! Its neck is so long and…erect.

COUNT That, St-Hilaire, is Atir, the animal's handler.

ALL FEMALE GUESTS Oui.

ST-HILAIRE She responds readily to his attentions.

ALL FEMALE GUESTS Oui.

The women, who are now focused on Atir, are suddenly startled by the giraffe's twenty-inch-long black tongue as she licks Atir's hand.

GUEST 3 Oh! Mon Dieu! Such a tongue! It's so long and black I thought it would eat me.

The Guests exit after the giraffe.

ST-HILAIRE The transport to Paris… I foresee major problems.

COUNT (*To St-Hilaire*) Ah, oui. I have a letter from Monsieur Drovetti. For the animal's safety, he urges that you should avoid the political unrest in Lyon and take a somewhat longer sea voyage via Gibraltar to the northern port of Le Havre.

Newspaperman mimes boat sinking.

ST-HILAIRE Far too dangerous.

COUNT May I suggest that the answer may be lighter than air. She must go by hot-air balloon. She already moves most naturally at an altitude above that of other creatures.

Newspaperman mimes balloon bursting. St-Hilaire just looks at the Count, not bothering to dignify the suggestion with further comment.

NEWSPAPERMAN The American Robert Fulton has a submersible
That's convertible.
A distinct possibility.
Just think of the publicity!
This ground-breaking expedition
Covered by a double-page edition.

St-Hilaire and the Count both stare at Newspaperman.

COUNT Of course, she could always remain here, in which case His
Majesty could visit her whenever he's in Marseilles.

ATIR No. Sogo Jan taama. (*Mimes walking*)

St-Hilaire looks to the Count for an explanation. The Count shrugs or shakes his head. Seeing that they don't understand, Atir tries again.

Sogo Jan… (*Points to giraffe*) …taama. (*Mimes walking*)

Preparation / Video-wall (fashion / measurements etc).

St-Hilaire organises the preparations for the giraffe's convoy. He consults with the Prefect and examines the animal from horn to hoof, taking measurements, analyzing even her droppings. Communication between St-Hilaire and Atir is made difficult by the fact that neither speaks the other's language. A Fashion Designer and his Assistants fuss around her, taking their own measurements as Sogo Jan is fitted like a fashion model for her debut on the catwalk. Newspaperman is on hand.

FASHION DESIGNER (*To Assistants regarding the fabric swatches he holds in his hands*) Idiot! I am designing for an African queen, not a French cow. (*With his hand held dramatically to his forehead*) Inspiration. (*Then fanning himself*) And air! I can't breathe. Stand back, stand back. Get…get off me. Sycophants! How can I create with you hanging all over me? (*To himself*) Breathe. Just breathe. (*To Assistants*) Ça va. Look! She is tall. She is statuesque. She is exotique! Go…

Puppeteer drops Fashion Designer's arm and begins to exit.

Not you. (*To Assistant*) Go and find me something that brings out the essence of her being.

ST-HILAIRE (*Attempting to communicate with Atir*) I need the measurement around of each of her hooves…hooves…sabots.

ATIR (*Pointing to hooves*) Ah. Sabara.

FASHION DESIGNER As you can see, the new longer neck-line is on the cutting edge of French fashion. It is the essence of what it means to be French: free, naturelle and yet mysteriously aloof. This beautiful creature will be my greatest triumph.

ST-HILAIRE Oui, and the tail.

Atir lifts her tail; droppings fall at his feet.

Collect that. I need it for my analysis.

Air hands him a handful of giraffe dung.

FASHION DESIGNER I cannot work under these conditions. Honestly. (*To St-Hilaire*) Pardonne-moi, Professor, but I, too, am a scientist, working in the science of haute couture. You. Yes. You. You asked to have this lovely creature draped with a cloak to protect her against the elements, and voilà! I am here. So would you mind… Excusez-moi. (*To an assistant*) Swatches! (*The assistant shows him material samples*) Non. Non! NON! Ouieee!!!!

NEWSPAPERMAN News flash! The latest fashion splash!
Necklines plunge! A bosom boom!
Longer necks, *au naturelle*
Is it fashion heaven or a fashioned hell?

Prefect's Stable

Day. Clothilde and Atir flirt behind the giraffe, each equally exotic to the other.

CLOTHILDE *Bonjour.*

ATIR I ni sogoma. I bi bamana men wa? [Hello. Do you speak Bamana?]

Titkallimi Arabi? La? [Do you speak Arabic? No?]

CLOTHILDE Parlez-vous français?

ATIR Bonjour?

CLOTHILDE Oui, bonjour.

ATIR Bonjour. Uh… Ismi Atir. [My name is Atir.]

CLOTHILDE Bonjour, Ismi Atir.

ATIR La, la. Atir. [No, no. Atir.]

CLOTHILDE Lala Atir.

ATIR (*Pointing to himself*) Atir.

CLOTHILDE Atir.

Atir points to her. She points to herself.

Clothilde.

ATIR Clothilde. (*Pointing to his tongue*) Lisan.

CLOTHILDE Lisan.

ATIR (*Pointing to his eyes*) 'Youn.

CLOTHILDE 'Youn.

ATIR (*Pointing to her lips*) Shifa.

CLOTHILDE Shifa.

Out of nowhere, Sogo Jan's head drops down, and her long black tongue licks Clothilde's chest, startling her.

Oh! Une grande langue noire!

ATIR Oui. Grande lisan. (*Continuing in Arabic*) Sogo Jan, they are very dangerous. Titkallimi Arabi? La? Très dangereux. Oui?

CLOTHILDE Oui. Très, très dangereux.

St-Hilaire and Count disturb the negotiations. Embarrassing moment.

ST-HILAIRE Pardonne-moi, Madame, Monsieur, but I would be very grateful to you if you would instruct me on the method of assuring the proper nutrition of this animal.

Atir doesn't understand. St-Hilaire picks up the milk pail and gestures toward the giraffe and then to himself.

ATIR Ah. Nono. Na, a mi. [Ah, milk. Come, drink.]

Atir takes the pail and attempts to feed the milk to St-Hilaire.

ST-HILAIRE No! No!

Clothilde giggles. Count gives her a look that beseeches her to control herself.

ATIR Oui, nono…haleeb. [Yes, milk (Bamana)…milk (Arabic).]

ST-HILAIRE No, the…

St-Hilaire gestures again toward the giraffe.

ATIR Ahh. Sogo Jan. Ana fahem. [Ahh. The giraffe. I understand.]

(*To Sogo Jan*) Na'yan, balma musso, a mi. [Come here, my sister, drink.]

Sogo Jan drinks, but she spurns St-Hilaire's attempts. She will only take food from Atir's hand.

(*Speaking sternly to Sogo Jan*) A mi! A mi! [Drink! Drink!]

Atir's hopes for an early return to Alexandria are dashed.

ST-HILAIRE (*To Count*) He seems to have a rather remarkable relationship with the animal.

COUNT Indeed, Professor. She won't take her milk from anyone but him, nor take one step without him.

ST-HILAIRE Then we have no choice. He will have to go to Paris as well.

Clothilde signs to Atir.

Madame.

They exit leaving an angry Atir behind.

ATIR (*To Sogo Jan*) Paris? I don't want to go with you to Paris. I am not your slave. You go. And give the King my regards.

Atir tries to leave, but St-Hilaire calls him back.

Sogo Jan is dressed in a transparent green rain-cloak. Fashion Designer fusses and beams. Sogo Jan looks questioningly at Atir who is laughing. St-Hilaire just shakes his head, feeling this indignity as if it were his own. Atir takes an amulet from around his neck and ties it around the giraffe's neck. Stolen moment between Clothilde and Atir. The entire entourage waved off by a tearful Clothilde and Grandville de Largemont.

NEWSPAPERMAN On the scene with this Special Report,
Your correspondent with the animal's escort.
With the eminent St-Hilaire as commander,
The caravan left Marseilles that day
To cheers from the crowd, which was very loud,
And protests from the creature's reluctant handler.
The Countess was tearful, distraught and distraughter,
But the object of her affection soon forgot her.
He hadn't much time to pine for her charms
As each day a new lady lay in his arms.
The King was excited and the Pasha delighted
As triumphant, the toast of all France made her way.
But things went sour. Atir became dour,
And nerves started to fray.
Letters got lost, communications crossed.
And no one was having a nice day.

Shed

ST-HILAIRE Esteemed Members of the Academy, these several weeks on the road have been difficult, but rewarding. I can at last report that the animal stands 4.72 metres from hoof to horn and weighs 1,092 kilos. In the wild she is a cud-chewing herbivore employing a prehensile tongue 48.26 centimetres in length, though this one takes only milk (twenty gallons per day). She appears to be neither predator nor prey, which defies the logic of nature and presents an interesting problem for science. (*Seeing Atir*) The security of the animal remains a constant problem.

ATIR (*To the giraffe*) This is a real problem.

ST-HILAIRE I must arrange for accommodations each evening and see to the needs of the animal and her sullen handler, (*Looking past the giraffe at Atir and speaking loud enough for him to hear*) who does not appear to take his responsibilities seriously.

ATIR I have to milk the cows until my fingers are cramped and look after this man who is so old he cannot walk. This is not my n'dakan. The nights are cold here. Every day he collects dung from you, but he never uses it to make a fire. If I were you I would ask what he is doing with all that dung.

ST-HILAIRE (*Stops writing to address the giraffe*) You know, I don't understand your affection for Atir.

ATIR (*Responding to his name with exasperation*) Oui.

ST-HILAIRE (*To Atir*) Nothing, Atir.

ATIR (*Responding again to his name*) Oui!

ST-HILAIRE Nothing!

ATIR (*To the giraffe*) And who can understand him? (*Making vaguely French-sounding commands in imitation of St-Hilaire*) 'Atir, Wayzhay voo!' 'Atir, Junna voovoo pa!' I am fatigued from hearing my name. And I am tired of taking care of you. I'm not your slave, and I don't want to go with you to Paris.

ST-HILAIRE (*To the giraffe*) He treats you like a stepchild and shows not the slightest concern for your safety. (*To himself*) Why am I talking to a giraffe?

Egypt; French Forest; Pasha's Palace

DROVETTI (*In Egypt, reading the message he is about to send the King via carrier pigeon*) Your Majesty will be pleased to know that the giraffe, which the Pasha of Egypt has sent, remains in excellent health on her long walk to Paris, and that in itself is reward enough for the months of planning and care I have given to that end.

The Pasha also praises Your Majesty's wisdom and neutrality in the unfortunate rebellion in Greece.

KING CHARLES X (*In the forest outside Paris*) This affair with the Greeks needs to be resolved before it becomes a problem for France.

DROVETTI P.S.: Has Your Majesty received any of three previous letters, which I sent via air mail?

KING CHARLES X All this talk of révolutions démocratiques has the people très agité. (*Shoots pigeon*) And no word from my consul in Egypt. What is his name?

MINISTER Bernardino Drovetti, Your Majesty.

The Queen is eating her pigeon pie.

KING CHARLES X Oui, Monsieur Drovetti. Any news from him?

MINISTER I am afraid not. Your Majesty may I suggest…

MARIE-THERESE Drovetti! BAH!

KING CHARLES X (*To the Queen*) What are you eating?

MARIE-THERESE Pigeon pie. Bonapartistes all: Drovetti, St-Hilaire, Mehmet Ali.

MEHMET ALI (*Palace, Alexandria, Egypt, dictating letter*) Dear Sultan, son of the Prophet, brother of the sun and moon, grandson and viceroy of Allah, ruler of the kingdoms of Macedonia, Babylonia, Jerusalem, Upper and Lower Egypt and Greece, emperor of emperors, sovereign of sovereigns; the hope and comfort of Muslims, confounder of Christians, etc, etc. I regret never receiving your previous letters, but you know how unreliable the mail can be in these parts.

Several bundles of letters sit on the stage.

Rest assured that the armies of Egypt are yours to command…

The bird, which has reached the forest, is shot by the King; it falls at his feet.

While we do not presume that your terrible might, invincible in battle, requires any assistance from us, we do understand that the Sultan has more important matters to attend to than swatting flies in Greece.

NEWSPAPERMAN Late-breaking news out of Africa!

Startled, the King fires, but hits something else on a shelf near Ali. He aims at the Newspaperman and takes pot shots at him throughout his speech.

Egyptian fleet sails for Athens, (*Gun shot*)
Greece! (*Gun shot*)
Does this mean War? (*Gun shot*)
Is lamb's wool fleece? (*Gun shot*)
Is the Pope a priest? (*Gun shot*)
Does A C E spell the end of Peace?

Gun shot. The King reloads his gun.

An emergency meeting called King Charles away
From a hunting expedition in the forest today,
Where dressed like a common poacher
Most unfashionably,
The talk of imminent war
Was discussed most irrationally.

The Queen enters.

MARIE-THERESE Charles! Not again! Where is your crown? You should be meeting with your generals and fabricating reasons to invade other countries. Why can't you be more pre-emptive, like America?

KING CHARLES X Why can't we all just get along?

MARIE-THERESE Because it's not profitable. (*Picking up the downed pigeon and discarding Drovetti's letter without even looking at it*) These birds are quite delicious. I had a lovely pie made of three others just like it recently.

NEWSPAPERMAN (*Obsequious*)
    The Queen was seen looking regal as ever
    Riding in the forest
    On her royal ass or horse,
    Follow by a chorus
    Of 'Long live the Queen!' No, no! 'May she reign forever!'

Back at the stable, Atir prepares for bed.

ST-HILAIRE (*Resuming his letter to the Academy*) We are nearing Lyon, which greatly concerns me, as the revolution is still very much alive there, and antipathy toward the King could pose a threat to the animal's safety. I have written His Majesty for permission to go by boat up the Saône and bypass Lyon altogether, but there is still no response.

Museum, Bamako

TEA LADY (*Reading St-Hilaire's letter*) The crowds are insatiable and the animal's handler is easily distracted. But Egypt could not have wished for a better ambassador.

ST-HILAIRE She has impeccable manners and makes a favourable impression upon all.

TEA LADY (*Commenting on the letter*) 'Impeccable manners'? But this is not science. It's a love letter.

The Storm

Into strange stable; music; video-wall – baroque storm; shadow puppet play.

A terrible storm develops. Atir is asleep in the stable.

Clothilde enters the stable holding an umbrella and a French coat for Atir. She looks around for Atir and notices him sleeping in the corner, a loose blanket covering him. She moves over to him. Puts the umbrella down and peeks under the blanket. Atir continues to sleep. Clothilde hangs the coat up and greets Atir from the entrance.

CLOTHILDE Atir.

ATIR Clothilde.

CLOTHILDE Bonsoir.

ATIR Bonsoir.

Atir wakes up and takes the umbrella away from Clothilde, kissing her hello.

CLOTHILDE (*Presents Atir with the new coat*) Pour vous.

ATIR Fransawi boubou?

CLOTHILDE Une boubou de l'haute couture. Paris est très à la mode. You cannot meet the King of France in those African clothes.

ATIR Merci.

He strips. Clothilde is trembling slightly. Clothilde seduces Atir, thrilled to be making love under the eyes of the giraffe.

After making love, Clothilde dresses Atir in the coat of a French dandy. Clothilde coaxes Atir to dance for her. He is a good dancer, but his African rhythms and her song don't connect. He soon realises that she has left him there alone. He picks up his old clothes and exits.

The Palace

KING CHARLES X Am I to be the last person in all of France to see my own giraffe?

MINISTER Your Majesty. (*Handing him a letter*) A letter from Monsieur St-Hilaire expressing concern regarding the route through Lyon. And we know there's little sympathy there for Your Majesty's neutral position on the Greek question.

KING CHARLES X (*Perusing letter*) He wants to sail up the Saône. But the cost…

MARIE-THERESE Charles! Are you fussing over that animal again? Just have them send the meat.

NEWSPAPERMAN Invasion!
International Political Equation:
The Turks take Greece,
Anti-Islamic sentiment peaks.
Mehmet Ali is
The most hated man in Europe,
Especi-al-ly
In Lyon, you see,
Where prognostications
In anticipation
Of the King's exotic creature say
The long-necked beast
From the east
Might soon be deceased.

Lyon

Lyon seems ghostly quiet. A Beautiful Lady enters. Two children are playing quietly with a cat. St-Hilaire, Atir and the giraffe enter the city.

ST-HILAIRE Atir. Be careful. This place is not safe.

The Beautiful Lady watches the newcomers. She catches Atir's eye and begins a flirtation with him. He walks a ways with her, leaving the giraffe to browse nearby.

A well-dressed, blind, black man with a doctor's bag stops to address Atir.

DOCTOR Taamala, segui i ko! You are on the wrong road. Look at you. Turn yourself around, black man, before it is too late.

Atir has understood only the first few words the doctor said, but is deeply disturbed by the encounter. The Mayor and Townspeople have gathered around the giraffe who shows signs of nervousness. The boy suddenly produces a toy guillotine and chops the cat's head off.

MAYOR (*To Atir and St-Hilaire*) Welcome, Monsieur...?

ST-HILAIRE (*To Mayor*) Etienne Geoffroy St-Hilaire.

MAYOR Welcome to Lyon! Home of the Revolution, capital of decapitations! Polito Politesse, mayor, at your service.

ST-HILAIRE Merci, but we really can't stay, since we are touring this animal, and crowds make her nervous.

MAYOR But Lyon loves animals. I will personally conduct this regal creature to the place reserved for royalty and other heads of state...

The Mayor opens up the Guillotine.

...brought to you by Guillotine, makers of fine French cutlery since 1789.

PEOPLE OF LYON (*Chant*) À la guillotine! À la guillotine!

ST-HILAIRE (*Still looking for Atir*) Atir. Atir?

The giraffe is spooked and starts lashing out at the Crowd then runs away. Chaos erupts. St-Hilaire is furious with Atir who runs offstage in search of Sogo Jan.

NEWSPAPERMAN This just in: Lyon designers find fashion a bore, Send new longer neck-lines to the cutting-room floor.

Storeroom / Palace

Paris music; video-wall (Mounted Heads / Hunting-trophy room in the palace).

The King enters the Storeroom (hunting-trophy room in the palace). One of the curiosity / trophy heads moves and startles him. It is only Madame Royale in a mask of heavy facial cream and hair rollers.

KING CHARLES X Mon Dieu! Marie-Thérèse! I thought you were a dead monstrosity.

MARIE-THERESE Beauty-rest, Charles, beauty-rest. Unlike you, I take my responsibility for maintaining the mystique of royalty seriously.

KING CHARLES X The people of France are eternally grateful, I'm sure. Perhaps you could speak to the Greek insurgents. The mystique of royalty escapes them. And that slippery viceroy in Egypt.

MARIE-THERESE Hounds and foxes, Charles. Hounds and foxes. Or in Egypt's case, lions and natives. It's time to let loose the dogs of war.

The King's Minister enters with a message, and Madame Royale quickly assumes a place among the King's trophies and monstrosities.

MINISTER Good news, Your Majesty. A letter from Monsieur St-Hilaire, denying the rumours that your most exotic animal was lost during the riots in Lyon. He assures your Majesty that it will arrive on schedule in your royal menagerie. And, please, may I make so bold as to compliment Your Majesty on his fine collection of frightening fetishes? (*Indicating the Queen*) That one is especially gruesome.

KING CHARLES X *Oui*, but there is a curse attached to it. Don't look at it; it will drive you mad. *Merci.*

Minister sneaks one last look, shudders, then exits.

MARIE-THERESE Fool. Protocol, Charles. Decorum! The King of France does not rush off to rendezvous with strange animals on the street.

KING CHARLES X No. He visits with them in the privacy of his study.

The Queen swaps her make-up and rollers head for her royal head. The Minister, bowing and scraping even more than before, enters to announce Drovetti. The Queen, now sitting where the gruesome fetish was, causes the Minister to do a double take.

MINISTER The Consul-General of His Highly Christian Majesty in the Valley of the Nile, Monsieur Bernardino Drovetti.

Drovetti enters and bows to the King and Queen.

DROVETTI Your Majesty. Madame Royale. Allow me to express my gratitude for the privilege of serving you and to say how deeply I regret that Your Majesty did not receive my letters, which I sent by carrier-pigeon. I have had the remaining birds – fat from dereliction of duty – sent to Madame Royale's kitchen, where I'm sure they will serve in a manner more to Madame's liking. Finally, with the imminent arrival of Your Majesty's giraffe only days from now, I bring you greetings from the viceroy of Egypt, Mehmet Ali. The pasha has offered to withdraw his forces from Greece in exchange for an alliance with France against the Turkish sultan.

KING CHARLES X Uhh…

NEWSPAPERMAN News Flash:
France goes to war!
Greek rebels score.
Egyptian fleet is trashed
When they clash with the French
In the port of Navarino.
But does His Majesty know
Who let the dogs out – woof, woof, woof.
Many boats lost
The Pasha pays the cost
For Greeks who seek to be
Their own boss.
What a great loss.
But who let the dogs out – woof, woof, woof.

All look questioningly at the Queen who just shrugs.

MARIE-THERESE Well. That's that. Come. It's time to eat your giraffe. Oh, dear! Did I say 'eat'? I meant 'meet'.

The Forest

Atir searches for the giraffe. Distraught and exhausted, he rips off his French clothes and throws them into the woods.

ATIR Sogo Jan!!!!

Atir starts to wail and mourn the loss of the giraffe. He is unaware of the giraffe which has found him. Sogo Jan, silently browsing in the trees above and behind him, lowers her large head to chew on his ear.

So.

He says nothing else for a few seconds while they commune in silence.

St-Hilaire enters. He has also been searching for Sogo Jan. The scene is emotionally charged. St-Hilaire crosses to the giraffe. He strokes her side and finally smiles.

ST-HILAIRE She's a magnificent animal, no?

Sogo Jan licks St-Hilaire's face.

But dangereux.

ATIR Oui. Très dangereux.

ST-HILAIRE (*Reflecting out loud*) Mankind is peculiar. We're always looking for marvels and monsters, the strange and curious. We seldom see the marvellous and monstrous in ourselves. We wander in search of the exotic. We dissect and analyse. But this marvel of creation is in itself enough.

ATIR (*Talking to himself*) They say walking helps to clear the vision. But the way is not clear for Taamala.

ST-HILAIRE Taamala?

St-Hilaire has heard that word before.

ATIR Oui. (*Indicating the place where his name is written in the giraffe's markings*) Taamala. (*Still reflecting to himself, as St-Hilaire cannot understand what he is saying*) That is how I was called in my village. It means 'the one who is always on the road'. But my village is gone now, and only blind men and Sogo Jan know my name…and my n'dakan.

ST-HILAIRE Atir?

ATIR Oui. Atir.

Atir indicates to the giraffe to follow St-Hilaire. St-Hilaire imitates the signals that Atir uses for the giraffe and for the first time, the giraffe follows St-Hilaire. This brings a smile to both Atir and St-Hilaire.

Paris

Exterior; video-wall.

NEWSPAPERMAN On this festive day…
(Sorry, please, but you're in my way)
Thirty thousand people
Line the Paris streets
In frills and pleats
Competing to get a glimpse
Of the arrival
Of the exotic creature
Whose survival
Of an epic two-year journey
From Nubia to here…
(Your hair is in my face, my dear)
To meet le Roi du France.

Enter a pregnant Clothilde with friends Fifi and Jolie.

CLOTHILDE Bonjour, Jolie! Bonjour, Fifi!

JOLIE / FIFI Bonjour, Clothilde!

JOLIE Oo la la! I love your hair.

CLOTHILDE À la giraffe! And the necklace, and the latest colours.

JOLIE 'Belly of giraffe.'

Fifi and Jolie ululate.

CLOTHILDE But my derrière is bruised from riding on the carriage floor all the way from Marseilles to accommodate my hair.

JOLIE Oh, your derrière has received beaucoup bruisings in the backs of carriages.

FIFI Who is he? Qui est?

CLOTHILDE (*Holding up the locket with the tiny portrait of Atir and the giraffe*) Look. That's him.

FIFI La girafe?

CLOTHILDE No, no Fifi. Not the giraffe. The African. The giraffe is a female.

JOLIE But, what if…you know? If the baby is brown? This time the Prefect will know it is not his.

CLOTHILDE Maybe I won't go back. He has his cabinet de curiosités. Maybe I will start my own collection of exotic specimens.

Drovetti and St-Hilaire enter. Clothilde begins a flirtation with Drovetti.

NEWSPAPERMAN You heard it first right here,
An epidemic soon to premiere,
From village to village
And town to town,
To ladies of high renown
Beaucoup babies born curiously brown.

CLOTHILDE Monsieur, you are so tall, so Italian, so…collectable. Will you do any excavation while you are here in Paris?

DROVETTI Does Mademoiselle have a site in mind?

CLOTHILDE Oui, but it's very hot there, in a valley that floods like the Nile.

NEWSPAPERMAN Infamous Italian tomb raider
Poised to be the next womb invader.
Details at eleven.

The French Court

Day. Music; choreography; back doors slide open.

Enter the dancers and castelets with great pageantry, followed by the King and Queen. Finally, Atir and St-Hilaire enter the court with Sogo Jan. Atir is dressed in his flowing, regal Sudanese clothes. St-Hilaire is dignified but tired and frail.

ST-HILAIRE Your Majesty, Madame Royale, I present to you La Belle Africaine!

More applause.

I must also commend to Your Majesty the giraffe's African guardian, Monsieur Atir. Without him, the animal would never have survived this extraordinary voyage of seven thousand kilometres.

KING CHARLES X Certainement, this is a créature extraordinaire. Merci, Monsieur St-Hilaire. And, s'il vous plaît, convey our appréciation to Monsieur Atir.

MARIE-THERESE Charles, if you dare address the savage…

KING CHARLES X (*Shouting defiantly*) An extraordinary creature. Well done, Monsieur St-Hilaire. And, s'il vous plaît, convey our appreciation to Monsieur Atir.

The Queen is mortified. The King welcomes his new acquisition.

Le Jardin des plantes

Night. The beautiful giraffe-house. Moon in the garden at night. Atir comes in, his bag packed to go. Sogo Jan stands still as a stone in the glass house.

ATIR So, now you are famous, Sogo Jan. This is a very fine house they have built for you. Lots of glass. I have two thousand francs from the King of France. I am returning home…a rich man after all. I am returning.

Atir pets the giraffe, then leaves with all his baggage. The giraffe seems lost and fidgets nervously. After a long moment, Atir returns.

I am not your slave.

Atir puts his bag down and lays down to sleep at the feet of the giraffe. She stands over him protectively. Nudges him to be fed.

(*Mumbling sleepily*) Tomorrow.

The giraffe nudges him again.

Tomorrow.

Sog Jan exits the stage, leaving Atir asleep there.

Storeroom, Museum Basement, Bamako

Dr Konate, assisted by his workers, is putting files back into the archives hanging St-Hilaire's coat in the closet. He wakes the sleeping Atir, who is once again Jean-Michel.

DR KONATE So? Did you find what you came for?

JEAN-MICHEL Maybe.

Long pause.

He never returned, did he.

DR KONATE You're here. A seed blown far from the tree can still become a forest.

Video-wall: gates of the Jardin shut, into Paris skyline. The giraffe walks across Paris skyline and turns into the Eiffel Tower.

JEAN-MICHEL I see.

End

Mervyn Millar was born in London in 1974. He is a theatre director and puppetry specialist. He has provided puppetry to major companies including the RSC, National Theatre Studio, NT Education, theatre-rites, Lyric Hammersmith, Bristol Old Vic, the West Yorkshire Playhouse, Liverpool Playhouse, and, frequently, BAC. He has created and directed installation and site-specific shows for wireframe and with Kazuko Hohki, and directed new writing and classics for the Steam Industry and others. He was formerly director of the Finborough Theatre where he worked developing new plays.

Also published by Oberon Books

THE ART OF DARKNESS

STAGING THE PHILIP PULLMAN TRILOGY

By Robert Butler

Robert Butler's intimate backstage story takes us into workshops, rehearsals and production meetings where, over six months, Philip Pullman's bestselling trilogy *His Dark Materials* was transformed into six hours of drama. It answers the all-important question asked by anyone who knows these epic books: how on earth are they going to do it? Lavishly illustrated with over fifty rehearsal and production photographs, this fascinating book is sure to appeal both to fans and to all those interested in how such an epic theatrical production is brought to life for a live audience.

ISBN 1 84002 414 3 • £12.99

Also published by Oberon Books

THE ART OF DARKNESS

THE STORY CONTINUES

By Robert Butler

A special illustrated supplement, to mark the triumphant return of *His Dark Materials* to the London stage, takes a further look behind the scenes at the making of one of the most exciting and innovative pieces of theatre of the new millennium.

'Daemons, cliff-ghasts, lovelorn witches, gyptians, harpies, armoured bears, soul-sucking spectres and tiny creatures riding dragonflies – the magical creations of writer Philip Pullman soared from page to stage yesterday in what could be the most spectacular theatre blockbuster ever.'

Observer

ISBN 1 84002 534 4 • £1.50

Ⓑ

Also published by Oberon Books

DARKNESS ILLUMINATED

DISCUSSIONS ON PHILIP PULLMAN'S **HIS DARK MATERIALS** AT THE NATIONAL THEATRE

Edited by Lyn Haill

Transcripts of Platform talks with Philip Pullman, Archbishop of Canterbury Rowan Williams, Nicholas Hytner, Nicholas Wright and lead actors Dominic Cooper and Anna Maxwell Martin and members of the production team for *His Dark Materials*, all chaired by Robert Butler, author of *The Art of Darkness*. These lively and entertaining debates throw light on the various aspects of adaptation and staging that brought Philip Pullman's hugely successful epic to the Olivier stage.

ISBN 1 84002 455 0 • £7.99

Also published by Oberon Books

THE COMING OF GODOT

A SHORT HISTORY OF A MASTERPIECE

By Jonathan Croall
Foreword by Sir Peter Hall

Fifty years ago Sir Peter Hall directed the English language world premiere of Samuel Beckett's *Waiting For Godot*. Now he has returned to this extraordinary classic, the quintessential absurdist piece that has become one of the most important works of modern drama. Jonathan Croall, who had access to rehearsals for this landmark anniversary production, combines an account of this theatrical journey with an informative history of the play that has intrigued, baffled, provoked and entertained all those who have ever come across Vladimir, Estragon and the ever elusive Godot.

ISBN 1 84002 595 6 • £9.99

WITH THE ROGUE'S COMPANY

HENRY IV AT THE NATIONAL THEATRE

By Bella Merlin

The National had never before staged Shakespeare's two most admired history plays; it was ten years since Michael Gambon's last appearance at the Theatre, and five years since director Nicholas Hytner had started talking to him about playing Falstaff. The plan was for *Henry IV Parts 1* and *2* – which Kenneth Tynan called 'great public plays in which a whole nation is under scrutiny and trial' – to open this year's Travelex £10 season. Bella Merlin follows the production from pre-rehearsal planning to opening night, charting the processes that make up two major productions in the Olivier Theatre, and provides a unique insight into the staging of two great Shakespeare plays.

ISBN 1 84002 560 3 • £12.99

Also published by Oberon Books

ARE YOU THERE, CROCODILE?

INVENTING ANTON CHEKHOV

By Michael Pennington

Acclaimed actor Michael Pennington retraces his ten-year exploration of Chekhov when preparing for the one-man show *Anton Chekhov*. As he describes its opening at the National Theatre and subsequent life on tour, television and radio, the actor and subject fall uncannily into step. Includes the performance script of *Anton Chekhov*.

'A classic depiction of theatre work at its most visionary'
Simon Callow

PB • ISBN 1 84002 458 5 • £12.99
HB • ISBN 1 84002 192 6 • £19.99

For information on these and other plays and books published
by Oberon, or for a free catalogue, listing all titles and cast
breakdowns, visit our website

www.oberonbooks.com

info@oberonbooks.com • 020 7607 3637